EMANUEL ROSEN was vice president of marketing for Niles Software, the maker of EndNote, for nine years. It was during that time Rosen noticed that the software spread to a large extent by word of mouth and started researching how buzz can be accelerated. The original version of this book, *The Anatomy of Buzz*, was a national bestseller and was translated into eleven languages. He lives in Menlo Park, California.

Additional Praise for
Buzz

"This book is the foundation upon which most buzz marketing knowledge is based."

—Guy Kawaski, Co-founder of Alltop.com

"Rosen's new edition with twelve new chapters (out of twenty-four) makes it the best contemporary guide to understanding and using buzz."

—Philip Kotler, S.C. Johnson & Son Professor of International Marketing, Kellogg
School of Management, Northwestern University

"Way beyond a revision, the book provides fresh insights and vivid case studies into how buzz is created and harnessed to propel business strategies."

—David Aaker, vice chairman, Prophet; author of *Spanning Silos*

"Before buzz had any buzz, Emanuel was onto it as the next big thing. *The Anatomy of Buzz* was a foundational book for our space, and now he does a perfect job building on all of those original concepts to present a state-of-the-art look at one of the most important societal factors of our time."

—Jonathan Carson, president, international, Nielsen Online;
cofounder, Nielsen BuzzMetrics

"The definitive handbook on word-of-mouth marketing, updated."

—Paul Marsden, Ph.D., author of *Connected Marketing*;
managing director, Clickadvisor

"This book is a true classic—the first book you should read if you want to really understand viral, buzz, and word of mouth."

—Andy Sernovitz, author of *Word of Mouth Marketing:
How Smart Companies Get People Talking*

"When I first read *The Anatomy of Buzz*, I found myself longing for more . . . and now I finally have it. In this long awaited update to his classic marketing text, Emanuel takes you deeper inside the idea of buzz and what makes a product or idea contagious."

—Rohit Bhargava, senior vice president of marketing, Ogilvy;
author of *Personality Not Included*

"As a word-of-mouth junkie I read everything I can find on the topic and I can honestly say that this book is the most comprehensive. The stories are fun and fascinating, the research is complete and compelling, and the balance of theory and application gives people everything they need to ignite, encourage, and measure powerful word-of-mouth campaigns."

—Greg Stielstra, author of *PyroMarketing* and *Faith-Based Marketing*

"A true word-of-mouth marketer himself, Emanuel Rosen collaborated with his readers over the eight years since *The Anatomy of Buzz*. His revised effort drills deeply into both the HOW and WHY of word-of-mouth. As with the original book, Rosen once again authors the quintessential word-of-mouth text."

—Stuart Sheldon, president, Escalate Marketing LLC-Atlanta Division; former director of brand activation at Coca-Cola North America

"Emanuel Rosen's update to *The Anatomy of Buzz* is truly a gem. With an easy to read style and wonderful examples to make it come to life, Rosen tells us what we need to know about why word of mouth is such a powerful force, and what savvy marketers can do to tap it."

—Ed Keller, CEO, The Keller Fay Group and author, *The Influentials*

Buzz

Buzz

Real-Life
Lessons in
Word-of-Mouth
Marketing

Emanuel Rosen

P
PROFILE BOOKS

This edition published in Great Britain in 2009 by
PROFILE BOOKS LTD
3A Exmouth House
Pine Street
London EC1R 0JH
www.profilebooks.com

Published in the United States of America in 2009 by
Doubleday, a division of Random House

This is a revised and updated edition of *The Anatomy of Buzz*, published in 2000

1 3 5 7 9 10 8 6 4 2

Printed and bound in Great Britain by
CPI Bookmarque, Croydon, Surrey

A CIP catalogue record for this book is available from the British Library.

ISBN 978 1 84668 248 3

Mixed Sources
Product group from well-managed
forests and other controlled sources
www.fsc.org   Cert no. TT-COC-002227
© 1996 Forest Stewardship Council
FSC

To Daria,

Noam, Yonatan,

Maya, and Mika

Contents

Why is buzz suddenly getting so much attention? The obvious
answer is that the Internet has caused the volume of buzz to
explode, but things are a bit more complicated than that.
Research shows that most word of mouth is actually
communicated in person. So how exactly has the Internet
contributed to the rise of buzz?

When I was writing the first edition of this book, people
doubted that it was possible to measure something that is as
amorphous, ephemeral, and intangible as buzz or word of
mouth. Today several companies are involved in measuring
both online and offline buzz.

Understanding what customers want to talk about is a key
factor in stimulating word of mouth. How do you find out?
And once you have this insight, what do you do about it? I
also discuss the importance of listening with your eyes.

Birds do it, bees do it . . . we all share information, but why?
And what can we learn from simpler forms of life, like ravens,
about why we buzz? What intensified the buzz among
Bedouins in Sinai? And if you view yourself as an expert on,
say, restaurants, will you share more information about a
positive experience or a negative one?

Some people talk more than others. I call these people "hubs."
I make a distinction between social hubs—people who talk
more because they know more people—and expert hubs—
people who talk more because they know more about
something. How do you identify these folks? And once you
do, what do you do with them? In this chapter I also discuss
the controversy surrounding the "Influentials."

People love to tell each other stories. What's the story of your business? If you don't have one yet, how do you find one? Is it something you simply create out of thin air? A good business story—a story that people will repeat and that will drive sales—should be anchored in fact.

People are hungry for something to talk about. And some people know how to supply the goods. One such person is Mechai Viravaidya, who's known as Thailand's condom king. You'll also read here about a movie premiere with an unlikely guest list of horses and about the power of gossip.

It can be as simple as involving a customer in creating a viral video or a much more complicated process that allows a customer to help design the product itself. When people are involved in creating something of their own, they are more likely to share it with others.

By giving exclusive information to a select group of people before an official launch, you are likely to get some extra mileage out of the news. When you hold information close to your chest, people want it. But as new research shows, you can take this idea only so far.

We constantly report to others about our social interactions. Anytime you can plug into this habit of ours, you'll stimulate talk. It's obvious how sites such as Facebook and MySpace benefit from this concept. Can it work for a soft drink? A scissors manufacturer? A book publisher?

Some people see word of mouth as the exclusive result of grassroots and guerrilla marketing efforts, when in fact a lot of buzz is generated by mass media. We'll meet a fascinating organization that uses mass media to stimulate discussion and to promote social change.

Introduction
to This Edition

(and a History of Its Title)

I started working on this book around 1993. I wrote a seventy-page draft and even came up with a title, *Start Spreading the News*. But at the time I was too busy marketing End-Note (a reference tool for researchers that our company developed) to go any further, so I put it to the side. Five years passed before I started rewriting the draft under a new title, which I really liked: *The Invisible Networks*.

In March 1998, with enough free time to work on this book, I flew to Albuquerque, New Mexico, to meet Everett Rogers, the author of *Diffusion of Innovations*, a book that had influenced me profoundly. We spoke for a couple of hours. Rogers didn't say much about my title. Otherwise, he was extremely supportive and generous and even offered to write a foreword.

Six months after our initial meeting, I met Rogers at the annual meeting of the International Communication Association in Jerusalem. Over coffee, he asked, "What's the title of your book again?"

"*The Invisible Networks*," I said.

"You're really writing about buzz. That's a good title for a book: *Buzz*," Rogers replied.

But I didn't like the word "buzz." I told him I thought it was too glitzy.

A couple of months later I sent a book proposal to an agent named Daniel Greenberg. He loved the proposal, but didn't like the title *The Invisible Networks*—he said it sounded like a book about Cisco. "You're really writing about buzz," Daniel told me on the phone.

The following day I called him with a new title—*The Anatomy of Buzz*.

After working on that first edition for another year, I saw that Everett Rogers and Daniel Greenberg were right—I *was* writing about buzz. Not buzz as in the latest news about Paris Hilton, but buzz as in the hum of everything that we tell each other about products, movies, people, books, ideas.

The book was published in October 2000. I've spent the past eight years writing drafts of two other books that I plan on finishing one day. But again and again I've found myself drawn back to buzz. I've given lectures on buzz, participated in panels about buzz. The more time passed, the more I liked the sound of the word "buzz."

Then, one day in 2007, the idea of publishing an updated edition arose. There have been many new studies and findings about the subject, and everyone involved felt that an updated edition was a good idea. When I first began the revisions, I thought I could probably finish them in a couple of months. A year later, I'm sitting here writing this intro.

What's new in this edition? First, lots of examples and research from the trenches. While I was desperately searching for case studies in writing the first edition, I had the opposite problem in writing this one—too much to choose from. The new examples and studies made me focus on concepts that I ignored (or almost ignored) in the first edition, such as the need to measure buzz, storytelling, the power of participation, ethical issues, conversation hooks, secondhand buzz, and visual buzz.

I also removed a lot of stuff. As I was talking to people, I developed a sense that few readers today need to be convinced of the importance of network thinking, online buzz, and word-of-mouth marketing in general. So you'll find less about *why* these concepts are important and more about *how* they are being used in the field.

The result wasn't what I expected when I started. Of the twenty-four chapters in the new manuscript, twelve are completely new (chapters 1–6, 13, 15–17, 19–20), only two have been largely untouched (chapters 9–10), and the rest fall somewhere in the middle.

So now that we had a new book, we had to find a new title . . .

I originally believed that *The Anatomy of Buzz, Second Edition* would suffice. But some people felt differently, and after some more thought I realized that they had a good point: this book is not simply a second edition. So we tossed around a number of ideas: *The New Anatomy of Buzz, Bride of the Anatomy of Buzz, Anatomy of Buzz 2: Electric Boogaloo*. We finally settled on *The Anatomy of Buzz Revisited*. In the UK, where fewer people are aware of the first edition, we decided to simply call it *Buzz*.

Everett Rogers is no longer here to tell me what he thinks about the new title. In the summer of 2004, I met him for the last time in Albuquerque. Lying on the sofa in his living room, he gave me a lecture on the economic development of New Mexico, a state that he loved and called home. He passed away in October 2004.

Remembering Everett Rogers should help us put things in perspective. There is a lot that is new in the word-of-mouth landscape, but the basic human behavior that Ev understood so well has not changed. Flipping through old editions of his book *Diffusion of Innovations,* I read so many insights that he and other researchers in the field saw years ahead of the rest of us.

Thinking about Everett Rogers should also remind us that, like any other tool, the communication methods discussed in this book can be used in many different ways and for different purposes. Everett Rogers dedicated his life to studying how positive change could be promoted in society. He wrote about communication methods for fighting AIDS and the diffusion of new technologies and new agricultural innovations in developing countries. I truly hope that this book will be used for promoting ideas, programs, and products that are similarly useful or valuable.

Emanuel Rosen

Menlo Park, California

June 2008

Buzz

Trigger

1

During the first few days of October 2004, Amy Rathke told everyone she met about the semester she had spent in Baja with the National Outdoor Leadership School. A senior at Willamette University in Salem, Oregon, she told her classmates about the spectacular views of ocean vistas. She told people at the dorm about climbing rocky canyons. She told her crew teammates about camping on beaches. She told the Willamette newspaper that they ought to write about the outdoor leadership school, known by its graduates as NOLS.

This is the foundation of buzz: in order to get people talking about your product or service, you must provide a great experience. And Amy Rathke had an undeniably great experience with NOLS.

But here's the interesting thing. Amy Rathke took her NOLS course in the fall of 2003, an entire year before that week in October 2004. If you were to plot on a graph how much she talked about NOLS in the months that followed her trip, you would see a very high level of talk right after she got back from Baja, followed by a little less talk with each month that passed, until gradually it tapered off. And then in early October you would see the line shooting up again and peaking on October 6, 2004.

What made her suddenly create so much buzz?

Before I go on, I need to define one term that will be used a lot in this book—"buzz." Some people think buzz is complicated and mysterious, but what I'm talking about is actually quite simple: person-to-person communication about someone or something. It can involve anything from computers to cars, movie stars to mobile phones. The basic building block of buzz is a comment. It can be transmitted through face-to-face or phone conversations, instant messaging, e-mail, blogs, or some other method of communication that someone is developing in his or her garage as you're reading this book. Some people use the word "buzz" to describe a spike in word of mouth—when something is talked about for a short period of time. In this book "buzz" refers to all the person-to-person communication—everything that is communicated verbally and visually—among current, previous, or potential customers.

Some buzz randomly springs up among people as part of their social interactions, and I'll discuss this kind of small talk later in the book. But I'm more interested in buzz that is *not* random—buzz that is triggered by something that a company does.

In Amy Rathke's case, that trigger was a bus.

Tootsie

Bruce Palmer was never too happy with the way many potential students first encountered NOLS. As the director of admissions and marketing for NOLS, he always felt that a bunch of glossy brochures on top of a table don't do justice to the school, which is all about being active in the wilderness. The idea of a road show percolated in his mind for a while. At one point he even started writing a plan involving a bus that would tour the country, spreading the word about the school. But that plan stayed on his hard drive, because it contradicted a fundamental value of the school—being environmentally responsible.

Then one day in 2003, two grads from a recent course, Lindsey Corbin and Logan Duran, visited NOLS headquarters in Lander, Wyoming, in an old school bus that had been converted to run on recycled vegetable oil. They were traveling from Middlebury College in Vermont to Conway, Washington, where they were going to drop off Thomas Hand, a friend from school, at his NOLS course. Their bus looked like a quintessential "hippie mobile," with a funky landscape scene painted on its exterior.

This wasn't exactly what Palmer had in mind, but as the students left, he and Brad Christensen, the school's Webmaster, looked at each other.

"You know, I think it would be kind of cool if we did something like that," Christensen said.

"Yeah. This was the only piece that was missing from my plan," Bruce Palmer replied.

The ideas started flowing. NOLS would get its own veggie bus, albeit one that looked a little more professional. It would have solar panels for electricity and a climbing wall on the side, and the crew who'd drive it would be trained to teach things like fly-fishing and wilderness medicine. Silk, the soy milk company, agreed to fund this project. Palmer and his team found a bus and tracked down someone who could convert it to run on recycled vegetable oil.

Soon the bus was on the road. The team called it Tootsie.

Running the bus requires constant scouting for vegetable oil. It's not hard to find used vegetable oil—almost any restaurant has it—but it *is* hard to find used vegetable oil that's good enough for Tootsie. Oil mixed with burger grease? Not so good. Oil with bacon juice? Sadly, no. Tootsie will only run on pure vegetable oil.

Seeking out this oil became a way of getting NOLS alumni talking. Alumni are notified before the bus visits their campus; sometimes they go along to find the oil and help filter it, a slimy and slippery job that always gives them something to tell friends back at the dorm: how the owner of this Chinese restaurant tried to talk them out of ruining a perfect engine, or how the entire staff of that restaurant came outside to take pictures. Back on campus, alumni often bring their friends to the bus to show them how it works—*and* to tell them about NOLS.

The bus's interior walls are decorated with a collage of alumni pictures. A photo of someone in climbing gear sticking the flag of Whitman College in the snow. Three young women in a boat and a scribbling in permanent pen: "Baja '03 La Tigrs." There are pictures of people in meadows and mountains, white rapids and calm waters, deserts and forests, all with their own codes and little inside jokes, telling a story that you may not get, but you can see by the facial expressions of those who do that it is incredible. There's something real about these pictures. They are not neatly framed. They look like what's on your friend's dorm wall.

Sometimes an alum finds his picture on the wall that was sent in by somebody else from his group. This always triggers some talk: "This was awesome. It's at base camp. We had the best lunch ever." And a story follows.

A man named Randy whom I met on the bus one day in upstate New York told me that back in 1984 he took some time off from college to do a spring semester in the Rockies with NOLS. He has fond memories of the school. Now, twenty-three years later, he brought his teenage daughter along to meet the NOLS folks. She's looking into taking a course too. Remarkably, Randy had been researching the possibility of getting a veggie-powered vehicle for about a year, and when he heard that NOLS had one, he felt yet another connection to the school and its goals.

NOLS grads really get into it. They put up posters all over campus. They go to nearby schools and talk to people. They send e-mails to groups that they belong to—the marching band or the chess club. On the day the bus arrives, grads don backcountry gear and huge backpacks, carry maps and compasses, and walk around campus to draw attention to themselves. They talk to people, hand out flyers, and chalk sidewalks pointing people to the bus.

Now back to Amy Rathke. Amy was too busy with classes and work on the day the bus visited Willamette to participate in any organized activities. She did stop by in the morning to say hi, though. And everywhere she went that day, she told people about the bus. "I was so excited to have the NOLS bus on campus," she remembers. Later that day, as she walked to the commons to get some food, Ashley Lewis, who worked on the bus, waved her to come over.

"Hey, hey!"

Amy went over to the bus.

"Everyone who came by today came by because they said *you* sent them," Ashley told Amy.

Tootsie triggers conversations. It reminds people of experiences they may have forgotten. Perhaps more important, the bus gives them an opportunity to talk about the school once again. It's not that Amy Rathke forgot about NOLS, but after she told all her friends about it, fewer and fewer occasions to talk about her experience presented themselves. Until Tootsie showed up.

Tootsie also turns heads on the street. One time a man who noticed the sign on the back of Tootsie announcing that it ran on vegetable oil followed the bus for one hundred miles on the way from Utah to Nevada because he had to know how. The bus, especially in its first couple of years, generated lots of media coverage too: eighty-five local TV news stories, twenty radio news stories, seventy-five newspaper stories, and features on CNN Radio, Fox TV, the Weather Channel, and CBS MarketWatch.

Is the bus the only way to generate buzz for NOLS? Of course not. About 80 percent of NOLS students hear about the school by word of mouth, which is largely fueled by students' experiences. But the bus starts conversations. Enrollment has been going up since Tootsie joined the marketing team, and Palmer believes that the bus has significantly increased the school's visibility, giving it further advantages when it comes to partnerships.

In the spring of 2007 in a parking lot in Charlotte, North Carolina, Tootsie encountered the grandfather of promotional vehicles, the Wienermobile. The excited bus crew posed next to the playful, hot-dog-shaped Oscar Mayer car.

The encounter reminds us that some aspects of word-of-mouth

marketing are not new. The Wienermobile has been around since the 1930s and yet still garners excitement. Mollie Conway, who drove one in the 1980s, told *American Demographics* about people running up to the Wienermobile and kissing it. One lady chased it for a block and a half.

What would happen if every company had some touring vehicle? Let's hope this doesn't come to pass. My point is not that every company needs to have a veggie bus. It's an excellent example of the kind of initiative that triggers conversations and reminds people about your product, but it's certainly not the only one.

Bob Dylan

In the opening segment of *Don't Look Back,* a documentary about his 1965 UK tour, Bob Dylan stands in an alley in London, singing "Subterranean Homesick Blues" and dropping cue cards with key words from the song. When he drops the last card, he steps off-camera. Two people who were talking in the background throughout the song (poet Allen Ginsberg and singer-songwriter Bob Neuwirth) follow.

In 2007 Dylan made this clip available to the public. Anyone could type his or her own text on those cards and watch Dylan sing "Subterranean Homesick Blues" while dropping the cards with the new text. So instead of loaded words such as "basement," "pavement," "medicine," or "government," a fan can write something like "Hey, Mark! What's up? Remember the ten dollars you owe me? Cheers from Joe!" and Bob will drop those words as if they were his own. Following the ten cards filled out by the user, the last four cards advertised a new boxed set that was to be released on October 1, 2007.

If you're a Dylan fan and you see an ad on TV announcing a

new boxed set, you'll make a mental note of it; it's even possible that you'll mention it to someone. But if you get a personalized video like this one from your friend Dave, it may prompt a different reaction. You always knew that you had a poem inside you, and wouldn't it be fun to write a few words yourself? (Surely it would be better than whatever Dave came up with.) Above all, it would look cool—all words look cool when the twenty-four-year-old Dylan throws them in the wind. Then you can e-mail them to a few friends from college, and to that girl from junior year. Wait, you'll write a special one for her . . . Over 250,000 customized messages were sent to friends, and these messages were viewed about 2.3 million times.

What makes this such a good trigger? A lot of things. First, the idea is brilliant: It lets Dylan fans personalize a classic. So is the execution. Consider the video's length, for example. The original is over two minutes long and includes sixty-four cue cards. This would have demanded a lot of the average person, so the creators cut it down to thirty seconds and ten cards. "It has to be easy," says Owen Matthews, of ten4design, the London-based company that created the viral video. "People don't want to spend ages putting something together." The best triggers are simple. All the work that went into this (the thirty-second video consists of about six hundred frames, and Matthews had to modify over four hundred of them manually) is invisible to the user, who simply types in a few words.

Not everyone liked it. Some people were simply opposed to any kind of viral marketing. Others were diehard Dylan fans who objected to the artist's involvement in such a blatant act of marketing. He'd already taken some heat for doing ads for Cadillac, Victoria's Secret, and other companies, but this video took things to a new level by allowing people to mess with the art itself. Someone told me it felt almost like Michelangelo encouraging people to climb up on the roof of the Sistine Chapel and stick their faces through holes where Adam's and God's faces had been.

But many others loved it. I sent this to a couple of friends who I knew were Dylan fans.

My cue cards asked them if they saw it and what they thought. One of them responded (through cards too): "Cool . . . Good to have Dylan to get us together . . ." Another one, the biggest Dylan fan that I know, wrote: "Oh, this is unbelievably cool!!!!!! Wow, I'm blown away. Thanks for sharing. It made my day."

She also said that she would be sending it out to friends. In other words, the trigger worked.

Built-in Trigger

In the last months of 1999 you could hardly go to a school in the United States without seeing some stamp-sized photos posted on binders, skateboards, and lockers. My daughter Maya, who was in high school at the time, had a picture stuck on her school binder of her friend Caitlin and herself. "Everyone had them all over their binders," Maya remembers.

In this case, visual buzz was critical. Those stickers served as visual comments that communicated a very specific message to kids about a new product called the i-Zone camera from Polaroid. In December 1999 the i-Zone became America's best-selling camera. Since then Polaroid has been swept away by a tsunami called digital photography, but our focus here is not on Polaroid's overall strategy but on how at a certain point in time it triggered buzz. In this respect, the i-Zone was a tremendous success, and not a coincidental one.

What triggered conversations among high school kids in this case were those stamp-sized photos. But in this case too, buzz didn't just happen by itself. It was the result of a series of design and marketing decisions. I'll focus here on just one. To understand the background for that decision we need to go back to 1997, a couple of years before the camera was released, to the busy streets of Tokyo.

Clifford P. Hall, Polaroid's general manager of new product development, was on a visit to Tokyo when he noticed a habit of local teenage girls. Two or three or even five of them would squeeze into a photo booth to take a picture. These photo booths, called *purikura*, were introduced in Japan in the mid-1990s and by 1997 could be seen everywhere. After the picture is taken, the machine prints a sheet with pictures that can be divided among the group. And, an important detail: The reverse can be peeled off, so you get not just a picture but a sticker.

"There were all these sticker booths everywhere," says Sandra B. Lawrence, who at the time was vice president for new product and product planning at Polaroid and also frequently traveled to Japan. "And kids had stickers on everything—on their books, on their little photo albums, on their cell phones."

Polaroid had been trying for years to bring young people back to instant photography. They knew that young people loved Polaroid partly because when they used the cameras, they could be a little naughtier than they could in pictures that needed to be developed by their parents. It was also clear to the company that social connection is an important driver of sales for teenagers—photographs are made to be shared. On their trips to Japan, the Polaroid executives saw how putting a bit of adhesive on the back of a photo takes this sharing thing to a totally different level. They started thinking about the camera not just as a photo camera but as a "*sticker* camera."

Few success stories can be attributed to one element. The i-Zone's cool design, its pricing, the promotion at Wal-Mart—these and other factors all played a role in its success. But the decision to add adhesive material to the back of the stamp-sized pictures made all the difference in the world in terms of buzz. Now, each time one of these stickers came out of an i-Zone camera, it acted as a visual comment about the i-Zone and triggered a conversation about it.

A trigger is not necessarily something that you slap on as an afterthought. In fact, the best conversation triggers are built into the product itself.

"I Love EndNote"

On August 15, 2007, a blogger from Madison, Wisconsin, named K8 made a public confession about some strong feelings she harbored toward a piece of software: "I love EndNote." She wrote, "This is serious love, although not quite on par with my love for shoes." The following day, someone named jordynn posted a comment on K8's blog saying that EndNote indeed is a big help and that it had shaved months off of her dissertation writing time.

What prompted these comments? Here we come back to the deepest driver of buzz—the user experience. For nine years, while I was VP of marketing for Niles Software, the company that made EndNote, between 40 and 60 percent of our customers told us they first heard about EndNote not from advertising, not from an article, not from a dealer, but from another person. And there is no doubt in my mind that the main driver behind this word of mouth was the customer experience: the fact that the software solved a messy problem of compiling bibliographies, the way the software felt, how easy the software was to use, how fast our technical support people responded to questions. User experience is the foundation of word-of-mouth marketing.

Some people miss an important point here. This "customer

experience" didn't happen by itself. It was the result of 1,001 small and big decisions. The outcome of many arguments and debates about the user interface. The result of many hiring and staffing decisions.

And throughout the years of marketing the product, we continually looked for ways to prompt additional conversations. Here's one example. When we introduced EndNote for Windows in 1995, we sent each user of EndNote for Macintosh one coupon that he or she could pass along to a colleague who used Windows. The coupon gave that person the opportunity to buy one copy of EndNote for $99. Our Macintosh users loved our software, and they knew that $99 was a great deal.

An acquaintance of mine who was the only PC user in a Mac environment told me that *nine* of her colleagues each gave her a coupon. Beyond just anecdotal evidence, we know that more than 20 percent of those coupons were redeemed. We triggered tens of thousands of conversations by making it easy for our customers to spread the word to their peers.

Here's how this idea works on a much larger scale. We all know about Ben & Jerry's Free Cone Day, a tradition that goes back to 1979. Once a year the company gives a free ice cream cone to anyone who walks into its stores. Now, if you give people free ice cream, of course they'll talk about it, but how can you trigger *additional* conversations? In April 2008, Ben & Jerry's put on Facebook a virtual ice cream cone which could be given as a gift to friends to remind them of the special day. Within hours, 500,000 Facebook users gave each other free ice cream cones! The virtual cones acted as conversation starters that drove people to the stores. As Katie O'Brien, who helped oversee the campaign for Ben & Jerry's, said, "We gave away 500,000 virtual cones, and in real life we gave away about a million."

. . .

Some people like to say that word-of-mouth marketing can be summarized by one simple principle: Delight your customers and they will talk about you. This is certainly the foundation of good word-of-mouth marketing, but this principle doesn't fully explain the word of mouth that was created about NOLS, Dylan, i-Zone, EndNote, and Ben & Jerry's.

Over the past few years a whole industry has emerged around word-of-mouth marketing. In conferences and meetings I sometimes hear about *the* way to do it. But I think these few examples demonstrate that there's more than one way to trigger conversations. In the case of NOLS, buzz was triggered by a veggie bus. Dylan fans were triggered by an invitation to participate. Buzz about the i-Zone camera was triggered by a sticker. Some talk about EndNote was triggered by a coupon. Ben & Jerry's built buzz around a Facebook giveaway. In short, there are many ways to get people talking.

"I Haven't Read This Book, but . . ."

2

A couple of years ago I read an excellent book by Stanford professor Morris Fiorina called *Culture War?* I was intrigued by the concept of the book, which questioned the notion of a polarized America, and wanted to read more on the subject. So I started looking for books with a similar theme, and as I did, the review of one such book caught my attention. It wasn't the content of the review that piqued my interest but the fact that the reviewer gave the book three stars (out of five) although she openly admitted that *she had not read it.*

As someone who's gotten some three-star reviews, I can tell you that they aren't much fun. You work hard writing a book and someone tells you that the result is just . . . okay. At the same time, you know that this is that person's opinion and you totally respect it. But a three-star review from someone who hasn't even read your book?

I became curious about this, so I decided to check if this is a rare occurrence or a trend. Since Amazon enables searching within its reviews, I searched for the phrase "I haven't read the book," and a new world was opened to me. One review I came across was written by a kid who was reviewing a book about fishing authored by his history teacher. "I haven't really read the book, but I don't have to," the young critic said. "I think this book is really informative, and the pictures are pretty cool looking. You did an awesome job," the kid wrote, congratulating his teacher, and he awarded him five stars.

A reviewer of a different book wrote: "This guy is my professor this semester"—again a teacher! "He seems to be a strict individual but not to a point of being unyielding. I trust that this book will be an engaging read." This reader gave his professor's book three stars. Why three stars and not four or five or one? Somebody who reviewed *The Truth (with jokes)* by Al Franken gives us a peek into the decision process of readers who don't read: "I haven't read this book yet, but I'll give it four stars. It is probably good but probably not as good as *Rush Limbaugh Is a Big Fat Idiot.*"

Reading reviews by nonreaders became a bit of a hobby of mine, and I now have a small collection of them. I should note that the collection is minuscule in size when you compare it with the vast number of reviews on Amazon that are written by people who read the books they are reviewing. But this incident

opened my mind to something more important—the link between consumer experience and word of mouth. How much
buzz is based on experience and how much of it is not?

Robert East is a professor at Kingston University in London
who has studied this phenomenon. For several years now, his
students have been delivering surveys to people's homes or
stopping people on street corners to ask them questions about
the products and services they talk about. In studies that Dr.
East conducted on word of mouth about cameras, leather goods,
computers, and cell phones, he found that 30 percent of the negative word of mouth was about brands that had never been
owned by the people who talked about them. So, for example, 33
percent of those who gave negative advice to a friend about a
camera had never owned that brand of camera.

While at first I was a little shocked by these figures, after
some thinking they made more sense to me. As we consider purchasing a product, we cannot help but form an opinion about it.
Since it's impossible for one human being to read all books, for
example, we use shortcuts such as reviews, comments from
friends, and media appearances by the author to form some initial opinion about a book. There's nothing wrong with this, of
course. The problem starts when we use these shortcuts to form
an opinion that we then pass along as if we had had the experience. In this sense, the reviewers on Amazon who tell us that
they have not read the book are being fair in that they honestly
admit that they haven't had the experience.

But I think that most people would agree that there is something problematic with reviewing and rating a book without
reading it, even if you disclose that fact. Why? In its purest form,
word of mouth is a filtering mechanism that we use in order to
find good products. In a society where every person recommends
only products that he or she personally tried and liked, good
products will quickly rise to the top. When people are using

other considerations (such as "This guy is my teacher") or simply relaying something that they heard, you get what can be best described as a buzz bubble, as depicted in another gem I found: "I haven't read this book, but judging from the online reviews below, I don't think it's a very good book" (one star).

What Can You Do about It All?

From a marketer's perspective, there is something scary about this phenomenon—that people who have never experienced your product or service (and maybe never will) are badmouthing it. What can a company do?

A good starting place is to look at different sources of buzz. In his book *The Ultimate Question*, Fred Reichheld classifies customers into two basic categories: promoters and detractors. Promoters are those who are extremely likely to recommend your company after some experience, and detractors are those who are not likely to do so. As East and others have shown, though, some word of mouth is generated by people who have never used your services, so I think it's useful to think about four groups of people: experience-based promoters ("I tried it. It's great"), experience-based detractors ("I tried it. It sucks"), secondhand promoters ("Jeff says it's great"), and secondhand detractors ("Joe says it sucks").

Your main goal is to maximize the number of experience-based positive comments. Why? Because research shows that these comments are more likely to bring sales. And that's why some of the triggers that I described in the first chapter are so important—you create reminders so that people who had a positive experience with your brand talk about it more. This will not stop the secondhand detractors from talking, but it will reduce the percentage of their comments in the overall mix.

What about the secondhand promoters? Their ability to create sales is not as high as that of the experience-based promoters, but it is not insignificant. They should be triggered to keep spreading the word, and, equally important, to actually use the product.

Another critical strategy, which I explore in Chapter 6, is listening to negative word of mouth. By doing so you achieve two goals: first, you can find unhappy customers (experience-based detractors), solve their problem, and possibly turn them into promoters. Even more important, you may identify problems in your system that will allow you to improve the experience of future customers and reduce additional negative comments.

What can you do about people who never tried your product and still say bad things about it, those secondhand detractors? First, you should listen to them too. They may be repeating a valid complaint, thus helping you identify a problem that is fixable. You can also try to find them and let them test the product, although this may be impractical in many cases. Perhaps the most important thing here is to build an immune system that will reduce the impact of their negative comments on the rest of your audience. There's a name for this immune system. It's called reputation, and it is affected by the consumer experience with your product and by what people have heard about you over the years. This is where advertising and public relations can help in setting the facts straight. Word-of-mouth marketing does not work in isolation.

The main point is this: A firm can and should be proactive about minimizing unjustified negative word of mouth and maximizing positive word of mouth. You can't afford to leave things to chance.

Positive or Negative?

Before you get too upset about people who badmouth your company without ever trying your product, you should know that recent research actually shows that most word of mouth is positive. The Keller Fay Group, for example, a marketing research firm that focuses on word of mouth, reports that 64 percent of conversations about brands are classified by their study's respondents as "mostly positive," a figure that is *eight* times higher than the 8 percent who classify the conversations as "mostly negative."

Why? One explanation is that negative word of mouth tends to suffocate itself. Dr. Barak Libai from Tel Aviv University explains that a product that typically generates negative word of mouth gradually limits its own potential to spread. An extreme example of this can be found in the case of Momenta, a computer that was introduced in the early 1990s. People who tried the new computer didn't like it and told their friends to avoid it. Those people followed their friends' advice. Some of them relayed the negative word of mouth to others, who avoided it too. Soon there were fewer and fewer people with Momentas and thus fewer and fewer people to spread word of mouth about them. Today nobody talks about Momenta, and you have probably never even heard of it until now.

Another explanation is that word of mouth is about solutions. Jon Berry, the coauthor of *The Influentials*, says that when asked for advice, people want to help by making a recommendation. Yes, they may also mention what to avoid, but ultimately, the person seeking the advice wants to know what to do. Again, this increases the volume of positive comments.

A third explanation has to do with the simple fact that we talk about our experiences, and overall we have more positive experiences as consumers than bad ones. I know this is hard to believe sometimes, but if you record all of your experiences as a consumer for one day, you'll see that it's true. The key is not to record only the time you call the phone company to discuss your bill, but to notice everything, from the delicious granola you have in the morning to the cushiony seats of your car, the sound of your car stereo, the speed of your highly functional laptop, your steaming cup of coffee, and so on.

While the fact that there's so much positive word of mouth may give you a warm and fuzzy feeling, it is not necessarily good news for your company. To understand why, let's look at a simple example. Suppose that you own a company called Brown and you're competing against a company called Green. You sample five hundred customers in your category. Seventy percent say that they spread positive word of mouth about Brown (your company) and 30 percent say that they spread positive word of mouth about your competitor, Green. When you get the results, do you do a touchdown dance around the office or do you crawl under your desk and into a fetal position?

The answer, of course, is that it depends. If Brown has a 95 percent market share and Green has a 5 percent market share, this is a reason for your competitor to be pretty happy, because it means that it gets tons of recommendations, even from people who use your product.

It's not enough to have "good word of mouth." As Robert East puts it, "To do well, a brand must get more [positive word of mouth] and less [negative word of mouth] than would be expected on the basis of market share." This again demonstrates the need for proactively increasing your positive word of mouth.

Words! Words! Words! I'm so sick of
words!
—Eliza Doolittle, in the song "Show Me"

The New Buzz

3 **So what exactly has changed**
since 2000, the year the first edition of this
book went to press? One thing is the volume. Back in
2000 there was already a lot of online buzz, but in the
past few years, with the advent of blogs, social networking sites, and the continuing growth of the Internet, the
volume of chatter has become astounding.

Another significant development is that "word of
mouth" is no longer just about words. The power of old

online buzz, mostly text-based, is now multiplied by visual buzz. After all, there's a huge difference between reading that a hotel room was dirty and actually seeing the dirty mattress and the used needles videotaped by an outraged guest. There's a difference between reading that you can build cool robots using Lego Mindstorms and actually seeing these robots in action on YouTube.

A trend I identified in the first edition but have since seen intensify is the beginning of a major power shift ushered in by the growing influence of Generation Y, the 60 million people born between 1979 and 1994, as well as those even younger. For Gen Y, asking for advice online is second nature. Word of mouth is how they shop.

Sharing everyday experiences online has also become a way of life for young people. In December 2007, the Pew Internet & American Life Project reported that 64 percent of those aged twelve to seventeen who used the Internet participated in one or more content-creating activities. Nearly half have posted photos where others could see them. And because these younger generations share more of their daily experiences with the rest of the world than older people, they also share more information about the products and services they use. As they gain buying power in the next ten years, expect buzz to become even more important.

In the early years, online buzz was transmitted from people's homes. This is changing too. An explosion of wireless communication devices has increased customer connectivity. Thanks to constantly evolving wireless devices, customers will become even more connected to a vast depository of opinions, often right at the point of purchase.

So what happens when millions armed with digital cameras, cell phones, and laptops share their lives on Facebook, blogs, Twitter, MySpace, and YouTube? Something interesting happens to buzz: People have more opportunities to observe and listen to each other. We often think of word of mouth as something that originates in enthusiasm, and that's certainly an important ingredient. But another big part of word of mouth is small-talk buzz—conversations about products that are simply part of our everyday interactions. This small talk can occur anytime, not simply when someone asks about a product, and new technologies that let us share our experiences increase small-talk buzz dramatically.

What Can You Do about All This?

At this point, it makes sense to return to NOLS, the organization I discussed in Chapter 1. Such a group could stand on the sidelines and watch this kind of small-talk buzz play out, or it could try to encourage even more of it. Making this decision wasn't easy for the school. The thought of encouraging students to post pictures online made everyone pretty nervous. What if students posted risqué pictures, the kind that might scare parents, or pictures that are against the school's "leave no trace" philosophy?

After the initial hesitation, the folks at NOLS realized that students can post risqué stuff online with or without the school's involvement. In the same way that students talk about NOLS in their dorm room, they also talk about NOLS on Facebook, MySpace, Flickr, and YouTube—with one huge difference: Their conversations, at least some of them, are public.

So NOLS chose to get involved. Amy Rathke (yes, the same Amy Rathke who back in 2004 told everyone at Willamette that the NOLS bus was coming) was selected as NOLS's first social network engineer.

After she graduated from Willamette, Amy spent seven months on the bus, touring the country and learning firsthand that she wasn't the only one who had so much love for this organization. It was Amy's job to manage this excitement online, and to get more people to post their pictures and talk about NOLS. So she started working on the school's blogs. She also put together an instruction sheet for how to post pictures on Flickr. (With all the talk about this tech-savvy generation, some people assume that they know everything. They don't.) She created a page on MySpace that allows NOLS alumni to befriend the school. She started promoting the NOLS alumni group on a Facebook page one alum had started.

Luke, a high school student I met on the NOLS bus, stores the pictures from his NOLS course on Facebook. There are pictures of him hiking and cooking and camping at the Wind River Wilderness course he took last spring. How do these pictures create buzz? Here's how he puts it: "People check it out and say, 'Hey, where did you go hiking?' And I say, 'Oh, I was out in Wyoming for a month.' 'A month? Where?' 'NOLS, it's this great course.'"

A big part of what the marketing team at NOLS does now is facilitate and trigger such conversations, making it easy for prospective students to meet alumni online. If you're considering taking a course, they will put you in touch with people you can talk with. Once you've enrolled, you join a small online group with the folks who will join you in the wilderness. Amy shows instructors how to blog. The marketing team does what they can to make it easy for people to share their experience with others.

A search for the word "NOLS" in Flickr.com in April 2008 found over 25,000 hits. It's a new form of buzz. It's visual. It's raw. And it's for the whole world to see. Actually, you may want to put the book down now and take a look at some of these pictures. They will tell you the story of NOLS better than any words that I can write. You'll see the people who participate and the amazing places they've traveled to. You'll see them climbing, hiking, sailing, laughing. The pictures are posted by students, by staff, by alumni, and together they create a living brochure that is searchable, authentic, and ever-changing. While you're at it, you may want to spend some time on the NOLS alumni group on Facebook. "Any NOLS alumni living in Beijing?" one person asks. "Heya! Any DC NOLS alums going to the reunion on Saturday?" Or "Anyone living in the Denver area who wants to get out climbing/hiking/skiing?" The page is brimming with life and stories, inside jokes and memories.

The Other Side

NOLS's experience online sounds like a walk in the park, but anybody who tells you that dealing with the online world is easy has never been flamed.

Back in the 1990s our company hosted the EndNote user group. EndNote users loved our software, a fact that was usually reflected in their postings. But they could also be merciless. These were academics, smart and eloquent people who knew how to be sarcastic when they wanted to. When they didn't like something we did, we heard about it. We once announced the Windows version of EndNote and were late in shipping it. Very late. We were (justifiably) criticized. ("Criticized" is an understatement.)

This is the other side of the new buzz, and it's not going to go away. Customers are brutally honest as they share information online—the good, the bad, and the ugly. Consider the following customer comment in response to a post on Toyota's official blog: "As a Toyota owner, I am absolutely DISGUSTED by your hypocrisy and your absurd double standards." Another one: "Shame on your shadowy works, and lame excuses." And another one: "Toyota, you have got mud on your face this time."

There were more than one hundred comments in response to that particular post, most of them negative. Toyota could have filtered out these messages. It didn't. Except for spam, obscene language, and off-topic postings, Bruce Ertmann, the corporate manager of consumer-generated media at Toyota, says the company doesn't filter anything out. We had the same policy with the EndNote newsgroup, and I can tell you that we would sometimes cringe while reading it, but we felt that this was the right thing to do and that really we had very little choice about it. If we didn't let our users express themselves in our forum, they would just find another forum.

Another example from Toyota's short experience with what is called CGM (consumer-generated media): In the spring of 2006, Toyota USA found out that in some of the earliest 2007 Camrys to come off the production line, transmissions were operating improperly. It was impossible to tell which cars the problem would show up in next—any 2007 Toyota Camry XLE was a candidate. In such cases, the car was safe to drive but not smooth, which was terribly upsetting to new owners.

Toyota could have waited by the phone for angry customers to call, but it wanted to do whatever it could to minimize the damage. It decided to be proactive about it.

This was just a short time after Bruce Ertmann started his new position as corporate manager of consumer-generated media. He contacted Edmunds.com, an information Web site for car owners, and asked it to set up a new forum dedicated to this particular problem. Ertmann quickly wrote an explanation of the problem in conversational English and posted it on the forum.

What followed demonstrates several things. First, people appreciate being listened to. "I am impressed by Toyota USA's response to this problem, and specifically to this forum" is just one example of a customer post.

The second is that simply listening won't get you too far. Yes, customers appreciate being heard, but ultimately they want answers. "What must be performed (after you take it to the dealership) to fix it? Has Toyota been able to resolve this problem for future-built Camrys? How will you be able to tell if your Camry might have the possibility for this problem?" are questions from just one customer.

Ertmann addressed each question with the patience of a Dear Abby. That was something that did not escape the attention of forum members, as one of them noted: "Some people have said that Toyota has gotten too big and arrogant, but after your (Toyota's) response to this issue (albeit, it seemed a little reluctant, which I hope will continue to improve) I happen to disagree. It has put to rest my doubts about Toyota caring for it's [*sic*] consumers."

More than anything else, the biggest lesson from this and other discussions is that what Toyota *does* is more important than what Toyota says. Yes, customers appreciate being listened to; yes, you get some brownie points for being proactive, but when the 800 number you refer a customer to doesn't give the answer, or when the transmission problem is not resolved, customers will continue to post and demand to see results.

There's a great scene in the musical *My Fair Lady* where Freddie, who's totally in love with Eliza Doolittle, starts singing a passionate serenade about love, the birds, his heart . . . Eliza cuts him off abruptly: "Words! Words! Words! I'm so sick of words!" She then offers two words of advice on how to win her heart: "Show me!"

Customers are not as sick of words as Eliza. They want to hear what you have to say and will grade you on your sincerity. But more than anything else, they want action. Since each person who encounters your brand can now post a picture, a video, or a story online, what you do matters a lot more than what you say.

The Wisdom of Crowds

Another trend driving the new buzz is the transformation of everyday people into "experts."

When Ruth Reichl moved from Los Angeles to New York City to become the food critic for the *New York Times*, one of the first restaurants she decided to review was the famous Le Cirque. It wasn't until her fourth meal at the restaurant that Mr. Maccioni, the owner of the restaurant, figured out who she was. Once he did, something very interesting happened: Everything improved—the seating, the service, the size of the portions. On visits when she wasn't recognized, Reichl had to wait for half an hour for a table. Did she have to wait for a table on the visit when she was recognized? "The king of Spain is waiting in the bar, but *your* table is ready," the owner told her as he escorted her to the best table in the house. Exceptional dishes like foie gras, lobster, and black truffles were rushed to the table. The raspberries in her dessert were three times bigger than they had been when she wasn't recognized.

In his office overlooking Columbus Circle, Tim Zagat, a tall, gray-haired man, has a twinkle in his eyes as he tells this story. With a ruler in his hand, he points to a page that is framed on the wall behind him—the alternative to reviews by food critics that he and his wife, Nina, created when they worked as lawyers in Paris in the late 1960s. Instead of relying on reviews written by professional critics, Tim and Nina Zagat asked friends for their opinions about various restaurants and compiled the results on a single page. In a different frame behind him, there's another page—the guide they started in 1979 in New York City as a hobby, which eventually became the famous Zagat Survey.

The concept didn't gain immediate popularity, at least not in some circles. When the Zagats sought to get their guide published in the late 1970s, publishers thought it was a terrible idea.

Nobody wanted to touch it, not even Simon & Schuster or Pren-
tice Hall, two publishing houses owned by Gulf & Western,
where Tim Zagat was the chief litigation counsel. "You know you
have a problem when direct reports turn you down," he says.

The Zagats decided to publish the guide themselves. After
printing a bunch of guides, they loaded the family station wagon
with boxes of books and started driving up Madison Avenue and
down Lexington, trying to convince bookstores to put the survey
on their shelves.

One thing became clear pretty quickly: While publishers
thought that nobody wanted to hear what nonexperts think about
restaurants, "regular" people very much wanted to hear exactly
that. The Zagat Survey did well right from the start, and after
some media coverage in the mid-1980s and strong word of
mouth, it became the bestselling book in New York City. This
doesn't prove, of course, that the survey reflects the truth better
than a review by an expert, but it does prove that *more people think*
that the survey reflects the truth better than a review by an
expert.

Does it? Tim Zagat points out that he has nothing against
restaurant critics. There's room for both. In fact, the Zagat Survey employs food critics in different cities as one way to detect
any unreasonable ratings. But having reviews by a large number
of people, he points out, has some advantages. One is depicted
in the story about Reichl: When critics are recognized (and they
often are), they are extremely likely to be treated differently, and
so they are rating a level of service that you and I are not likely
ever to experience.

In his book *The Wisdom of Crowds*, James Surowiecki lists four
elements that make it likely for a group judgment to be accurate:
aggregation, diversity of opinion, decentralization, and independence. Aggregation is, of course, what a system like Zagat is all
about. Diversity of opinion means that each person in the group

should draw from some private information. In the case of a restaurant review, it comes from the fact that each person's experience is unique, based on several factors. Each of the ninety-seven people who reviewed Le Cirque on Zagat.com after it moved to its new location had a unique experience in terms of the time visited, the food ordered, the waiter serving, and so on. Decentralization refers to people's ability to specialize and draw from local knowledge. On one page of reviews of Le Cirque on Zagat.com, I find reviews submitted from New York, Turkey, Arizona, New Jersey, California, Florida, Washington, D.C., and Texas. All of these reviewers saw the restaurant from slightly different angles. Independence means that the opinions of participants should not be influenced by each other's opinions. The fact that Zagat reviewers don't consult with each other before they rate is an advantage.

What about manipulation? In the same way that a restaurant owner can treat a critic better, he (or his competitor) may post reviews online. In the war against manipulation, a rating system has several weapons. Perhaps the most powerful one is the number of participants. "So many people participate in the survey that the number of people who may have personal interest is insignificant," says Nina Zagat. The 2008 San Francisco Zagat guide is written by 8,161 people. If a particular restaurant does not get enough reviews, a dash appears instead of a number. If there are fewer than one hundred reviews, an upside-down triangle denotes caution. Another powerful weapon possessed by a rating system is simply knowing the normal behavior of respondents. This allows the people who run the survey to detect any oddities and examine these reviews more closely. People do sometimes try to game the system, and at Zagat there's a team, and not a small one, that's always on the lookout for suspicious things. In the end, I agree with Nina Zagat that the numbers make a difference. Once a survey like this reaches a certain number of people, it becomes almost impossible to manipulate the outcome.

We see the world through filters. Ruth Reichl is a filter. Zagat is a filter. It's not that people no longer trust the Ruth Reichls of the world. A person like Reichl brings tremendous knowledge, and a wonderful way of expressing herself to reviewing. But people want additional filters—multifaceted filters, tools that aggregate the opinions of numerous consumers and present them in one place.

Today we have dozens, if not hundreds, of similar aggregation mechanisms. Yelp hosts reviews of local businesses. Sites such as reddit, del.icio.us, Fark, and Digg let users vote for the best content on the Web. MenuPages stores menus and user reviews of restaurants in New York City. TripAdvisor stores reviews of hotels and attractions.

These tools are far from being ubiquitous, even among young people. A 2007 study of 1,060 students at the University of Illinois in Chicago found, for example, that only 4.4 percent of them visited Digg, and fewer than 1 percent visited Yelp in the past year. Still, there are clear signs that counting on other people's opinions is on the rise. Another 2007 study found that one in four Americans who use the Internet read a review online at least once a month, and 11 percent post ratings and reviews.

The power of these tools doesn't come from their ability to calculate averages, but more from their ability to aggregate so many details in one place. After reading enough reviews of a new electronic gadget, you get an idea of what to expect. To this day I'm thankful to the reviewer on Amazon who explained that on the Olympus digital voice recorder that I bought, the Hold button is also the On/Off button. It would have taken me forever to figure this one out without that helpful hint.

Farther down the road, if enough people submit ratings of products, such tools can cause a real consumer revolution, giving customers accurate information on failure rates of products and customer satisfaction levels. The answer to a question like "Which microwave oven is least likely to break?" exists out there. The problem is that it is currently scattered over several million brains. Aggregated buzz tools could summarize it in one place.

What this means to businesses is that the need for quality will keep increasing. It will also call for higher standards in customer service. Irate customers don't have to wait for these tools to post horror stories online—they can complain online in other ways today. But if service ratings become standard, they will become a competitive tool for companies that get high ratings. For example, before you open a checking account at a bank, you may take a peek at one of these sites to see how customers rate your bank on service. The level of detail these tools will allow goes far beyond what any magazine could ever achieve. Once they're ubiquitous, you'll even be able to compare levels of service in a range of branches in your neighborhood or chart how consistent service has been. (On Yelp, for example, you can already see how a business has been rated over time.)

Overall, aggregated buzz tools are good news for companies with high-quality products and excellent service and bad news for companies that try to get away with less than the highest standards. This doesn't mean, unfortunately, that bad companies will disappear. But the rise of democratic measuring tools is likely, over time, to improve the quality of products and services we use.

The Value of Implicit Recommendations

In 2007 a marketing research company called Marketing Evolution conducted a study to examine the inner workings of campaigns conducted on social networking sites such as MySpace. The study focused on two campaigns, one for Adidas, one for Electronic Arts, and involved a sample of 11,266 people. The main question it was trying to address was this: Where lies the value in such a campaign? Rex Briggs, the CEO of Marketing Evolution, expected to see most value coming from e-mail referrals. This is how things worked in Philips Norelco's edgy Shave Everywhere campaign, which he had studied previously.

I'll focus here on the Adidas campaign. If you visited the Adidas MySpace page around that time, you would have seen two virtual soccer teams, Predator and F50, both made up of famous players. As a visitor, you were asked to choose one team. On the left side of the screen you could see Predator F.C., the red team, which featured David Beckham and some other famous players. On the right side of the screen you saw F50 Club de Futbol, the green team, which featured Arjen Robben and others. Each team had its own signature shoe with special soccer cleats. Visiting each team's portion of the Web site, you could view and rotate the shoe associated with it, the F50 or the Predator.

The two teams had different attitudes as well. Predator F.C.'s motto was "Pure Game." The text highlighted the unbreakable bond between players and things like power and precision. Over at F50, they were talking about soccer as an art, about mavericks running to the beat of their own drums. So you had to decide: Did you see yourself as a Predator or an F50?

Since there was an online competition between the two groups—the winning team would be the one with the most members—you had an incentive to go out and tell all your friends to come to MySpace and join your team.

But buzz is not only about telling. Some recommendations are implicit. You see a Nike poster in a friend's dorm room; perhaps you don't even talk about it, but you noticed it. As Briggs and his staff started analyzing the data, they found that similar implicit recommendations on MySpace profiles were more significant than e-mail referrals. Briggs calls it the "momentum effect"—people affiliate themselves with the company by adding Adidas to their personal page on MySpace, prompting others to do the same. There were several ways a MySpace member could make such a recommendation. He could change the whole appearance of his personal profile by downloading the Adidas "skin," or wallpaper. He could add Adidas to the list of his friends, or he could add an Adidas logo to his page, and so on. Then, when his friends visited his page, they would be exposed to the message in the same way that you are when you visit your friend's dorm room.

Focusing only on those people who changed their opinion in a statistically significant way after being exposed to the campaign, and extrapolating to the number of visitors, Marketing Evolution concluded that 4 million people had a better opinion of Adidas after they were exposed to things that their friends posted on their personal page (or forwarded to them within MySpace). Compare that to about 19,000 people who improved their opinion of Adidas after being referred by a friend through e-mail.

Writing e-mails is relatively hard. Thinking of how to say something that won't make you sound stupid is time-consuming. Adding an icon to your personal profile, however, is quick and easy.

When Marketing Evolution factored in the cost of maintaining a custom community such as Adidas's on MySpace and calculated the return on investment, they reached a number of $0.40. In other words, it cost Adidas forty cents to bring a customer to a high intent to purchase. Briggs comments that this is one of the best returns he's ever seen in marketing. He notes that the results may be an exception and that more research is needed to determine the average of a number of such campaigns.

Still, the story illustrates that the best results don't always come from verbal buzz. Sometimes the biggest value is created by giving your audience a way to affiliate themselves with your brand. Much more research is needed in this area, but I suspect that a significant part of the value of the new buzz will be found not in words but through implicit recommendations like those in the Adidas example.

This phenomenon has existed for many years in the offline world—bumper stickers, branded T-shirts, and branded baseball caps all serve a similar purpose. The online world simply offers more ways to do it and enables you to affiliate yourself with more products. You can wear only one T-shirt at a time, but on Facebook you can cheer for your favorite band, operating system, book, political party, and so on, simultaneously. Some of these icons and links will trigger conversations; at other times your friends will learn about these brands simply because those little markers are there.

Technology

Does technology affect word of mouth?

The dissemination of the telephone in the twentieth century made it possible to talk with people regardless of their location. Then came e-mail, which enables you not only to talk to people anywhere in the world but to talk to many of them at the same time. Now kids hardly use e-mail—they instant-message and text-message, and they post on their friends' Facebook wall. The Web and blogs allow you to broadcast your opinion.

So technology has affected the number of people we can reach. But has it affected word of mouth itself? We have more oppor-tunities to talk, but do we talk about different things? I doubt it. We still talk about ourselves. We talk about our experiences. We brag about our little (or big) victories. We seek advice and solutions. We gossip. We connect.

But some things *have* changed. Look at music. Our ability to share a song with another person is not something that can be compared with our experience on the phone. It's something new. Our ability to share video and pictures, to record our voice and broadcast it, to be part of virtual worlds such as Second Life, to record text that is searchable—all these things change not only the frequency of communication but also its nature.

You can be sure that in ten years communication technology will be different. It's hard to tell now exactly how, but it will have changed. It will be even richer. It will be available anytime anywhere. You might be able to incorporate yourself in a movie and send it to a friend. You might be able to create a convincing avatar of yourself and send it out to tell all your friends about your favorite book. Technology might change in ways that we don't yet see.

One thing is clear. People will have even more opportunities to share their experiences with others—which directly translates to more buzz.

Despite an ever-expanding array of advertising platforms and sources, consumers around the world still place their highest levels of trust in other consumers.

—from a 2007 Nielsen study in forty-seven countries

Why Is Buzz on the Rise?

Why now?

4

Why do we hear so much about buzz and word of mouth? As I discussed in the previous chapter, the Internet has obviously played a major role in the rise of buzz. And yet research shows that most comments about products—about 74 percent of them—are transmitted the old-fashioned way, in face-to-face conversations, and about 17 percent are transmitted by phone, which means that only about 9 percent are transmitted online. So how *exactly* has the Internet, and technology in general, contributed to the rise of buzz?

On the most superficial level, technology has affected the *visibility* of buzz. Even though online word of mouth represents only a small segment of all buzz, it has made buzz visible to marketers. In the past, even marketers who recognized the importance of word of mouth could easily ignore it. Today, buzz is much more in your face. It's hard for a brand manager to disregard a negative blog post that appears at the top of Google's search results. It's hard for a hotel owner to dismiss a negative review on TripAdvisor. It's hard not to pay attention to a movie about your product posted on YouTube. Word of mouth can no longer be ignored.

Marketers also pay attention because they know that this is the beginning of something bigger. Think of all the people on the street with cell phones glued to their ears. You didn't see them in the United States ten years ago. What are they talking about? They talk about life—about who does what with whom and why. They talk about what their boss just told them or why they need to get a new job. They talk about their weekend plans or their trip to the doctor's. In the process, however, they also talk about the stuff they use, the movie they saw last night, the restaurant they're going to, the car they want, what they're going to wear for the concert on Saturday night . . .

And it's not just cell phones, of course. As more people around the world get high-speed Internet access, more people spend more time connected and therefore have more opportunities to talk. As I pointed out earlier, social networking sites such as Facebook, MySpace, LinkedIn, and Bebo give us more opportunities to observe what others are doing. It's easy to ask a quick question via e-mail and even easier by instant messaging.

But perhaps the most important way in which technology has contributed to the rise of buzz is by serving as an accelerator.

People tend to live in social clusters—areas in networks where people are more densely connected to each other—and the Internet has a way of bridging groups.

Let's look at EndNote as an example. Some customers heard about EndNote on the Internet, but from talking to many of our customers over the years, I know that many of them heard about our software not from someone at the other end of the country but from someone at the other end of the hall, or someone they met at a party on campus, or at the lab. Someone at a university would hear about EndNote online and would then tell some people at the cafeteria about the great new software he'd found. One of these people would then post the news in yet another bulletin board or newsgroup, and the news would jump to another university. In other words, it's the combination of online and offline communication that is so powerful.

Something similar happened with the spread of Hotmail. In a story that's achieved mythical status, we always hear about that famous line that made Hotmail viral ("Get your free e-mail at Hotmail.com"), but that line is just one part of the story. The word about Hotmail spread both electronically and through face-to-face conversations. After the first user from a certain town subscribed, the number of subscribers from that town would increase rapidly. The same phenomenon took place in the spread of Facebook and MySpace. Both online and offline communication spread the word.

In any area in life, there's someone who comes up with the "Which one's more important?" question. Which one is more important, speed in developing new products or quality? Which one is more important, long term or short term? And of course there are people who will ask, Which one is more important, online or offline word of mouth? Jim Collins and Jerry Porras talk in *Built to Last* about the "tyranny of the OR." They point out that highly visionary companies liberate themselves from this question. Buzz is another area where this concept applies: It has become such a powerful force these days because of the *combination* of online and offline communication. So when someone asks you, What's more important, online buzz or offline buzz? the correct answer is both.

It's not technology alone, though, that makes word of mouth so important today. To explore an additional reason, I want to tell you about a punk song.

The Song That's a Hit and a Dud

"Lockdown" is a song by a Milwaukee-based punk band named 52metro that perhaps can help us understand one reason that people turn to buzz today. What's so interesting about this song is that it got to the number-one position on a certain online forum because it had been downloaded more than any other song in that forum. At the same time, on a different online forum consisting of very similar people, that same song was downloaded many fewer times. On that second forum, it got to be number forty (out of forty-eight songs).

How could one song rate number one and number forty by two extremely similar groups of people?

Between October 2004 and March 2005, banner ads started appearing on the popular teen Web site Bolt.com. The ads invited readers to click on the ad so that they could listen, rate, and download music. Participants who came to the site saw a list of forty-eight songs by relatively unknown bands.

What the participants did not know was that they were subject to several different conditions. Some participants in the experiment saw just the names of the songs and the bands. For members of this group—the control group—deciding whether to download a certain song was based solely on how much they liked it.

All other participants saw another piece of information. They saw how many people had downloaded each song before them. The researchers created eight "worlds," and users only saw how many people from their world had downloaded a particular song. The researchers, Matthew Salganik, Peter Dodds, and Duncan Watts, didn't manipulate the results. When each world began, all the songs were set to zero. But then something interesting happened. The songs that got downloaded more often by early visitors got downloaded more often by people who visited the site later. A snowball effect was created. What happened to a song early on had a huge impact on its destiny.

Overall, 14,341 people took advantage of the offer and downloaded songs from the site. Faced by a list of forty-eight unknown bands, most visitors clicked on songs that had even the smallest clue that differentiated them from the others: Someone else liked them. This is exactly what happens in so many other areas today. Inundated with choices in the marketplace, we are starving for clues that tell us what's good. We are hungry for buzz.

This is not necessarily new. Consumers in the Western world have been inundated by a wealth of choices for many years now, but it's getting worse. Information overload is nothing new either, but this phenomenon too doesn't show any signs of letting up.

Another issue contributing to the rise of buzz is skepticism. I remember once standing at our booth at a trade show. We were about four weeks away from releasing a new version of our software. A young scientist stopped by the booth, and I showed him how the new software worked. He was impressed, but when I told him that this version was going to be released in a month, he turned around before I could say anything, muttered

"Vaporware," and walked away. It didn't matter to him that I'd just showed him a working version (which had been under development for more than a year). As far as he was concerned, this software didn't exist, and he obviously didn't believe that it was going to be released in four weeks.

Who is considered the most credible source of information about a company? In the 2007 Edelman Trust Barometer, an annual study of credibility and trust conducted in eighteen countries around the world, the top-rated source in the developed world was "a person like me" (along with "doctor or health care specialist"). The CEO of a company was rated number eight and a public relations executive number ten. Similar results were found in developing countries, although there a "financial industry analyst" was number one, followed closely by "a person like me" or an academic. Here too a CEO was rated number eight and a public relations executive number ten.

We are skeptical of information that comes from companies. But we trust people like ourselves.

There are other factors behind the increased attention to word-of-mouth marketing. "In the past thirty years, and particularly in the past ten years, we've seen an exponential increase in media clutter and media fragmentation," says Piers Hogarth-Scott, the cofounder of Yooster, a word-of-mouth marketing and research company. People have so many media outlets vying for their attention that it becomes harder to reach them. Marketers also discovered that even when they reach their audience, people are not engaged in the message.

How then do you engage people? Integration, a marketing research firm based in Cyprus, has conducted hundreds of market contact audit studies, which examine the impact of all forms of contact between top brands and consumers. After reviewing hundreds of studies, Integration determined that word of mouth is the form of contact with the highest capacity to engage consumers. Marketers understand that if they can somehow stimu-late positive word of mouth, they'll engage people in their mes-sage.

Yet another factor contributing to the increased attention paid to word of mouth has been the wide adoption of the Net Promoter Score (NPS) by corporations. NPS is calculated by measuring the percentage of people who are extremely likely to recommend a company (promoters) and subtracting from that number the percentage of people who are very *unlikely* to recom-mend (detractors). There's been a debate about the ability of NPS to predict growth, but one thing is clear: Suddenly everyone is talking about recommendations, which has increased the per-ceived importance of word of mouth.

Indeed, research from all over the world validates the impor-tance of buzz. Nielsen conducted a survey in forty-seven markets around the globe and found that "despite an ever-expanding ar-ray of advertising platforms and sources, consumers around the world still place their highest levels of trust in other consumers." Consumer recommendations were rated as the most credible form of advertising among 78 percent of the study's respondents (26,486 people).

So marketers are paying attention. In 1996 the expression "word of mouth" appeared in *Advertising Age* twice. Both times the story was about brands that got strong word of mouth and were now adding advertising to the mix. Ten years later, in 2006, "word of mouth" appeared in seventy-four articles in this weekly magazine. Marketing publications such as *Adweek* and *Brandweek* show a similar trend.

I'm glad that the marketing world is finally listening. But I also suspect that sooner or later (if it hasn't happened already) somebody will announce the decline of word-of-mouth market-ing or "the death of buzz." As in other fields, trends in market-ing go in and out of fashion, and business magazines have an ongoing need for cover stories that show the triumph of the latest new thing over older ideas and methods. But people will always rely on their peers for information, and the factors that make buzz so important today—communication technology, information overload, skepticism—are not likely to disappear.

In bed, typing this tweet on my iPhone
3G in Safari. It finally feels like 21st
century.

—one of 1,665 mentions of iPhone on Twitter
during the last hour of the day Apple
introduced the iPhone 3G

Can Buzz
Be Measured?

5 **When I worked on the** first edition of

this book, I could find hardly any marketing

research firms that studied word of mouth. With very few

exceptions, research companies ignored word of mouth.

When I tried to discover why, people explained that it

would be prohibitively expensive to measure. Others

doubted that it was even possible to measure something

that is as amorphous, ephemeral, and intangible as buzz.

They had a point: How can you measure something

that happens among consumers in private conversations? Even if people gave you permission to listen to their conversations, how could you keep track of something that's so unpredictable and chaotic?

Seven years later, I'm walking down Church Street in New Brunswick, New Jersey, toward a three-story brick building at the end of the street. On the third floor of the building, a small startup called the Keller Fay Group is dealing with the challenge of measuring buzz.

One of the people behind this effort is Brad Fay, a tall blond man in his forties. In his office, which overlooks an old church, he sits at a desk cluttered with papers and memos. Fay's eyes shine when he invites me to explore buzz in America with him.

"What do you want to see?" he asks. "You can pick any brand, any category."

I choose automotive. Fay pushes some buttons on his laptop and the computer crunches the data for a few seconds.

A chart that depicts the level of the conversation for the different brands appears. We notice that Toyota and Chevrolet ran neck and neck for a while in 2007, until for some reason buzz about Chevrolet peaked in April. Fay points out that Volvo had a low level of conversations but that when you look deeper into the data, you find that 77 percent of the conversations were positive and only 5 percent were negative. He says that this is way above the average. In 1,903 conversations where Ford was mentioned, only 52 percent were positive and 14 percent were negative (the rest were neutral or mixed).

How can Brad Fay tell me all this? Does he eavesdrop on people's conversations in shopping malls? Does he analyze blogs? Does he read other online forums? None of the above.

Mission Impossible

When Brad Fay and Ed Keller started thinking of a way to track word of mouth, some of the initial ideas that came up can best be described as odd. One was to have volunteer customers carry a digital recorder around their necks as they went about their day. This idea was quickly dismissed for obvious ethical and legal reasons.

There was also a practical problem. Lots of conversations don't relate to marketing, and the focus of this research is marketing-related conversations, especially those in which a particular brand is mentioned. This means that even if there were no privacy issues, researchers would have had to sift through thousands of hours of recordings to find these branded conversations.

The solution they found was to rely on participants to report on their conversations. Every day 100 people from all over the United States keep track of their conversations for twenty-four hours and report them into a database. The following day 100 other people do the same thing. There are 700 new reports every week. About 3,000 fresh reports a month. And 36,500 reports a year. As this book goes to print, there are about 60,000 entries in the system.

To make sure people don't forget the conversations they had throughout the day, Keller and Fay created a two-page conversation diary that helps participants take notes. When they have some free time, participants sit in front of their computer and answer detailed questions about each conversation: How many people participated? Was it mostly positive or negative or mixed? What brands were mentioned? Was there any reference to other sources of information? Was there a strong recommendation to buy or try the product?

With a database of thousands of reported conversations, you can start measuring a lot of things. You can check, for example, how much buzz your brand is getting among teenagers, or women, or residents of California. Is your brand mentioned typically on its own, or is it usually compared with other brands, and if so, which ones? Can you see changes in the level of the conversations as a result of certain marketing activities?

"When you do something significantly different with your advertising, it does show up," Fay says. After Super Bowl 2007, Keller Fay and the media specialist company MediaVest found that Coca-Cola, Bud Light, Taco Bell, and Honda enjoyed the highest increase in post–Super Bowl word of mouth. For Coca-Cola, for example, the estimated increase in daily brand mentions was 9 million.

MediaVest also used the database to look at buzz surrounding retailer ads for Wal-Mart, one of its clients. The firm found that magazines were not mentioned frequently in buzz about certain retailers, but ads in newspapers were. There were also significant differences among the retailers when it came to which media worked best. For Target it was mainly newspaper and sales promotions; for Costco it was mainly promotions and point-of-sale displays that were mentioned in conversations.

There's also an open-ended question in the Keller Fay study that allows participants to describe their conversations in their own words. A fifty-six-year-old woman reported talking with a friend about the fact that the colors on Herbal Essences hair coloring don't always come out as shown on the box. A forty-year-old woman shared a conversation she had with her son, who feels that she spends too much time on MySpace. A thirty-seven-year-old man revealed that his friend "misses his Beemer." A twenty-four-year-old woman talked with a relative about a friend who had an accident driving a BMW M3. The car flipped several times and he walked away without a scratch. "Superior automakers," she comments.

What is America talking about? The first thing that you learn from this database is that we talk a lot. In the course of a week, every American has more than one hundred conversations about the fifteen categories that Keller Fay tracks, including automotive, food, and household products. Each American will talk about roughly seventy brands a week, or ten brands a day.

Another thing one learns from the data is that people don't only talk about cool stuff. People talk about their lives, and they recommend or seek advice about the brands around them. This goes against the common belief, fed by the media, that people pay a disproportionately high amount of attention to things like the iPod or Xbox. These products get talked about, but people also talk about Home Depot, Wal-Mart, Chevrolet, and other less glamorous brands.

In general, big brands get more buzz. This is not surprising, really, because people talk about their experiences, and more people experience more commonly used, high-market-share items.

But that's not all I learned from my time at Keller Fay. Most conversations about brands, at a ratio of eight to one, are positive. About half of such conversations are with a partner or a family member. In nearly one in two brand conversations, people refer to things such as advertising, editorial coverage of a product, a Web site, or a point-of-sale display.

What about Online Buzz?

With all the chatter on blogs and other online forums, the Internet seems to offer a great opportunity to listen to and measure buzz. Indeed, around the year 2000 several startups rushed into this space, developing tools to analyze and get insight from online buzz. But if most buzz happens in person and only 10 percent of it is happening online, some people question the usefulness of the Internet as a measurement tool for buzz. Can online buzz serve as a proxy for offline word of mouth?

I spent the day before my visit to Keller Fay at an event on Madison Avenue in New York City organized by Nielsen Buzz-Metrics (now Nielsen Online), a company that measures online buzz. Judging by the crowded room and by the Fortune 500 companies that were present, it's safe to say that many people believe in the value of measuring online buzz.

Why are marketers interested? First, even at just 10 percent of the conversations, there's a lot of online buzz, and the percentages are higher for younger demographics. There are also those who argue that the percentage is actually higher because consumers underreport their online activities. Second, we are very likely to see an increase in the share of online communication in coming years. Third, regardless of the question of online buzz serving as a proxy for offline word of mouth, Nielsen has conducted some studies that show a correlation between online buzz data and sales of products.

Exploring online conversations about your company is something that should be done, with or without the help of a company like Nielsen. Search engines for blogs such as Technorati and Google Blog Search have existed for several years now. Sites such as YouTube, MySpace, Twitter, and Flickr are easily searchable. Listening to what people are saying about your brand online is like participating in a huge ongoing focus group. What are customers talking about when they talk about your product? What other features do they want? What issues are important to them?

Nielsen and other companies measuring online buzz, such as Cymfony, BrandIntel, Biz360, and MotiveQuest, take this listening to the next level by quantifying and analyzing their findings on a regular basis. Nielsen's software, for example, searches the Internet for messages that contain certain brands and keywords.

The software then analyzes the material: Are the messages written by someone young or old? Male or female? Are they positive or negative?

How can a machine determine whether a message is positive or negative? By recognizing patterns. "If you show the machine a thousand comments that are positive toward Colgate-Palmolive and a thousand comments that are negative toward it, then it learns to spot the difference," says Jonathan Carson, president, international, Nielsen Online and BuzzMetrics founder. At around 80 to 90 percent accuracy, the recognition is not perfect. With some additional manual work, its success rate can be improved.

The early clients of BuzzMetrics signed up for this type of consumer insight. "The idea that thousands and thousands of their customers were online, interacting with each other and talking about the products, was quite interesting for them," says Carson.

Measuring online buzz can also help in forecasting. "The premise, we think, is very intuitive," Carson says. "A consumer is oftentimes going to talk about a product before they buy it." In one project, the company measured buzz about low carbs and the Atkins diet and found that it was a strong predictor of sales of the products associated with these diets. When the researchers dug further into the data, they also found that focusing on the most influential consumers—those who created a lot of online content and whose content was cited most often—can improve the results. "That study found that those influencers were as far as fourteen months ahead of the sales of those associated products."

Another study conducted by BuzzMetrics and BASES (a Nielsen Company service) revealed that sales forecasts could be improved by adding buzz to the mix. At first researchers tried to predict sales of a group of consumer packaged goods (CPG) products based on media spending, distribution, and initial consumer scores alone. When they added after-use data on product satisfaction, the prediction improved. And when they added buzz data—in this case, the number of monthly blog postings in the first year of the product—their forecasts significantly improved.

Everybody in this business understands that these are early experiments. Seven years ago, I'd have been amazed at the tools available today. In seven more years, as data increase, tools improve, and new insights emerge, we may look back at today's tools and smile.

Measuring a Buzz Campaign

In recent years we've seen detailed studies aimed at measuring the effectiveness of specific buzz campaigns. In 2003 a company called Rock Bottom was trying to build buzz for its restaurants and breweries. But how do you know if the campaign is generating buzz and, more important, if it's leading to sales?

From April to June 2003, 1,073 people participated in a study conducted by David Godes of Harvard Business School and Dina Mayzlin of the Yale School of Management. Each participant filled out an extensive survey about his or her social activities and knowledge about beer and food. The participants then received via regular mail an information packet that included background about Rock Bottom and some suggestions for creating buzz for it (when to talk, what they might want to say). Participants were directed to a Web site where they were asked to report in detail about any word-of-mouth activity they'd generated in an online form. Over the next thirteen weeks participants were buzzing and reporting.

After thirteen weeks, the two researchers got two sets of

data. First they got all the information reported by participants. Second, they got Rock Bottom's weekly sales data for each of the fifteen markets where the chain operates. Armed with all this data, the researchers looked for a correlation between word of mouth and sales.

Did it work? Yes. The proactive effort was associated with higher sales. The way the two researchers put it (a bit more tentatively): "The firm can, it seems, create exogenous word of mouth among consumers that has significant and measurable effect on sales." This is an important finding that shows how a company can proactively create word of mouth, which in turn leads to an increase in revenue. But a more interesting finding of this study was that some people were more effective than others in creating the kind of buzz that leads to sales.

The 1,073 people who participated in the study did not all come from the same source. Six hundred and ninety-two of them were BzzAgents. BzzAgent is a word-of-mouth company that maintains a panel of volunteers who spread the word about products. The other 381 participants were people who signed up for Rock Bottom's loyalty program (every time they ate or drank there, they earned points that they could exchange for rewards). Based on the extensive data collected about the participants, they could be broken into several groups. Some of them were more socially active; some of them knew more about food and beer. For the Rock Bottom loyalty program members, the researchers also knew their past purchasing patterns. Some could be considered "heavy loyals" and others "light loyals"—people who were part of the program but actually didn't visit the restaurant too often.

The surprising finding of this study was that the heavy loyals didn't bring in a lot of new sales. One explanation is that these people had already done their buzzing prior to this campaign and had already exhausted their reach. The light loyals brought more business, but it was the nonloyals, for whom Rock Bottom was totally new, who brought in the most. In fact, each word-of-mouth discussion by a nonloyal yielded incremental category sales of $192.

My conclusion from this study is not that loyal customers are not important. It is that the importance of different segments can fluctuate over time. Time is a dimension that has been largely ignored in the discussion about word of mouth. Certain people can create a lot of buzz for you at one point and much less buzz a year later.

Some measurement efforts have gone beyond the macro level and the link of buzz and sales. In a study conducted by Dr. Walter Carl from Northeastern University, the focus was on trying to measure and understand the flow of buzz. And it gets pretty detailed. Consider this: On October 15, 2006, Teresa, a thirty-four-year-old mom who lived in Rensselaer, New York, sent an e-mail to ten of her friends and family members about Sonicare Essence, a power toothbrush from Philips. She said in her e-mail that she initially thought it would be just like any other toothbrush but was really surprised when she had a chance to try it out and found it especially helpful for her teenage son. The following day, Laura, a thirty-four-year-old acquaintance of Teresa's from Kingston, New York, reported that she had read Teresa's e-mail and that she was very likely to buy the toothbrush. She also reported that she had already told Bryan, an acquaintance in his thirties, and Joshua, a relative, also in his thirties, about Sonicare Essence.

Though names and specific locations have been changed, this is an actual thread. How do we know all this? The research team gave Teresa "a conversation card" with a unique conversation number and a Web site URL. The card contained smaller, detachable cards, which Teresa was asked to pass along to anyone she talked to about this toothbrush. If she communicated with people online, she simply had to give them the conversation code and the URL.

So, for example, when Vivian, another friend of Teresa's, who lived in Indianapolis, got Teresa's e-mail, she went to the Web site, entered the conversation code, and answered the questions presented to her. She did not report telling anyone else about the toothbrush. Abigail, on the other hand, a thirty-nine-year-old acquaintance of Teresa's from Los Angeles, reported that since she had gotten Teresa's e-mail she had already bought her own Sonicare Essence. During the course of her participation in the study, Abigail reported telling ten other people about the product.

Some people hold the romantic (and naive) view of word of mouth that each one of the ten people who got the e-mail from Teresa would tell another ten people, who would tell another ten, and so on. If this were true, Teresa's message would reach over a million people in just six easy steps. As we have seen in the example, this doesn't happen. Laura told two, Abigail told ten, Vivian told none.

The details we get from such a study are very specific. The thread that started with Teresa reached thirty-seven people in fifty-two days. The seven out of ten people who responded were from a wide geographic spread: New York, California, Indiana, and Wisconsin.

The campaign (also managed by BzzAgent) started on November 7, 2006. The company invited agents according to certain demographics (they had to be older than twenty-five and live in North America). Within two days, 30,000 people in the United States and 3,000 people in Canada signed up. Each participant was then shipped a Sonicare toothbrush (no wonder so many people signed up in just two days) plus five $10 mail-in rebates to give to other people. Three thousand of these people participated in the study run by Dr. Carl. Each of them got, in addition to the toothbrush and the rebate coupon, some conversation cards and a conversation code. The conversation partners contacted by BzzAgents (people like Laura, Abigail, and Vivian) filled out not just one survey but four: one right after they heard about it, and three additional surveys after one, three, and six weeks. Based on what they told him, Dr. Carl was able to determine that on average, this group of people each told 3.64 other people about the product.

In addition to the relay information that Walter Carl was interested in, BzzAgent captured some other data. The study found that 95 percent of agents told at least one person about the power toothbrush they got for free and that on average each one of them told 9.4 other people about it. Based on this, BzzAgent and Dr. Carl calculated the number of people who heard about the product to be 294,690 (33,000 × 0.95 × 9.4). When multiplying this by the average number of people who heard about the toothbrush in each time period and adding the agents themselves, and those who heard from the agents, they concluded that the total reach of the campaign was 1,400,641 people.

Is this an accurate number? We can't know for sure. It's an early study in a new field that relies on the reporting of agents. Still, the data collected by BzzAgent were validated by the conversational partners that reported to Walter Carl. In addition, the study didn't take into account the many people down the line who may have passed on the word, or any buzz that may have occurred *after* the six-week study.

In the past few years there has been a proliferation of research that measures word of mouth. A Carnegie Mellon University study that analyzed over 15 million recommendations exchanged among 3.9 million customers of a large retailer found that 1 out of 69 book recommendations and 1 out of 136 music recommendations resulted in a sale. In another study researchers from the University of Connecticut and Ohio State University analyzed a referral campaign for a telecommunication company and concluded that the return on investment of the campaign was around 15.4 times the cost. (Interestingly, they found here too that the most loyal customers were not the strongest advocates.) Other examples that involve buzz measurement are scattered throughout this book (the Adidas and Bob Dylan campaigns are just two). For those who are interested in learning more, the Word of Mouth Marketing Association (www.womma.org) has already published four volumes on the topic. And while we still have a lot to learn about word of mouth and how to measure it, we've come a long way since the 1990s, when some marketers unequivocally determined that word of mouth cannot be measured.

Insight
and Buzz

6 **When Shirley Polykoff was a** kid, she was proud of her beautiful blond hair. She loved being a blonde, and at age fifteen, as her hair started to darken, she started visiting Mr. Nicholas's beauty parlor, not far from her parents' apartment in Brooklyn. "Mr. Nicholas and I maintained a pleasant fiction," she would write years later. "He didn't bleach my hair. He just lightened the back a little to match the front." Mr. Nicholas understood his customer.

When Polykoff got a job as a copywriter at Foote, Cone & Belding in 1955, she started working on the Clairol account. Hair coloring wasn't socially acceptable in America at the time. The women who dyed their hair were actresses, models, some career girls like Polykoff herself, and a group known as fast women.

Polykoff was going to change that. In order to do so, she first made several observations. She understood that women wanted to get rid of gray hair but that fear of family disapproval prevented them from coloring their hair. She understood that words like "bleach" and "dye" were scary for women.

The line that she came up with for the campaign became a classic. "Does she . . . or doesn't she?" The ads all featured photographs of regular women, often with their kids, with beautiful blond or red or brown hair. The text called to mind a real conversation. "These ads were one woman talking to another, but in the oblique way that people tell you intimate details about themselves," she later explained.

Polykoff also understood that the ads should run not only in fashion magazines read mostly by women, but in magazines like *Life* that are read by the entire family. After all, other family members were the ones who needed to approve of hair dying for it to become acceptable.

Fifty years later, a marketing team at a group called Tremor was trying to gain insights relating to another Clairol product, Herbal Essences—with one big difference. Their objective was not to write another ad. They were trying to create a conversation piece.

Tremor is a business unit of Procter & Gamble that was started in order to stimulate word of mouth. It provides services both to P&G brands (Herbal Essences is one of them) and to outside clients such as movie studios and other manufacturers.

The stigma that was once associated with hair coloring was long gone, but the Tremor team was trying to identify the issues that teenagers deal with when they think about dying their hair. Their research showed something interesting: Fear of disapproval was still a big issue, but this time it was not their family's disapproval they feared as much as the opinions of their peers. As it turned out, young people are scared of what their friends will think about their choice of color. And this gave Tremor an idea for a conversation piece.

What would be a good conversation trigger in this case? What would get teenagers talking to each other about hair coloring and dispel the fear they had about the color choice?

What the Procter & Gamble team ended up creating was a colorful booklet with a hole in the middle. To use the booklet, you put a lock of your hair through the hole to determine the current color of your hair. For example, if you're a blonde, you compare your hair with different shades to determine if you're a light blonde, a medium blonde, or a dark blonde. Once you determine the exact color of your hair, you flip to a page where you can see how your hair will look after being dyed with specific Clairol Herbal Essences. If your hair is light brown, for example, how will it look with Chilean Sunset? Or with Plush Plum?

What do you do if you're a teenage girl and you get something like this in the mail? You probably go to the mirror and try it out, but you discover very quickly that, first, it's not easy (I tried), and more important, standing in front of the mirror by yourself doesn't give you what you really want, which is the help of your friends in choosing the color. If you're a teenage girl who's concerned about what your friends will say about your choice of hair color, this is a perfect conversation hook.

In addition to the color guide mailer, which was sent to several thousand teenagers, P&G built a micro site devoted specifically to the Herbal Essences program that invited visitors to involve their friends in choosing the perfect shade.

Did teenagers talk about Clairol Herbal Essences hair colors as a result of this campaign? According to Tremor, 82 percent of participants shared the materials with five or more members of their social network. That little booklet started a lot of conversations, and national sales volume increased compared to the previous year.

How do you find such a hook? Some people would recommend that you take your creative team, sit in a room, and start brainstorming. Maybe add pizza and beer to the mix. Ideas will emerge.

For Steve Knox, the CEO of Tremor, word-of-mouth marketing starts with understanding what the consumer wants to talk about. "This is really about hard and deep consumer research to uncover, from the consumer's standpoint, what is 'talkable' about your brand," he says. "What is it that they talk about? What would cause them to go talk about it? It's about a lot of listening and stimulation to uncover that unique insight. I wish I could tell you it was easy, but it's not," he adds.

Tremor's methodology involves both quantitative and qualitative methods. The firm's research usually finds six to eight insights about what may be "talkable." It also uses a quantitative predictive methodology that helps identify the message that most consumers would want to talk about.

Knox argues that consumers don't object to advertising if it's relevant to them. But the message they share with their friends will be different from the original marketing message. A BMW owner is not very likely to tell his friend that he is driving "the ultimate driving machine." He is much more likely to talk about the car in a way that is related to his life. In the case of Clairol Herbal Essences, P&G's research found that the message the consumer wanted to hear from advertising was that it works, it produces vibrant colors, and it smells good. This was totally different from the conversation she wanted to have with her friends, which was all about getting reassurance regarding her color choice. The result was that little booklet.

A lot of marketing research still focuses on finding the right message that will persuade a person to buy a product. That's understandable. Everyone wants to find the next "Does she . . . or doesn't she?" The marketing research done by companies like Tremor has a different focus: finding the conversation.

How the Clay Stayed in Cranium

Sculpting with clay is one of the most popular features of Cranium, the megahit game: You make something out of clay and your team members have to guess what it is. "We are still laughing about the fire hydrant I had to construct . . . and how I got Freddie to guess it by including a dog with his leg raised," one woman wrote on her blog. Another blogger wrote how a friend sculpted a Razor scooter that she almost shoved down her partner's throat when he didn't get what it was. When people have to sculpt things like a dimple or a taco, there's going to be some fun.

When Richard Tait worked on developing Cranium with his partner, Whit Alexander, he thought that including clay was a bad idea. He doesn't like clay. "I hated that activity. I didn't want to put it in," he said at a recent conference.

Then one night he was sitting in someone's living room, watching people playing with a prototype of the game that included clay. Tait saw the eyes of one guy in his forties opening as wide as a four-year-old's as he dug his fingers into the clay. Tait was fascinated by the guy. He was having so much fun! "The clay is in," Tait told everyone after this experience.

In the first part of this chapter we saw how listening can help you identify the right hook to improve word of mouth. Listening helps increase buzz in another, more straightforward way: If you listen—if you truly listen—you have a better chance of improving your customer experience and thus increasing word of mouth.

In the case of Richard Tait, he listened with his eyes. Observing how your customers use your product can sometimes be the most effective way to hear them. Intuit is famous for its "follow me home" sessions, where employees observe customers using their software out of the box. A few years ago the QuickBooks division sent more than five hundred employees on three days of follow-me-homes. A similar initiative in the TurboTax division led to major changes in the software. As software developers add features, those features are likely to frustrate users—and not because users are stupid. I had my own eye-opening experience after sitting next to my wife one night as she was using a beta version of EndNote 3.0 for the first time. Daria is a Stanford University professor, but she had no clue how to start using that version. I sat next to her, recorded her actions, and e-mailed my report to our development team. A few months later, based on the input from dozens of other users, we had a version that was easier to use.

Whenever I start talking about listening in my presentations, I see blank faces. People get more excited by the silliest viral ad than by yet another guy talking about listening to your customers. And yet if you truly listen to your audience and improve their experience based on their feedback, you will probably create better word of mouth than by enlisting any other strategy.

There are two ways in which this kind of listening can improve your buzz. First, if you help the customers who complain, you have a chance of turning them into advocates. The more important reason is that listening can help you uncover problems in your system. And if you solve these problems, you may not only save your relationship with the customer who is on the phone right now, you'll also prevent a lot of future customer frustration.

There are so many ways to listen: Pick up the phone and talk to customers, meet them at retail outlets or on the street, read what's being said about you in blogs, run focus groups, set up a private online community, run surveys, measure your Net Promoter Score, talk to the folks at your call center, sit with them and listen to conversations they are having. Hear customers complain, praise, suggest. You can be assured that once they hang up the phone, these callers say pretty much the same things to their friends.

Anyone who's run an online survey knows how exciting it is to see the results accumulating in real time right in front of your eyes. These days there are so many innovative ways to listen, some of which I discussed in the previous chapter. Here's another: A company called CRM Metrix recruits several hundred people to answer an online survey about your product. The questions you come up with can be related to word of mouth, a new product idea, or choosing a slogan—anything that requires you to listen carefully.

Let's look at a hypothetical example. Suppose that you want to find out what people care about when they talk about soup. You offer several possible answers: that it tastes good, that it's not too spicy, that it's nutritious and good for you. People will start rating the importance of these factors, and a few will write their own answers. Someone may write "that the ingredients are locally grown," and these words will now appear on someone else's survey as one of the options. Some people may choose it. Others will not. The key point is that if it resonates with enough people, if it strikes a chord, it will bubble up to the top and get your attention. Laurent Florès, the CEO of CRM Metrix, stresses that this process lets you identify not only your customers' favorite idea but also their favorite choice of words. "It lets you select not only which idea resonates the most, but which *statement* best supports the idea," he says.

The Customer as the Enemy

And another thought about listening: Listen to your employees. I'm not only talking about listening to their ideas and suggestions. Listen to what your staff is saying about your customers. Ask them what they say to other employees. Are they engaged in long lamenting sessions about customers?

Listen with your eyes too. Is there a lot of eye-rolling and head-shaking when people talk about their dealings with customers? Trust me, customers notice. And these things have a profound effect on word of mouth.

Naturally, customers can be difficult. Some make unreasonable demands, some are rude, some want to get everything for nothing. But customers can also be a pleasure to deal with, reasonable, polite, and respectful. The truth is that most companies have a mix of customers. The interaction between your staff and your customers creates stories—stories among your customers and stories among your staff. In the same way that you want to listen to what your customers say and increase the positive stories among your customers, you also want to listen to your staff and increase the positive stories that they spread to other employees. If you let the negative stories take over, you may gradually develop a culture in which the customer is the enemy.

When Jackie Huba and Ben McConnell, the authors of *Creating Customer Evangelists,* moved to Austin from Chicago in 2007, they bought new stuff from at least a dozen vendors—expensive stuff: office furniture, computers, electronics. But of the twelve vendors from whom they bought, only one asked for their feedback.

I've yet to meet a businessman or businesswoman who says that he or she doesn't listen to customers or that listening to customers is not important. And yet we all know that listening, especially true listening, is rare.

I asked Ben why. "I think that the real answer is fear," Ben said. "I think that companies deep down are scared to know what the true answer is to how they're doing." And of course people in business have only so much time and so many resources; they are inundated with projects and meetings and agendas. Adding another task to this—listening—is beyond what many managers are ready to do. Yet what you will hear from customers—even if it hurts—is likely to give you the most valuable insight into your business and how to make people talk about it.

Having more pairs of looking eyes
increases the likelihood that all birds
will be fed, and on a continuous basis.

—from a scientific report explaining why
ravens share

Why We Talk

7 **When Jimmy Carter was growing**

up in Plains, Georgia, he remembers, men

would often knock on his family's kitchen door and ask

for food or a drink of water. Those were the years of the

Great Depression, when thousands of people were mi-

grating from the South, looking for work. Carter remem-

bers these men as polite; many of them offered to do

some work in the yard, like cutting wood, in return for a

sandwich or some leftover chicken. When Carter's mom

was home, nobody was turned away. Mrs. Carter and her kids would talk to the men, find out about their lives and where they were headed.

One day a neighbor, Mrs. Bacon, came to visit and sat with Miz Lillian, as Carter's mom was known, in the Carters' kitchen. Miz Lillian commented on the number of people who had recently knocked on their kitchen door asking for food. Mrs. Bacon said she was thankful they never came in *her* yard. This was more than a bit perplexing for Lillian Carter. How could it be that so many men passing through Plains would knock on the Carters' door but not on their neighbor's door? How did they find out about the generosity of the Carter family?

The next time a small group of men knocked on their kitchen door, Miz Lillian asked for an explanation. Why did they come to the Carters but not to their neighbors? The men tried to avoid answering, but Miz Lillian wouldn't let it drop. Eventually one of the men told them about a set of symbols that were marked on a family's mailbox to indicate that family's attitude. In the case of the Carters, the symbol said that you wouldn't be turned away or mistreated at this home.

When the men left, the family went outside and indeed found some scratches on the mailbox. "Mama told us not to change them," Jimmy Carter wrote years later.

Why do we exchange information? On the surface it seems pretty simple. The man who told the Carter family about the secret code—let's call him Harry—was looking for these codes because he was hungry, and the man who left the marks on the mailbox in the first place—let's call him George—did this to help another human being. Digging a bit deeper, we can see that the answers are not clear-cut. Exploring them in this chapter will allow us to understand better why we talk about products and services today.

Why Do Ravens Buzz?

We'll come back to discuss the specific motives that Harry had to seek information and George had to leave those marks behind. But first let's look at the big picture and explore why engaging in such an exchange seems to be part of our nature as human beings.

A hint to the answer can be found by looking at the communication patterns of a simpler life-form—in this case birds. Dr. Bernd Heinrich of the University of Vermont studies, among other things, ravens. And ravens, as it turns out, have their own buzz. Dr. Heinrich and his colleagues wanted to know how ravens find out about food in the cold winters of Maine, and they ran some experiments to study the issue. They obtained the carcass of a cow from a farmer, then went into the forest and put the carcass out in the snow. They waited in a nearby cabin or behind a snow-covered spruce blind. After a few days a common raven appeared in the sky and discovered the carcass.

This bonanza of food could feed a single bird for the entire winter. But to the surprise of Dr. Heinrich and his colleagues, the raven flew away without taking a bite. A few days later the raven was back, this time with dozens of other ravens. The scientists repeated this experiment twenty-five times, and the results were always the same: When one or two ravens detected food, they came back several days later with family and friends in tow.

But isn't a raven better off keeping the secret to itself? Apparently not. "Having more pairs of looking eyes increases the likelihood that all birds will be fed, and on a continuous basis," the scientists explained. We're all familiar with similar behavior among ants and bees. Bees (which really should get the credit for inventing buzz) communicate through dancing. A honeybee that finds a patch of flowers goes back to its hive and performs a dance that tells the other bees where to go. A black carpenter ant that finds food sprays a secretion that excites the other ants to follow it to the food source.

The fundamental reason we talk is no different from the reason ravens communicate about food. Sharing information is an effective survival mechanism for ravens, bees, ants, and people. This is one way to explain George's behavior. He left those scratches on the Carters' mailbox as part of a survival mechanism that increases the chance of everyone getting a meal. With very little additional work by each individual, the task of finding food becomes easier.

We talk because we are programmed to talk. Those of us who are lucky enough not to worry about our next meal still talk so much about it—food is the number-one topic of discussion among people (according to market researchers at Keller Fay). And when it comes to certain survival issues, like hunting for a job, we *do* count on tips from others—studies have shown that most people find out about their jobs through other people. This reliance on others as sources of information becomes most obvious in crisis situations. With every food scare, for example, people all over the country start warning each other about the brand or the product category.

Grooming

Another explanation for talking is our need to establish alliances. What we're really doing when we're communicating with each other, according to Robin Dunbar, the author of *Grooming, Gossip, and the Evolution of Language*, is very similar to what apes and monkeys do when they groom each other: establish and maintain alliances and social ties. In small groups of primates, members of a network can manage alliances through grooming. Dunbar theorizes that as groups became larger, grooming every other member became impractical; language, he suggests, evolved as a much more efficient tool for managing alliances. Whether one agrees with Dunbar's evolutionary theory or not, the result is pretty clear: We constantly groom each other with words.

Moreover, we don't use highbrow concepts like quantum mechanics to accomplish this "grooming" but simple phrases like "So he said," or "She told her boss," or "Did you see John's new car?" In fact, we are "fascinated beyond measure," as Dunbar puts it, with the minutiae of everyday social life. Dunbar and his colleagues have found that about two-thirds of people's conversations revolve around social issues: "Who is doing what with whom, and whether it's a good or a bad thing; who is in and who is out, and why."

Products are caught in the middle of this "grooming" process. Consumption is such a major part of our lives that products and services are always good conversation pieces. "What aftershave are you wearing?" the assistant at the dentist's office asked me the other day. "So what did you use for the stuffing?" someone asked over Thanksgiving dinner. It's easy to incorporate products into small talk. When you're at a hotel and you want to start a conversation with someone, asking about a good local restaurant or about the laptop the person is using makes more sense than asking about the meaning of life.

Marketers tend to see their products as the focus of word of mouth. But when two young women are shopping together, they are buying and connecting at the same time, and often it's the *conversation* between them that matters most. Today it's about your product. Tomorrow it's about something else.

Can this need to connect explain George's behavior? It's very possible. Although he may be traveling through Plains, Georgia, by himself, he learned the signs from other people whom he now perhaps uses as a reference group. There's also a real possibility that at one point George would have met some of the men who followed him; it would have been rewarding for him to tell them that he was the one who left the mark at the Carters'.

Making Sense of French Cheese

A friend of mine who used to live in the Sinai desert told me how every afternoon the men of a Bedouin tribe would gather in the *mag'ad*, a central tent used for social gatherings. They would sit all afternoon and into the night around a small fire and talk. What would they talk about? "Everything: life, food, where to buy what, what's the best price for gas and cigarettes, where to go next." Bedouins are nomads who are in constant search of good grazing sites for their herds of sheep, goats, and camels. The *mag'ad* became their MySpace hundreds of years before computers were invented. A guest from another part of the Sinai Peninsula would stop by to report some rainfall where he lived. The men would discuss that, because it meant that in two to three weeks they could expect good grass around that area, and it might be time to move on. Word of mouth has always served two functions: to spread information ("There's rain not far from here") and to analyze it ("Maybe we should go there").

A few years ago a ship that was on its way to Saudi Arabia sank not too far from the coast of the Sinai desert. Entrepreneurial Bedouins got some boats and started to make trips to the sinking ship to bring merchandise to the shore. Buzz in the *mag'ad*s around Sinai became intense. For weeks the shipwreck was the main topic of conversation: what you could get from that ship, who would give you the best price, and so on. Suddenly the Bedouins, who usually eat pita bread, olives, and rice, had to figure out the difference between La Vache qui Rit and other brands of French cheese. There was a lot to talk about.

In a way, living in Western society is like having hundreds of such sunken ships loaded with merchandise all around us. We are constantly bombarded with new products that we need to make sense of. With so much to talk about, getting opinions from others helps us make sense of the world.

Why Customers Seek Information

Now let's focus on Harry and try to understand his motivation for seeking information. The most obvious motivation is his hunger. To satisfy this need, Harry could simply knock on the first door and ask for food. This, however, could be very time-consuming. Looking for signs that were left by other men would save him time and a lot of walking. Human beings are always on the lookout for shortcuts, and this is a huge reason that we seek information from others. If you know that a MySpace friend spent three hours customizing her profile and now knows all the ins and outs of how to do it, you can save a lot of time by simply asking for her advice. If a customer is looking for the best mutual funds and he knows that a reliable friend has spent three days researching this topic, why not ask for the friend's advice? Most people have better ways to spend their time than reading about tax-exempt income funds. We love to get honest advice from other people, because it simplifies our lives.

Beyond just saving time, Harry was looking for those signs to reduce his risk. The men who traveled around the country were facing a myriad of potential problems, and they had special signs for all of them. A triangle with hands meant that the homeowner had a gun; two circles (handcuffs) meant that the police in this town weren't friendly; sharp teeth meant that there was a vicious dog in the house.

Asking for advice about products and services can also reduce risk. Customers are scared (and rightly so) of being ripped off, buying something they won't be able to use, or simply paying too much. Checking with friends before they invest their hard-earned dollars, especially on big-ticket items, is a good way to reduce this risk.

And perhaps a bigger risk than being chased away by a dog or an armed man is the risk of being humiliated. Imagine that you lost your job tomorrow and had to walk to other people's homes and ask for food. It would be humiliating enough to ask, but probably even more so to have doors shut in your face. You obviously would try to minimize the number of times you're turned down. The hobos had several signs that denoted generosity. A picture of a cat meant that a generous woman lived in the house, a top hat meant that a generous man lived there. These signs were a godsend to an ego-bruised homeless person.

As consumers, we talk to reduce psychological risks. Nobody wants to look stupid to a salesman who enjoys knowing so much more than you do about cell phones or software or cars. We also want to avoid the feeling that we made the wrong decision, and we hate to admit it to our close friends and family. Asking for their input in advance is a sure way to reduce this risk.

Why Do Customers Share Information?

Understanding Harry's motivation is pretty straight-forward: He's hungry; he wants to find food quickly, with minimum walk and risk. But let's go back to the more difficult question: Why did George leave that sign on the Carter family's mailbox? He was walking out to the road with a full stomach. What made him stop by the mailbox to leave some scratches for some anonymous men who might walk by there in the future looking for food?

While it's true that leaving these signs increased the chance for all men to be fed while minimizing risk, this doesn't explain this behavior at the individual's level. If anything, George had some good reasons *not* to share the information, because some of the men who followed him might have been competing with him for food down the road. Indeed, there are situations where consumers do not share information. In one experiment, two researchers, Jonathan Frenzen and Kent Nakamoto, offered participants information on a sale at a department store. When the discount offered wasn't deep and there was no limit on how many people would be let in for the sale, people were very likely to share the information. But when the researchers presented participants with a scenario of deep discount and limited access (such as top-of-the-line business suits at 50 percent discount, and only the first ten customers would receive the discount), the likelihood of sharing information, especially with people they were not close to, dropped significantly.

I once overheard a conversation between a customer and a receptionist at a spa tucked away in a redwood forest in Northern California. The customer was telling the receptionist that this place was her little secret, which she wouldn't share with any of her friends. She loved the fact that the place wasn't crowded, she loved it that scheduling a massage was so easy. The receptionist, who knew that the place was struggling, was trying to throw in hints to encourage the woman to tell all her friends about it. The customer had no incentive to do it. It would have been a good idea to implement a word-of-mouth program in this case while addressing current customer concerns (perhaps something like "Refer a friend and get priority in booking"). The place closed down after a few months.

More Reasons to Talk

In other cases we use products to send messages to the people around us. By announcing to the world what book we read, where we ate last night, or what electronic gadget we bought, we tell others about our wealth, sophistication, and smarts. Look at soft drinks: "Everyone knows I drink regular Coke," one woman told Susan Fournier of the Harvard Business School, who has studied people's relationships with brands. "If they were to see me with a Diet Coke, they would be . . . surprised. Because I sort of make a statement when I don't drink Diet that I don't do what everybody else does, that I don't really care about the extra calories that much." By drinking regular Coke, this woman is telling her networks that she doesn't need to pay attention to calories. Words are often the currency we exchange to manage an important asset: our reputation. And products help us do that.

We tend to recommend books or movies that convey messages that we ourselves want to send to the world. "We're always trying to convince other people of our own views, and a good book can be a wonderful way to do that," one customer said to me in explaining why he posted a review of the book *Cold Mountain* on Amazon.com.

This hidden agenda or mission helps explain why people give books as gifts. It's a way to connect that reaffirms the values and taste that the gift giver and the recipient share. Janice Shank from California, for example, sent copies of *Cold Mountain* to her brother, her sister, and two friends in Switzerland. She sent copies of two other books she loved, *The Perfect Storm*, by Sebastian Junger, and *The Fisherman's Son*, by Michael Koepf, to five other people. "Books for me are a vehicle for connection," she explains.

Often we can benefit directly from talking about products. Sometimes this is true because of what economists call "network externalities"—the fact that certain products become more valuable as more people use them. These network effects are easy to see in interactive technologies. If you're the only person in the world who owns a fax machine, its value to you is zero. To increase that value, you are likely to encourage others to get their own fax machines. The same effect took place in the diffusion of things like e-mail, MySpace, and Facebook. By encouraging friends on campus to start using Facebook, a student is making it easier for himself or herself to share information with them.

Snakes in Detroit

"It all started in one of those little clothing factories in Taiwan. A box of newly made coats ready to be shipped to the United States was left open accidentally. A poisonous Asian snake thought it would be a good place to lay its eggs. Somewhere on their way to a Kmart store in Detroit, Michigan, the eggs hatched. Several weeks later a shopper at Kmart decided to try on one of these coats. She slowly put her arm through the sleeve and didn't think much of the pricking sting she felt. When her arm started swelling several hours later, she was rushed to a hospital, where her whole arm had to be amputated."

This story, overheard on the streets of Detroit, is an urban legend. Not one word in the story is true. There were no eggs in the shipment of newly made coats, and consequently no customer in Detroit claimed she was bitten by a snake. A reporter from a local radio station spent a day digging through hospital records but found no victim. Yet Kmart's publicity director received more than ten calls from news reporters who were investigating the story after hearing it from people in the city.

A chapter on why we talk about products wouldn't be complete without an exploration of negative buzz. Rumors are often based on people's most basic anxieties. Nobody knows where the rumor about Asian snakes started, but there is speculation that it was no accident it spread successfully in Detroit. It's possible that the rumor had its roots in Detroit's worries about Asian car imports.

What does this mean? Sometimes we talk to let off steam or to vent anger. A common source of negative buzz comes from a negative experience a customer has had with a company. Unhappy customers will try to ease the internal tension they feel by getting even. And they do! Studies have shown that negative information is given more weight in the purchase decision and spreads faster than positive information. The Internet gives customers the ability to tell even more people about their negative experiences, as Pete Blackshaw clearly demonstrates in his 2008 book, *Satisfied Customers Tell Three Friends, Angry Customers Tell 3,000*.

Tension is also often created as a side effect of the purchasing process. Especially with expensive products, customers may feel discomfort after making the purchase, a phenomenon known as cognitive dissonance or buyer's remorse. To reduce the dissonance, they will talk to others and try to justify their decision. A person who has bought a new car is likely to tell others about the advantages of the particular brand and cite information from reliable sources that supports his or her decision. By seeking information before they buy, customers increase their chances of feeling satisfied later on, thus reducing the potential for tension.

Competitors often benefit from spreading negative buzz. When the gas industry was threatened by Edison's electric lighting, it belittled the significance of the innovation and exaggerated its dangers. When Federal Express was losing money in its early years, some competitors sent customers copies of news articles that mentioned the losses. Negative comments often come from those who are already invested (financially or psychologically) in a different technology. When George Eastman introduced paper negatives, which were supposed to replace bulky and fragile glass negatives, he encountered a lot of . . . well, negative buzz from the current user base at the time. An article from the *American Journal of Photography* in the spring of 1886 describes the reaction users had to the innovation. They complained, among other things, that the paper would rot in time and that the odor of the castor oil used was "disagreeable." But when they were asked by the author of the article if they had actually tried the new negatives, "the answer has generally been: 'Nope; but so-and-so has, and he don't appear to think much of them'—or something to that effect." In all these scenarios, people talk to benefit from the outcome financially (sometimes in indirect ways).

Self-Enhancement

When Andrea Wojnicki started working on her doctorate in marketing at Harvard, she decided to explore what goes on in consumers' minds when they participate in word of mouth. She ran ten one-on-one interviews with consumers, each lasting two and a half hours, where she asked people to talk about their thoughts and feelings when sharing information about products and services with other people. To prepare for the interview, participants were asked to go through magazines and cut out any pictures or photographs that illustrated to them any thoughts or feelings that they had when they shared information about products and services with others.

One woman, for example, brought a page she had cut out from a catalogue showing some photos of jewelry. "When I share information with my girlfriends about, say, hair products, I feel like I'm giving them a little jewel, it's like a little gem that I'm giving them. It's a gift," the woman explained to Wojnicki.

All other participants started the long interview by explaining their word of mouth in a similar way: They want to be helpful, they like to help. After some time, though, they all also talked about the fact that there's something in it for them too: "It makes me feel like a cool cat," one said, or "It makes me feel like I'm on the cutting edge." Some of the participants revealed that part of the motivation just moments into the interview. For others it took an hour. But they all ended up explaining that word of mouth was a way for them to express their personal identity and to feel better about themselves at the same time.

Andrea Wojnicki was intrigued by this insight and made it the main topic of her dissertation. She came to the conclusion that self-enhancement played a major role among experts. To illustrate the point, I'd like you to meet two guys, Andy and Jeff. Andy sees himself as someone who knows a lot about restaurants. Jeff doesn't. Now, when they have a bad experience with a restaurant, which one of the two is more likely to tell more people about it, Andy, the expert, or Jeff, the nonexpert?

In a paper that Dr. Wojnicki coauthored with David Godes, they reported that when people share information with their friends about a negative or dissatisfying restaurant experience, people who see themselves as experts and those who don't see themselves as experts tell an average of six people about their experience. In other words, there is no significant difference between how much word of mouth will be generated by Andy and how much word of mouth will be generated by Jeff.

Here's my next question: When Andy and Jeff have a *good* experience at a restaurant, which of the two is more likely to tell more people about it, Andy, the expert, or Jeff, the nonexpert?

In this case there is a *very* significant difference—it's definitely Andy. People who see themselves as restaurant experts tell *over twice as many* friends than people who don't see themselves as experts. These results, Wojnicki and Godes argue, can be explained by the motivation of why the experts talk. Part of the way Andy sees himself is as someone who knows about restaurants. When he has a bad experience, he shares it with some people, but pretty much with the same number of people as Jeff. However, when he has a *good* experience, every time that he talks about it, his self-image as a restaurant expert who has made a good choice will be enhanced, which is why he's motivated to talk about it again and again and again. This also has a practical implication. Dr. Wojnicki points out that when experts are reminded of their positive experience and of the fact that they are experts, they are likely to generate even more word of mouth. Finding satisfied experts among your customers and reminding them of their expertise will generate more buzz.

Now back to our traveling hobo George. George's need to enhance his self-image may be the best explanation for why he left markings on people's front gates. Perhaps George lost his job and felt helpless. It is hard to rely on the kindness of strangers. As he walked away from a house toward the street, George had an opportunity to feel better about himself—to share his own expertise about that particular residence. He stopped, made the marks, and continued with a full stomach and a somewhat restored ego.

By now you may have picked up on some similarities between the hoboes' language and today's Internet. Both are loosely connected networks of people who don't really know each other but actively help others by giving them advice and information. There is no one way to explain this behavior. Some people talk to justify their purchase decision; others use products or brands as a kind of symbol for who they are or what they believe in. Some people simply want to connect. And others have altruistic motivations, which is another way to explain George's action. When he experienced generosity, he wanted to be generous too.

Regardless of the motivation, all these stories illustrate one thing: Talking is not an incidental activity we engage in when we don't have anything better to do. It is rooted in the basic needs we share with other living creatures. We *need* to talk, and we don't need much encouragement to do it. Which, come to think about it, is pretty good news for anyone who's trying to build buzz.

> What we shall call opinion leadership, if we
> may call it leadership at all, is leadership at
> its simplest , . . not leadership on the high
> level of a Churchill, nor of a local politico, nor
> even of a local social elite.
>
> —Elihu Katz and Paul Lazarsfeld, in *Personal Influence*

Hubs

8 **Sean O'Driscoll knows not to** refer to Microsoft MVPs as evangelists. They don't like it. But occasionally somebody from Microsoft who comes to speak at the annual summit of the nonemployees deemed "most valuable professionals" by the company uses the "E" word, and it never goes over very well. "I've seen Microsoft people stand in front of an audience of MVPs, both offline and online, and refer to them as Microsoft evangelists. And this is a very hazardous moment. This is where your audience turns from listeners to tigers," he says.

The word "evangelist" is commonly used in high tech to describe someone who passionately promotes a certain technology. Why don't MVPs like it?

Microsoft presents its MVP awards to those it feels have made an exceptional contribution to technical communities worldwide. They're the folks on a newsgroup who answer your question about the latest virus or who have a blog on how to use Microsoft Excel. There are currently about four thousand of them in ninety countries. You can't sign up to be an MVP—it's an invitation-only honor. We all know someone like this, someone who knows more than the rest of us about Windows or about using Microsoft Word on the Mac and who is happy to help us figure out these products. And you probably have friends who are equally knowledgeable about other areas—digital cameras or cooking, fashion or sports.

I call these folks hubs—people who talk more than average about a particular product category. Later in this chapter I'll discuss "social hubs"—those who talk more because they know more people—but for now let's focus on "expert hubs"—those who talk more because they know more about something. The MVPs are a perfect example.

MVP Susan Bradley is such an expert hub. She's a regular on technical online forums and writes a blog that gets about two thousand visits a day. She posts on her blog so much that sometimes when she Googles for a solution to a tough technical problem, she ends up finding the answer on her own blog!

So what's wrong with using the word "evangelist" when referring to someone like Bradley? To her, an evangelist is someone who sticks to the party line—a person for whom Microsoft reigns supreme. "That's not what an MVP does," she says. When a real MVP is asked about a new product, he or she gives you a spin-free answer. "The best MVPs out there—and I would argue the best for Microsoft as well—are the ones that say, Here's where it works, here's where it doesn't work, and here's the workaround, and yes, I gave them feedback and they need to fix this."

The issue of allegiance is not unique to Microsoft MVPs. Most hubs gain their status not from their source of information but from the people who listen to them. A hub who blindly praises everything that some company does will lose credibility pretty fast. And this is why MVPs don't like the "E" word: They are afraid that labeling them "Microsoft evangelists" will hurt their credibility among their listeners or readers.

This is a key insight: Hubs are not fans. Their first loyalty is to the people around them.

Before Bradley started using Microsoft's software, she used Novell's server software, and she says she will switch again if something better comes along. So if people like her are not fanatic loyals, why does Microsoft want to talk to them? Why does the company give them software, invite them to its Redmond, Washington, headquarters for four days every year (all expenses except for travel paid)? Because these folks communicate every year with numerous Microsoft customers and potential customers. It makes sense to help them in the task that they took on themselves.

It makes special sense because of the MVPs' independence. "The credibility that they have in those community conversations comes from their independence," says O'Driscoll, who's been running the MVP program at Microsoft since 2002. These hubs are not part of Microsoft, they don't work for Microsoft, and sometimes they are critical of Microsoft. Which makes them much more trustworthy when they say good things.

Why Hubs Exist

From time to time I hear people who question the existence of hubs. They say that this is a nice theory but doubt that hubs are for real.

So I went looking for more real-life examples. I talked about hubs with Jia Shen, whose company, RockYou, makes widgets and small applications for social networking sites such as MySpace and Facebook. Among the teenage users of MySpace, Shen observed certain girls whom he calls "supernodes"—girls who know every one of their three or four hundred friends, girls who are always updating their page, often with widgets that RockYou provides, such as SlideShow or Horoscope. Each girl is also the person that all her friends turn to when they want to customize their page.

I told Shen that some people think that hubs don't exist. He looked surprised at first. Then he said something that sounded completely unrelated: "In the end, people are really lazy."

What does being lazy have to do with hubs? His point was that the girl who's continually customizing her page on MySpace accumulates a lot of knowledge in this area; her MySpace friends seek her advice because it saves them lots of work and time. This is an important point. Expert hubs are not necessarily cool or charismatic or persuasive. We seek their advice and knowledge not because we're easily influenced but because we are, on some level, lazy.

Think of it as a division of labor. Each of us specializes in something. We can be extremely industrious in gathering information about our specialty area, but when we want to learn about something else, we want the bottom line, and so we turn to expert hubs—people who've already gained expertise in that field.

This is why I prefer the term "hub" to others. The term "opinion leader," which is often used in this context, calls to mind someone whom others seek to follow, implying something more grandiose than is often the case. The term "influential" suggests a skill at persuasiveness that some hubs may possess but others do not. The terms that Malcolm Gladwell used in his 2000 book, *The Tipping Point*, "mavens" and "connectors," are better. The problem is that the word "maven" in the marketing literature refers to someone who's an expert in multiple domains. A connector is a person who spans several social groups—again, something that some hubs do and some don't. You'll still see all these terms in my book when I'm quoting researchers or firms, but when possible, I'll use the more neutral term "hub."

"Champions" and "evangelists" are terms used to describe raving fans, a group of people described in Jackie Huba and Ben McConnell's book *Creating Customer Evangelists*. Some of what NOLS alumni do when the veggie bus is on campus—walking around in backcountry gear, handing out flyers, and chalking sidewalks—falls into this category. You definitely should work with these fans and cultivate the relationships, but keep in mind that a single customer's satisfaction has little to do with how many other people listen to that person. There are certain brands (Harley-Davidson and Apple come to mind) that are so strong that some hubs totally shift their allegiance to the brand. But they're the exceptions; this is not the case for most brands, even high-quality ones. Certainly not for Microsoft.

Peter Kellner is another MVP. He has curly gray hair and thin-rim glasses. He's soft-spoken, unassuming but confident. When he explains something to you, you don't get the feeling that he's talking down to you. He's also the kind of person who has a hard time containing his excitement when he gets into something new. After he sold his small software company in 2000, he got into biking. For Kellner, this meant a two-hundred-mile ride every third Saturday and a twenty-seven-day cross-country trip from California to Georgia.

In 2003, ready to get back to programming, he began looking around for a development platform. He had previously used Oracle and Sun software, but he looked at what Microsoft had to offer and liked what he saw.

When he was making his first steps in the new environment of the Web development framework ASP.NET, he posted lots of questions on its online forum. "People were amazingly helpful," he says. Slowly, as he gained knowledge, he felt that he could and should start answering questions himself. His rule of thumb was, if he asked a question, he should also answer one.

He also started going to meetings. He was particularly excited about Code Camp, grassroots meetings organized by software developers. He attended four or five of them around the country but was surprised to see that the camps weren't available in the San Francisco Bay Area. So he decided to organize one. About eight hundred people came to the first Code Camp he put together at Foothill College in Los Altos, California.

Kellner's involvement in the online forums did not go unnoticed, and forum organizers invited him to be a moderator. Somebody at Microsoft whom he met at a show suggested that he write an article for a technical publication. He wrote five.

Like Susan Bradley's, Kellner's loyalty to Microsoft is not a given. When he organized Code Camp, he also invited representatives from both Oracle and Sun to speak. At the same time, he feels that the MVP program strengthens his relationships with Microsoft. If he were ever considering switching to another environment, he says, this relationship would be a factor. He has about forty Microsoft employees as friends on Facebook. "It's a loyalty builder for me," he says. He refers to this as the " 'Have you drunk the Kool-Aid?' question." In other words, has he become such a fervent believer in a product or company that he's willing to overlook all its flaws? And his answer is "I kind of have, but that doesn't mean I don't think anymore."

Sometimes being a hub means walking a fine line between independence and access to information. Being close to a company gives a hub certain privileges, not the least of which is having early access to information. But being close to the source comes at a price. If a hub is perceived as being too intimate with the company, he loses his credibility. For marketers it's important to understand that this tension is there and will always be there. If you expect hubs always to say good things about you, or pressure them to do so, you may turn off potential advocates— or you may end up with avid fans that nobody listens to.

The MVPs are an example of expert hubs who know a lot about a certain category. Social hubs, in contrast, are people who talk more because they are more connected. In every group, there are those who are especially charismatic, trusted by their peers, or more socially active. Remember the Herbal Essences hair-color guide that was sent to teenagers? That conversation piece was given to teenage girls who were part of a panel of "connectors" created by Procter & Gamble. While Tremor reports that in 2006 an average teen had around thirty-five names in her instant-messaging buddy list, one teen connector had between 150 and 200 names. The company also enlisted a panel of mom connectors. The research indicates that while an average mother talks to five people a day outside of work, a connector mom talks to twenty-five to thirty a day.

Working with panels of connectors is by no means the only way to reach social hubs. If you own a small business, it's not too hard to know who is most active and connected in your community. In their book *The Influentials*, Ed Keller and Jon Berry show that people who participate in town meetings, head the PTA, and are involved in other community activities also tend to make more product recommendations.

Why are hubs so important? Because they are credible with their audience and they can build buzz quickly. Dr. Barak Libai from Tel Aviv University says that in most cases an excellent product will ultimately be adopted by people even without the recommendation of network hubs. Hubs simply *accelerate* the process, which in some industries, such as entertainment and media, is absolutely key to a successful launch. "The acceleration is a major part of the value of word of mouth and of opinion leaders," Libai says.

Characteristics of Hubs

Can you easily identify hubs by their demographics? I wish I could tell you that they are all thirty to forty-five years old, have an average household income of $55,075, and watch PBS every Wednesday night. Of course, it's impossible to pin down such precise information, because there are all kinds of hubs. A video games network hub could be a twelve-year-old boy. A network hub for medical equipment will have a totally different profile. Still, several characteristics typical of network hubs emerge. Let me offer an easy acronym you can use to remember them: Network hubs are ACTIVE. They are Ahead in adoption, Connected, Travelers, Information-hungry, Vocal, and Exposed to the media more than others.

Ahead in adoption. Network hubs are usually not the first to adopt new products, but they are at least slightly ahead of the rest in their networks. They are not on the cutting edge in the marketplace as a whole, but they want to be ahead of their friends. Tremor, for example, found that the teen connectors feel that they "stay cool" if they are the ones who bring new stuff to their social networks. But don't misunderstand this. Hubs don't automatically adopt every new product they come across. They can be early adopters of certain products and early rejecters of others. Conversely, not every early adopter is a hub. Just because someone was one of your first customers doesn't mean she talks to a lot of other people. Still, hubs are often the first to adopt new products in their network.

Connected. Network hubs are by definition connected. *How* they are connected may vary. One hub may be heavily connected within her clique. Another may be connected to several other clusters, serving in effect as an information broker among these different groups. Often hubs will have ties within a core group of peers and also be connected to an outside source of information. Ultimately hubs have lots of connections. In the teen space, as I just mentioned, Tremor found that a teen connector has at least four times as many names in her instant-messaging buddy list than an average teen.

Travelers. Sixty-nine percent of the "influentials" described by Keller and Berry are eager to see new places—a full nineteen percentage points higher than among the total public. There's also support for this idea in early studies. For example, a classic study for the pharmaceutical company Pfizer in the 1950s found that opinion leaders attended more out-of-town scientific conferences and visited more out-of-town medical institutions than others. However, out of the six characteristics of hubs, this one has the weakest support. I suggest that we think of this group as cosmopolitan rather than measuring them on travel alone.

Everett Rogers defined cosmopoliteness as the degree to which an individual is oriented outside a social system, and he argued that opinion leaders are more cosmopolite than their followers.

Information-hungry. Because they often serve as local experts, network hubs always want to learn more. This is especially true of expert hubs, who are expected to provide answers to people. It is worthwhile to keep this in mind when you communicate with these hubs. Colorful writing can help, but what's really important is hard facts about products. The knowledge that these hubs accumulate in a certain category helps build their credibility.

Vocal. The most important characteristic of hubs—their defining characteristic, really—is that they are vocal. Some of these people blog, some of them participate in online forums, some of them just talk to lots of friends. Thirty-eight percent of people Keller and Berry define as influential made a recommendation about a car in the past year, while only 21 percent of the total public say they have done the same. Fifty-four percent of these influentials say that they have recommended a vacation destination to another person in the past year, while only 24 percent of the total public say they have done so.

Exposed to the media. Because network hubs are information-hungry, they read more. One study found that financial opinion leaders are more likely than others to read publications such as *Money, Barron's,* and the *Wall Street Journal* and watch TV programs such as *Wall Street Week.* Other studies have demonstrated similar results among hubs who are interested in politics, fashion, and medical innovations. But buzz doesn't follow neat patterns, so don't expect all network hubs to learn about new products from the media and then pass it on to their "followers."

This "trickle-down" theory used to be the common belief among researchers, but it doesn't always work that way.

Where Can You Find Hubs?

How does Microsoft find its MVPs? It uses a combination of analytical tools, referrals, and lots of manual labor. It uses tools designed to find people who give answers that end an on-line forum thread with a definitive response. These automated searches are bolstered with hours of actual reading of news-groups, blogs, and Web sites. The tone of a person's postings is important too. "Read the manual, you idiot, it's on page 42" may be a technically accurate answer, but it won't get you into the program.

There are essentially four ways of identifying hubs.

Letting hubs identify themselves. One group of network hubs is easy to find—they're the ones who come to you. Many of these people are already e-mailing your company about the products they like and how to make them better. Your job here is to recognize them, and you may be surprised by how many companies don't. These people will come to you for something they like more than anything else: information. They may spend extra time at your booth during a trade show. They may call to ask questions that go beyond what a regular customer would ask. Some of your employees may feel bothered by this intense interest, but they need to understand that network hubs thrive on information.

Identifying categories of hubs. The previous method will help you find only some of the hubs—those that approach you. Yes, network hubs are information-hungry, but what if their hunger for information is fed by your competitors, or what if they're not *that* hungry? You need to use other tactics too. The most commonly used method is to identify categories that may include potential hubs. For example, readers of a fashion magazine are likely sources for information about the latest fashions. This is an important method, and the only reason I don't expand on it here is that it is well documented and widely known: The use of trade magazines, conferences, and trade shows is a sure way to reach opinion leaders.

Spotting hubs in the field. Identifying hubs by category usually allows us to find people in trades that use our products—teachers, nurses, physicians, for example. Such people are important, but they aren't always the street-level network hubs we're looking for. To find the grassroots network hub, you need to go out into the field. How do you spot them in the crowd? Their category knowledge is one way. Because they're hungry for information, they usually know more than the average person. The fact that they're vocal is another way to spot them. If someone blogs frequently about your category, she may be a hub. If lots of people link to her blog and comment on her posts, then you know she is. Pay attention not only to the editor of your trade magazine but also to those who frequently write letters to the editor. For its MVP program, Microsoft searches for people who give great answers. But often what you're really seeking are people who consistently ask good questions and raise important issues that resonate with other customers.

Identifying hubs through surveys. There are three broad means of identifying hubs this way: sociometric methods (you ask all members of a given network to name the people from whom they seek information), informants' ratings (you ask people in a particular network to observe who the hubs are), and the self-designating method (you ask people about their own behavior). Not surprisingly, the last method is the most popular, because it's the easiest and cheapest to implement. Because this method is based on self-reporting, however, it is not as reliable as other methods.

Is there a way to avoid the bias that occurs in self-reporting? Matchstick is a word-of-mouth agency in Canada that specializes in seeding products. When it surveys people, there's always a danger that respondents will overstate their involvement with the category in order to get free stuff. One way to reduce the problem is to test the respondent's knowledge in the category. When Matchstick is trying to identify influencers in the fragrance category, it asks people to list some brands they know. "If they don't know the cool fashion-forward fragrance brands, then they don't fit our profile," says Patrick Thoburn, the cofounder of the company. Dr. Karen Stenner of the Word Of Mouth Company in Brunswick Heads, Australia, explains another way: "One of the ways that you reduce overreporting is that you ask extremely specific factual questions." The company doesn't just ask "Have you recommended the product?" but also "To whom have you recommended it? In what store did you buy the product?"

Hubs and Time

Being a hub isn't usually a lifetime position. Ed Keller and Jon Berry report that there is a great deal of fluidity among influentials. They found that about a third of the influentials they uncovered had only qualified for that status for less than a year (measured by participation in eleven specific activities). Another third had been active between a year and five years, and about a third had been involved for more than six years.

Some people show a consistent interest in a given category.

More than half of that last third were involved in those activities for over ten years. Likewise, a significant segment of expert hubs naturally want to maintain the knowledgeable status they have worked so hard to achieve.

But people's interests change, and so do circumstances in their lives. Even among expert hubs there is fluidity. Sean O'Driscoll says that about 75 percent of MVPs are reawarded every year. The 25 percent who are not renewed for one reason or another stopped behaving as hubs. People get a new job that doesn't allow them the time they once had; they find new passions; or sometimes they get sick. Hubs are dynamic. You're looking not for someone who was relevant five years ago but for someone who is talking or is going to talk about your product right now.

Just one example: When Matchstick was looking for people to help spread the word about the Chrysler 300C in Canada, it sought hubs who were not only well connected but also in the market for a car in the next six months and therefore more likely to talk about the category.

How Should You Work with Network Hubs?

Once you identify those hubs, what do you do with them? "Early access is key," O'Driscoll says. "They want prerelease stuff that other people don't know. And if you repackage what people already know, they will throw you under the bus, because they've already read everything. They've already scoured the Web."

Microsoft MVPs sign nondisclosure agreements, which allows Microsoft to involve them at an earlier stage. Microsoft has found that the same people who are very helpful in online communities are quite vocal in prerelease product sessions. And when the product that they were initially not allowed to talk about is finally released, is it any wonder that they talk and talk and talk? This type of ongoing conversation with hubs can be extremely beneficial when maintained over time.

Buzz needs ammunition, and hubs need a constant supply of stuff to talk about. After all, how many times can you tell your friends that you now drive a Jeep? But if you come back from a two-day, action-packed Jeep Jamboree, you'll have a lot to talk about. The jamboree is an off-road weekend trip designed for Jeep owners only. Although this activity is not designed exclusively for network hubs, it is very likely to attract them. The Jeep Jamboree tradition goes all the way back to 1953, when the first fifty-five Jeep vehicles took on the Rubicon Trail, driving from Georgetown, California, to Lake Tahoe. The 155 passengers and drivers who participated had something to tell everyone back home: The nine-mile trail took about nine hours to complete!

What else can you do? Give them the facts. Don't worry about boring network hubs. They are willing to read a lot about stuff that interests them. Never assume that your hubs already know about your latest product review. They may have missed it, or they may have noticed the one bad review you got in a different publication. Although many hubs consider themselves independent thinkers, they are just as easily influenced as the rest of us by others. Keep them up-to-date as the product passes certain benchmarks or wins awards. Also, make sure hubs have a way to broadcast their support of you. Both icons on their blogs and a T-shirt that they wear can serve as conversation starters that will let them tell others about your product.

Connecting to Passion

In August 2007, Judy Porta, a volunteer at a nonprofit organization in Berkeley, California, told me that American Express had made a five-year commitment to give $5 million for historical preservation in the United States. A month later, at a community center in Chicago's Chinatown, another woman pointed out to me the generosity of American Express. These individuals are not financial experts. Yet they talked about American Express. A lot.

How did American Express motivate these two women to talk about their corporate giving program?

American Express, like other companies, has been giving money to community projects for decades. But information about this kind of giving often stays in glossy brochures or in nonprofit boardrooms. For this particular project, however, American Express chose a slightly different strategy, one that would get the public involved and spread the word about the company's preservation initiative. As this book goes to print,the campaign has been executed in San Francisco, Chicago, and New Orleans.

In the campaign's first stage, a long list of potential preservation projects in each area was put together. In San Francisco, for example, the list included historic buildings such as the Japanese YWCA Building, the Angel Island Immigration Station, and the Fox Oakland Theater. These were not high-profile projects of preserving landmarks like the Golden Gate Bridge, but rather involved fixing up local community buildings with storied pasts that desperately needed a face-lift.

Then a group of experts narrowed down the list to twenty-five candidates. Out of these projects, American Express promised to fund thirteen. Which ones? In terms of promoting buzz, this was their masterstroke: They let the public decide.

"It became like an *American Idol* for historical buildings," says

Marc Schiller, whose company, Electric Artists, ran the campaign. American Express established a Web site called Partners in Preservation, where you could vote as well as post pictures and personal stories about your favorite historical site. One important point was that you could vote more than once. In fact, you could vote once a day for a period of six weeks.

What happened next is not hard to imagine. Each of these projects involves not just an architectural structure but also a community that cares deeply about its future. And at the heart of each such community there's someone—often more than just one person—who's a hub.

Judy Porta is part of the Friends of First Church Berkeley, a nondenominational organization dedicated to the preservation of the church, which was designed in 1910 by the noted architect Bernard Maybeck. Porta created a postcard with a picture of the church on the front and some text with the American Express preservation project Web site address on the back and mailed it to about a thousand supporters, encouraging them all to vote. She also wrote a detailed e-mail and sent it to about thirty people who she knew cared deeply about the building.

These people started forwarding the e-mail to everyone they knew, asking them to vote and vote often. Porta, who strikes you more as a friendly grandma than as a viral marketer, was amazed by the power of the Internet. You didn't have to be a San Francisco Bay Area resident to vote, and she started getting questions and e-mails of support from Maybeck fans all over the country. At some point her e-mail was forwarded to alumni of Principia College in Illinois, who also started voting for the church; Bernard Maybeck designed Principia's campus. "It was the e-mail to those thirty people that did it," she says.

Dozens of other organizations in San Francisco, Chicago, and New Orleans launched similar initiatives, encouraging their supporters to vote. And every time someone reminded a friend to vote, he or she also passed on the news that American Express was giving $5 million for historic preservation.

Judy Porta is not an expert hub. Is she a social hub? She certainly served as one when it came to information about the American Express preservation program. Sometimes hubs are just people in the right place at the right time, and even if they don't fit the ACTIVE hub profile, they may spread the word for you.

Passion and interest should not be ignored when you look for people who will spread the word. "Category knowledge and category enthusiasm are the key predictors whether or not a customer is likely to recommend," says Dr. Paul Marsden, a social psychologist and market researcher who specializes in word of mouth.

Influencers under Attack

The role of hubs is often exaggerated. The concept seems so simple that some people assume it is the *only* way to spread the word. It is not. And because some people overstate the importance of hubs, the concept occasionally comes under fire.

In 2007, Dr. Duncan Watts, a sociology professor at Columbia University, wrote that recent work he had done with his colleague Peter Dodds shows that influentials have far less impact on the formation of public opinion than is generally believed. In a *Harvard Business Review* article, Watts positioned his work against Malcolm Gladwell's bestselling book *The Tipping Point*, in which Gladwell argues that "social epidemics" are driven by the actions of a tiny minority of influentials. *Brandweek* followed quickly with a headline: "Buzz-Kill: Columbia Prof Blasts Influencer Model." *Advertising Age* followed with "Sorry, Malcolm, but the Tipping Point Might Be More Myth than Math." In February

2008, *Fast Company* had another catchy title: "Is the Tipping Point Toast?"

The academic debate about influentials has been going on for decades and probably will continue for a few more. I don't know if it can be resolved unless someone successfully breaks down the concept of influence into several sub-ideas. After all, the way a new toy spreads among kids may be different from the way a new philosophy gains popularity. But I want to make sure that marketers don't dismiss a valuable method because of a few catchy headlines.

So what *is* Watts arguing? He doesn't seriously question the existence of influential people. The idea that some people are more influential than others "is almost certainly correct," he writes. His main claim is that you don't need to find these people if you want to create far-reaching influence or, in his words, a "global cascade." Such global cascades of influence, he argues, are usually driven not by influentials but by a critical mass of easily influenced individuals. He also points out that although the results of his research do not exclude the possibility that influentials can be important, they suggest that the influentials hypothesis requires more careful specification and testing than it has received—and I certainly agree.

How does he support his argument? Dodds and Watts built a computer model that consisted of 10,000 simulated people, each of whom has something we could refer to as an "influence threshold"—a number of neighbors who must buy into an idea before he or she will do so. For example, if one of these people has a threshold of four and he hears about a new idea from three neighbors, he won't adopt the idea. Once a fourth neighbor tells him about the idea, however, he becomes "infected." Watts also took connectedness into account: Some of these people were more connected than others. The top 10 percent (in their number of connections) were defined as the influentials. At this point, one person was picked randomly (he may be an influential or an average Joe) to begin the flow of information, and Watts and Dodds watched what happened. Were lots of people "infected," or just a few?

After repeating this experiment thousands of times, each time starting with a different person with a different level of connectedness and a different influence threshold, the researchers could see some patterns. The surprising thing was that in most cases, societywide cascades started with a regular person and not an influential. Although the authors noticed that when an influential started a trend it spread much further, most global cascades were started by people with few connections.

Should Microsoft Cancel Its MVP Program?

So should you call a halt to any program you use that involves hubs? Should I send advance copies of my book to random bloggers rather than to the more influential ones? Should Microsoft cancel its MVP program? I don't think so. Watts's study is a good reminder that word of mouth is not created only by hubs. But it does not prove that connecting with your hubs doesn't work.

Threshold models have been used in diffusion studies for years, and they certainly reflect real-life behavior patterns. But models have to simplify things. Sometimes oversimplify. Watts himself referred to his model in one discussion as "almost comically simple." Of course, just because models can be simplistic is not a reason to dismiss them. It doesn't mean that we can't learn from models, but we can also learn from real experience.

Learning from experience is not without problems either. Duncan Watts believes that it is extremely misleading. He points out that narrative explanations usually are based on a biased selection of events and overlook the possibility of multiple or indirect causes in favor of simple linear causation. Still, there are many examples from the trenches that show that working with hubs can be effective, and while we should keep in mind their limitations, I believe that we can definitely learn from these stories.

In the mid-1980s, Brian Maxwell, the late cofounder of the energy bar company PowerBar, decided that he would reach athletes through influencers—in this case, coaches and leading athletes. "That's really a model that we use, the whole idea of there being influencers and finding them," he told me in a 1998 interview.

Watts may argue that the real reason for the success of PowerBar had to do with conditions in the marketplace: A lot of people were ready for this idea, as they'd been looking for something to eat while training. This may well be true, and it gave the company a good starting point. But Maxwell still needed to accelerate the process. Without money to advertise, he chose to spread the word through other tactics, including hubs, which proved to be very effective for PowerBar. Would his campaign have been as effective if he'd focused on random athletes instead of coaches to help convince everyone that this strange-tasting glob was good for them?

Another example of the effectiveness of hubs is *The Purpose-Driven Life*, by Rick Warren, which sold 20 million copies in its first two years. Greg Stielstra, who was senior marketing director at the publishing company Zondervan, describes in his book *PyroMarketing* how *The Purpose-Driven Life* was promoted through twelve hundred pastors in churches around the country. In an interview with the *Washington Post*, Warren described these pastors as cultural gatekeepers who are often overlooked. "People do not realize how much influence they have," he said. I discuss this campaign further in Chapter 14. For now, one point: Would this book launch have reached the same results by working with just anyone in the church? I doubt it.

When I asked Steve Knox about this debate, he declined to refer to any specific company or person, but he emphasized that Tremor's model of working with teen and mom connectors has proven to have measurable business results. The two characteristics that Tremor uses to identify its connectors are how connected and vocal they are. "We know our model works," he said.

Research also shows that opinion leaders can be effective not only in disseminating information but also in changing people's behavior. At least in certain domains, the decision of whether to adopt or not involves many more factors than how many of your neighbors have been "infected." The following experiment illustrates how influence works in these situations.

In the mid-1980s, Canadian physicians were abuzz about the use of cesarean sections. In response to concerns that the surgical procedure was often used when it wasn't needed, causing unnecessary risks and expenses, the Society of Obstetricians and Gynecologists of Canada issued guidelines that unambiguously recommended a lower rate of cesarean births. The guidelines stated that the fact that a woman had had the procedure before was not a reason to reach for the scalpel again. About a year after the guidelines were sent to all practitioners, a group of researchers headed by Jonathan Lomas from the Centre of Health Economics and Policy Analysis wanted to see if doctors were aware of the guidelines and whether they had changed their practices. A survey that they conducted found that most practitioners—94 percent of them, to be exact—said that they knew of these guidelines, and 56 percent reported that they had discussed them with a colleague. But when the researchers checked the monthly discharge data from hospitals to see whether there was a reduction in the number of cesarean sections as a result of the new guidelines, the answer was no.

It's not that the physicians disagreed with the guidelines—about 85 percent of practitioners said they agreed with them. In fact, many physicians claimed that they had changed their practices. "I think they truly were under the impression that they had changed their behavior," says Lomas. "But in fact they hadn't."

Lomas and his colleagues were intrigued and decided to search for the most effective way to influence these physicians. They tried several methods and eventually found that the best way to change people's behavior in this case was to work with local opinion leaders.

The first step was to identify the network hubs. To do this, the researchers sent out questionnaires to physicians in each hospital asking them to nominate colleagues in the area who matched the "opinion leader" profile. When the opinion leaders were identified, they were invited to participate in a workshop that explained the rationale behind the guidelines. In the weeks that followed the workshop, the researchers asked the physicians to do a little "marketing." They asked each physician to mail a personal letter to his or her colleagues with some material from the workshop, to follow up with another letter, to host a meeting with an expert on the topic, and in general to talk with colleagues about the issue. The results were impressive: The vaginal birthrate in the cases handled by physicians who were educated by opinion leaders was 85 percent higher than that in groups where different strategies were tested, including simply mailing out the guidelines a second time and promoting the reduction of cesarean sections at medical staff meetings and via an extensive audit procedure.

One problem with applying Watts's model to marketing is its implicit idea that a global cascade is a "success" and a local cascade is "failure." (Anything less than one thousand adoptions was considered a local cascade.) This may be the case with large-scale social change (for instance, with voting for a presidential candidate) but not necessarily in business. Of course, it is every marketer's dream to achieve a global cascade (and in certain markets achieving dominance is indeed a must), but most marketers are happy with any strategy that shows returns that exceed alternative strategies.

In the end, it really depends on how much it costs you to reach these influentials and what you get in return. In fact, this is what Watts and Dodds themselves say: "Whether or not the additional impact of influentials justifies paying special attention to them—versus, for example, focusing on some other group, or even recruiting individuals at random—is therefore a matter that will depend, possibly delicately, on the various costs associated with different strategies, and the particular details of the influence network." It's a subtle and well-put analysis, and a far cry from the headline "Columbia Prof Blasts Influencer Model." But then, "It Depends" never makes for a good headline.

Watts's work reminds us that not all buzz is created by hubs. (And I can think of some cases when I've needed this reminder too.) Keller Fay says that its "conversation catalysts"—another way of describing influentials—consist of about 15 percent of the population and are responsible for 30 percent of buzz, an acknowledgment that 70 percent of buzz is generated by nonhubs.

This is important. It means that marketers should work on all fronts and that they can do a lot without first locating hubs. In fact, we've already discussed some cases in this book. The NOLS bus triggers talk among all NOLS alumni, not only among the most influential ones. You don't need to be a hub to download the Adidas logo on MySpace or to forward the Bob Dylan video to someone. There are many other examples of products that I describe in this book that spread without the help of hubs—Nintendo's Super Mario Brothers 3, Hotmail, *The Blair Witch Project*, Kodak, Polaroid, Windows 95, to name a few.

Having said that, if Keller Fay is correct and 15 percent of the population is responsible for 30 percent of the buzz, that means that you may reach more people by working through those hubs. Moreover, if some people have a natural propensity to talk more *without* being triggered to do so, they might talk to even more people when triggered to talk. And that's the idea of hubs in a nutshell: Find those who talk more about your category, listen to them, and help them talk about you.

It's a Small World. So What?

9

It's possible that your physician went to school with someone who collaborated on a research paper with a colleague of my dentist. Or maybe a cousin of my neighbor works on the same floor as a good friend of your seventh-grade teacher. Research shows that we're all connected by a chain of no more than six mutual acquaintances, but what does the concept of "six degrees of separation"—also known as "the small world phenomenon"—mean to marketers?

A lot has been written in recent years about social networks, those interpersonal information networks that connect us to each other (not to be confused with social networking *sites*, like MySpace and Facebook, which are just one way we connect). In this chapter I'll focus on ten principles at work in social networks that I think are most relevant to understanding buzz.

Principle 1: Social Networks Are Invisible

Are social networks still invisible in the age of social networking sites such as LinkedIn, MySpace, and Facebook?

Let's first address this question by thinking about the world before social networking sites.

In the same way that we can't tell that the world is round just by walking on the surface of it, we don't have the right perspective to see the huge social networks of which we are a part. We know our friends, and we may know of our friends' friends, but that's about where our social horizons stop. The networks are just too complex. Even in a small network of only 100 people, there are 4,950 possible links among them. In a network with just 1,000 members, there are almost half a million possible links! As if this weren't complicated enough, the networks keep changing. People in our society constantly form new friendships, change jobs, move—all factors contributing to the fluidity and invisibility of the networks.

Even in the most familiar environments we don't seem to see the networks very clearly. Studies of informal networks at the workplace show that managers have a difficult time describing workplace networks. "Although they may be able to diagram accurately the social links of the five or six people closest to them, their assumptions about employees outside their immediate circle are usually off the mark," say David Krackhardt and Jeffrey

Hanson, the authors of a study of how informal networks operate in the workplace. It is true as well for online communities, as
illustrated by Stacy Horn in her 1998 book *Cyberville*. A few
members of Echo, the online community Horn founded, once
complained to her about a clique they identified on Echo. So
Horn asked them to name members of this in-group. "The answers were amazing," she writes. The complainers pointed to
members who barely communicated with each other. "They as-
sumed friendships between people who were either indifferent
or who actively disliked each other."

Okay, but is this still true today? Your network obviously becomes a little less invisible to anyone who can look up your profile on Facebook and see who your friends are, but I don't think
that the networks are truly exposed, and certainly not to the
marketer. One reason is privacy. People don't necessarily want
strangers to know who their friends are. Anyone who ever tried
to do what's called "snowball sampling" knows that people are
reluctant to give names of friends. Indeed, there are many on
Facebook and MySpace who mark their profile as private, so that
the list of their friends is blocked to unknown viewers. People
also don't necessarily want to share everything with their friends
or acquaintances. Facebook learned this the hard way in the fall
of 2007, when it introduced its Beacon service. This feature notified users' friends about their online purchases, and users got
confused and concerned about how to approve what information
(if any) they wanted to share. After more than 50,000 Facebook
users signed a petition against Beacon, Facebook's founder,
Mark Zuckerberg, apologized and called it a big mistake.

Then there's the question of coverage. Out of all the real-life
links that exist among a group of people, how many are reflected
on a social networking site? There are people who don't use
these networking sites at all or are very light users who've included only a small portion of their real-life connections. Real-

life social networks can also be very dynamic, and it will be interesting to see how comprehensive the social sites' coverage becomes over time.

There's also the issue of "tie strength," which is currently not reflected on networking sites. Harald Katzmair, the founder of FAS.research, a company that specializes in social network analysis, points out that this is one reason for a lot of noise in the data that come from these sites. An example of this kind of noise: Somebody you meet at a trade show asks you to befriend him. As far as the system is concerned, this guy is your friend, but several months later you don't even remember who he is or how you met. This kind of loose tie looks exactly the same as a close friendship on many networking sites.

The bottom line is that large sections of social networks are still invisible to the marketer. The extent to which they will stay invisible depends on user preferences, technology, and cultural standards. There's a range of attitudes around privacy among consumers, and so the cultural norms that are developing around this issue may be different according to where in the world you live, your age, and other variables. But one thing is clear: The individual should have full control of his or her private information and who can access it.

Overall, I think that marketers are still in the dark when they look at a social network, and that's a good thing. Word-of-mouth marketing is not about exposing a social network against its members' will but about encouraging people to tell their friends about what they like.

Principle 2: People Link with Others Who Are Similar to Them

Picture a family taking a stroll on a Sunday afternoon: mom, dad, teenage boy, young girl, and a dog. Now imagine another family coming from the other end of the street: another mom, dad, teenage boy, young girl, and a dog. They wave. Obviously the two families know each other. What do you think will happen when they meet? Most likely the adults will talk to the other adults, the teenage boy will talk to the other teenage boy, and the two girls will talk to each other. Even the dogs will sniff each other before they do anything else.

It's human nature for people to make contact with others like themselves. Scientists love to talk with other scientists. Rich people associate with other rich people. If you're into mountain biking, you're likely to hang out with other bikers. This tendency for people to like and associate with those who are similar to them is called "homophily," and it is one of the fundamental principles of social networks.

As innocent as this principle may sound, it is the main factor that can limit the acceleration of buzz. When PowerBar was first introduced, the high-energy snack spread quickly among runners, cyclists, and swimmers. As a triathlete, Jennifer Biddulph, who cofounded the company, knows people in these sports. Brian Maxwell, a world-ranked marathoner, also counted many leading athletes as friends. "We'd talked to a lot of serious athletes who were our friends and had given them samples of the bars we were working on in our kitchen," he told me in 1998. But each sport has its own social networks, and although some people help to link different sports, a company can't rely on them alone. Swimmers talk to swimmers, golfers talk to golfers, windsurfers talk to windsurfers. Maxwell realized that buzz about PowerBar wouldn't spread easily between runners and golfers, for example. "We really had to plant separate seeds in each area," he noted. When they marketed PowerBar to tennis players, they hired a tennis player. "She was not a marketer, but she knew tennis," Maxwell recalled. They gave her a certain number of complimentary bars and a marketing budget, and then they set her free to market to her network. She sent bars to tennis people she knew, called tournament directors, placed bars in tennis shops, and so on.

The homophily principle has two basic implications. The first is that people who are similar to each other tend to form clusters (a concept I discuss further in Principle 3). The second implication is that the more similar your employees are to your customers, the easier the communication between them will be. Nintendo used this concept when hiring video game enthusiasts as "game counselors." These counselors, typically just a few years older than the children they advised, were well placed to understand the kids' feedback and to raise excitement about new games. The homophily principle also affects the type of people who apply to work for a company. "You'll find that in a running shoe company, a lot of people are what we call running geeks, people who just like to run 10Ks and hang out with runners," says Helen Rockey, a former executive at Nike and Brooks Sports.

Principle 3: People Who Are Similar to Each Other Form Clusters

Why do Hell's Angels travel in packs? Why do the girls in second grade play together? Because people tend to interact with others who are similar to them. The results are clusters—sets of people who share similarities in some dimension of their lives and, as a result, frequently communicate with one another.

Millions of unique clusters are formed according to dimensions such as age, sex, education, occupation, social class, area of interest, geography, and ethnic background.

Clusters and cliques are so common, in fact, that when we don't see them, we're perplexed. A study of social networks in a prison found that the inmate networks always clustered around race, geographical origin, and the type of crime the inmates had committed. Russ Bernard, one of the researchers, says, "In the hundreds of groups among the living units we studied, the cliques always made sense." They did come across one exception: The researchers discovered three men who formed a tight network despite the fact that they didn't seem to have anything in common. As the researchers and the prison staff were contemplating this special case, the three prisoners escaped together. Common goals can also tie people to each other.

Clusters can informally adopt products together. In marketing EndNote to the academic market, we often came across university departments that defined themselves as "all Macintosh" or "all PC." Software usage followed the same pattern: You could find a cluster of WordPerfect users in one university building and a cluster of Microsoft Word users in another. Everett Rogers and Lawrence Kincaid observed this same phenomenon when they studied the adoption of family-planning methods in Korea. The Korean government promoted three types of family planning: oral contraceptive pills, vasectomy, and IUD. In surveying twenty-five villages, Rogers and Kincaid found that villages tended unofficially to select one particular method. In fact, the researchers started referring to some villages as "pill villages," to some as "IUD villages," and to one as "the vasectomy village." Explaining these clusters was easy: After one local network hub chose a method, she began to spread the word about the advantages of that method and consequently influenced the rest of her village.

The good news for companies is that if your product becomes the standard within a cluster, it makes it very difficult for competitors to uproot you from this position. There is a reinforcing effect, as network members tell each other about the product and as your company develops relationships with members of the network. Of course, this is *bad* news when it's your competitor's product that has been adopted.

Another implication of this principle is that sometimes a product becomes so closely associated with a certain cluster that people in other clusters hesitate to adopt it. In the early 1970s, for example, the Birkenstock brand was adopted in alternative-lifestyle clusters, so much so that wearing Birkenstocks became a political statement. It took the company years to convince mainstream customers to wear the sandals.

Principle 4: Buzz Spreads through Common Nodes

We all belong to more than one cluster or clique, which is one way buzz spreads. To understand this idea, we need to examine the "small world" or "six degrees of separation" concept, the idea that any two people are linked through a chain of no more than six other people. The focus here shouldn't be on the number six. The main point is that experiments have demonstrated that any person can be reached through a limited number of steps. The key reason for this is that none of us knows exactly the same people as someone else. We are usually connected to our family through one cluster, to our colleagues at work through another, and to our friends from college through yet another cluster. In this way clusters are connected to larger networks, ultimately linking people who belong to distant clusters.

The social psychologist Stanley Milgram was one of the first people to study how people are linked to each other. Milgram asked people from Wichita, Kansas, and Omaha, Nebraska, to pass on an envelope to a target person, the wife of a divinity school student in Cambridge, Massachusetts. Each participant in the experiment was given an envelope and a brief description of the target person (where she lived, what she did, and so on). If the participant knew the target person on a personal basis, he or she could mail or give her the envelope directly (none did). Otherwise, the participant was asked to pass it on to someone who they thought was likely to know her or get the envelope closer to her. Four days after the experiment started, someone stopped the target person on the street in Cambridge, handed her an envelope, and said, "Alice, this is for you." This particular envelope originated with a wheat farmer in Kansas, who passed it on to the Episcopalian minister in his hometown, who forwarded it to an instructor at the Episcopal Theological Seminary in Cambridge, who handed the envelope to Alice. Most envelopes in this and later studies had a longer trip. In one study where people were asked to pass on an envelope from Omaha, Nebraska, to someone in Sharon, Massachusetts, it took, on average, about five intermediate people to get the envelope to the target person.

Incidentally, in 2002 researchers from Columbia University (including Duncan Watts, whose work I discussed in the previous chapter) repeated this experiment on the Internet. Thousands of people signed up as volunteers to pass messages to certain target people. I volunteered to try it and got two names. One was a guy in Croatia. I forwarded his name to a friend, but the (virtual) envelope got stuck somewhere on its way. The second person was a potter and musician from New Zealand. To reach him I forwarded the message to Ken Williams, EndNote's distributor in Australia. Ken sent it to someone in New Zealand. The message circled for a while in New Zealand and finally reached the target person. There were five people between us.

To see how the small world phenomenon helps buzz to spread, let's focus on one tiny section of a network. In following the buzz about the book *Cold Mountain* (a book I discuss in the next chapter), I met Jody Denison, who lives in the San Francisco Bay Area. She loves books and belongs to two book clubs. Denison heard about *Cold Mountain* from members of one club, the Diablo Book Club, and relayed the information to her friends at the second club, the Crow Canyon Book Club. Essentially, she served as the link between the two clusters.

What does all this mean to marketers? While it is true that buzz spreads through mutual acquaintances, the degree of control that marketers have on this process is very limited. Let's assume that the following path exists between you and me: Your gardener's cousin is taking dancing lessons with a neighbor of my optometrist. Could I have gotten the word about my book to you through our mutual acquaintances? I doubt it. When you first hear the concept of five or six degrees of separation, it doesn't sound like much of a separation, but it is. "When we speak of five intermediaries, we are talking about an enormous psychological distance between the starting and target points," Milgram wrote in 1967. "We should think of the five points as being not five persons apart, but 'five circles of acquaintances' apart—five 'structures' apart. This helps to set it in its proper perspective."

Principle 5: Information Gets Trapped in Clusters

I once promised a new customer of EndNote that I would give her a quick demo of our software and help her install it on her computer. On the designated day I arrived at her office and quickly installed the software on her Mac. We had hundreds of users already at the medical center where she worked, so I was a little surprised when she asked me if anyone else around there was using EndNote. She was equally surprised to hear that hundreds of people in the same medical center were already using the software. The mystery was resolved after we talked further. She was a surgeon involved mostly in clinical work. Most of the users of EndNote at that university at the time were Ph.D.'s whose work focused on research. There was a significant gap between them.

Ronald Burt of the University of Chicago defines this type of a gap as a "structural hole"—"a separation between nonredundant contacts." It is important to realize that oftentimes different information circulates on either side of a structural hole. The surgeon with whom I talked about EndNote certainly knew of the Ph.D.'s at her facility, and may have occasionally interacted with them. But most of her daily contacts were with other surgeons. When we look at a diagram of a network, we first notice the connections. But sometimes you can learn just as much from paying attention to the absence of ties.

It is important to identify the gaps between different clusters and to find ways to spread the word about a product to people on both sides of any structural holes. Of course, in real life this neat theory is complicated by the fact that no one is handed a chart of such social networks. All you see is people. Still, trying to identify these gaps—even just knowing that they exist—can be valuable.

Principle 6: Network Hubs and Connectors Create Shortcuts

Imagine a woman from California traveling to Germany for her vacation. She stays at a health spa, where she takes yoga classes. One morning she asks her yoga teacher about a certain brand of Scandinavian wooden sandals that she believes would be good for her feet. The yoga teacher tells her about another kind of sandal, with a cork sole instead of a wooden one. The woman finds these sandals, buys them, and discovers that they're exactly what she was looking for. When she returns to America, she tells others about the sandals' benefits.

While no one planned this link, this shortcut was a significant event in the history of the German manufacturer of Birkenstock sandals. The woman who made that trip to Germany is Margot Fraser, who became not only a satisfied customer but also the company's exclusive distributor in the United States, with estimated sales of more than $120 million. Margot Fraser's tie with that yoga trainer is an example of a spontaneous shortcut that connected two clusters and accelerated the diffusion of the product.

Shortcuts that connect clusters may explain the small world phenomenon, according to Duncan Watts and Steven Strogatz, who have used computer simulation to analyze this phenomenon. What's surprising, according to Watts, is that it takes very few shortcuts to turn a big world into a small world. It only took one person to connect two clusters in Germany and California and dramatically accelerate the diffusion of Birkenstock shoes. The point is, however, that without these kinds of shortcuts, the networks would be much slower to spread the word.

As I pointed out in the previous chapter, it's important not to overstate the importance of hubs. Shortcuts are created by non-hubs too. Connectors such as Fraser are not necessarily directly linked to a lot of people. What distinguishes them from hubs is that they can connect two or more clusters. Fraser was originally from Germany, so she speaks both German and English and is familiar with both cultures. Connectors like her who straddle the world are best positioned to create shortcuts. (It's worth mentioning here that unlike Gladwell, I define connectors simply as people who connect different clusters, even if they don't know lots of people.)

Another example of people who tend to create shortcuts is venture capitalists. To spread the word about a product to startup companies in Silicon Valley, try getting the attention of local venture capital firms. The partners in these companies work with many startups and serve as a communication channel among them. A message that they value will find its way to their contacts quickly.

The first implication of this principle is that companies can deliberately create shortcuts by having people within the company link with individuals in remote networks. In so doing, companies accelerate the natural diffusion process. The other implication is that companies can identify people who have the most potential to create shortcuts. The automotive industry, for example, has for years been aware of the importance of accountants, realtors, and lawyers in spreading the word about their cars. Because of the nature of their daily work, these people often serve as a bridge between cliques and clusters in the local community.

Principle 7: We Talk to Those around Us

The Internet does cross geographical boundaries, but this does not mean that geography no longer matters. Physical proximity is still key in the way buzz spreads. Back in 1999, my assistant, Haim Zaltzman, asked students to name three people with whom they discussed the singer Lauryn Hill, and we found that the vast majority of communications were with people who lived close by. There was relatively little communication about Lauryn Hill with people off-campus, although all the students had e-mail accounts and access to a phone. Ongoing research by Keller Fay has some similar results. In 2007 the firm reported that 74 percent of all comments are transmitted through simple face-to-face conversations.

Barry Wellman and David B. Tindall of the University of Toronto reported that while residents of Toronto had global ties, most of their ties lived in or near metropolitan Toronto. Thomas J. Allen from MIT, who studied communication among employees in seven R&D labs, measured the walking distances between each of the technical people in these labs and asked them to keep track of whom they communicated with for several months. The results showed that the closer people were to one another physically, the more likely they were to talk. Although these two studies were conducted before the Internet era, the Keller Fay data confirm that this fundamental aspect of human behavior has not changed. It's simply more convenient and natural to talk with those who are around us.

When you think about it, this makes perfect sense. First, remember that most people hang out with people like themselves—perfect candidates for a conversation. Add to that the fact that it's still easier to talk than to type e-mail, and then factor in the fact that a lot of "product talk" is incidental—small-talk buzz that's motivated by a grooming instinct. Although the Internet allows people to connect with anyone around the world, and many do, physical proximity is still an excellent predictor of those with whom you will share information.

What are the implications for marketers? In the same way that regional dialects continue to live on in the United States despite decades of national TV, local and regional influences remain important despite the Internet. Since people talk to those around them, when marketing a product or service you hope will have national or global appeal, it is important to create a presence in every geographical location. This means that traditional marketing focused on Zip Codes, database marketing, and brick-and-mortar sales outlets are still key in spreading the word.

Principle 8: Weak Ties Are Surprisingly Strong

In the late 1960s Mark Granovetter, a graduate student at Harvard, was interested in how people found out about their jobs. One question that sparked Granovetter's curiosity was how the shape of people's close networks helped them in their job search. He asked his interviewees to name the five people with whom they spent most of their time and to draw a diagram of how these people were linked to each other. It was basic knowledge that most people find out about jobs from other people rather than from advertising, so Granovetter asked his interviewees to identify the person who referred them to their last job. To his surprise, that person was never on the diagram of close friends. When he asked them to tell him about the friend who *did* refer them to the job, they would often correct him by saying "Not a friend, an acquaintance."

Granovetter went on to survey 282 professional, technical, and managerial workers in the Boston suburb of Newton, and he found that most of these people—about 56 percent—found their jobs through a personal contact and that this personal contact was usually *not* a close friend. In fact, of those who found their job through a personal connection, only about 17 percent had learned about their last position from close friends or family. Most people found out about it from people outside their immediate close network—people they saw occasionally or rarely, such as former workmates or old college friends.

This phenomenon, which Granovetter called "the strength of

weak ties," goes well beyond just the job market. Your closest friends—those who move in the same social circles as you do—are likely to be exposed to the same sources of information as you are. Therefore, they don't usually bring you fresh news. On the other hand, people outside this group are much more likely to hear things that you do not. In this way, weak ties with distant acquaintances are most apt to bring in information that is new.

Remember the Rock Bottom study that examined who creates the most buzz for these restaurants and breweries? Among other things, that study concluded that word of mouth through acquaintances had significantly more impact than word of mouth with close friends and relatives. Keep in mind that the company studied the impact of incremental word of mouth—the new word of mouth that happened as the result of this campaign—so don't jump to the conclusion that word of mouth among strong ties is never important. At that time, though, the buzz that went to acquaintances brought more sales.

What is the takeaway to a marketer? Strong-tie buzz has a different impact from weak-tie buzz. A chat between a husband and a wife will spread the word within a certain cluster, whereas a conversation with an old roommate from college is more likely to spread the word from one cluster to another. Which one is more common? Strong-tie buzz seems to be much more prevalent. Keller Fay reports that 27 percent of conversations are with a spouse or partner, 25 percent with another family member, and 10 percent with a best friend. Added together, these numbers are nine times higher than the 5 percent of conversations that take place with acquaintances and 2 percent with strangers. It's not that one is more important than the other, but keep the difference in mind and try to think about which type you're trying to stimulate.

This principle also has clear implications for the way we

gather data about the world: Since we tend to form networks with individuals who are similar to us and are likely to be exposed to the same sources of information, people outside these networks are important in bringing in fresh data. Don't listen only to your close network—it is likely to rehash what you already know. Diversify your connections.

Principle 9: The Net Nurtures Weak Ties

It's easy to maintain weak ties on the Internet, or at least easier than by phone. Calling someone on the phone is somewhat intrusive and time-consuming. Dropping people a friendly note via e-mail is an easy way to keep in touch without placing too much obligation on them. On Facebook, you don't even have to e-mail people, because you can see what they're up to on your newsfeed. You can also quickly create new ties online and use these ties to acquire information. Many people in newsgroups and online forums either maintain very weak ties or don't know each other at all. In the past ten years there's been an explosion of weak ties on the Internet. "I can have hundreds and thousands of these kinds of connections, because they don't take a lot of time and energy to maintain," says Valdis Krebs, an expert on social networks.

This explosion in weak ties, however, should not lead us to the conclusion that technology will soon link everyone on the planet. Our own operating system, the brain, is capable of managing only so many links at any given time. The fact is that we can't (and probably don't want to) maintain links with an unlimited number of people. One proof is that despite the fact that many of us live among millions of other people in major metropolitan areas, "we still know only about the same number of people as our long-distant ancestors did when they roamed the plains of the American Midwest or the savannahs of eastern Africa," the psychologist Robin Dunbar says.

It is difficult to determine how many links each one of us can handle. It's even hard to figure out how many links we actually do maintain. Scientists have delineated three levels of links. At the most intimate level, the number seems to be eleven or twelve. These numbers consistently come up when people are asked to list the names of those whose death they would find devastating. At the next level you find people with whom you feel comfortable—people you wouldn't be "embarrassed about joining uninvited for a drink, if you happened to bump into them in a bar," as Dunbar puts it. Dunbar argues that "the figure of 150 seems to represent the maximum number of individuals with whom we can have a genuinely social relationship." Finally there are acquaintances, people you know but are not too close to. The average of those seems to be between 500 and 1,500.

The increase in weak ties on the Internet can explain why information travels much faster today. The Internet creates millions of shortcuts of weak ties that bridge social clusters. There are many pieces of information that wouldn't warrant a special phone call to distant friends but that you can include in an e-mail message and send to several of your acquaintances or mention on your blog, if you have one.

The fact that there is a limit to the number of ties one can maintain means that clusters are here to stay. Because we can manage only so many links, and because we prefer to form links with those similar to us, we will probably continue to cluster around people like us.

Principle 10: Networks Go across Categories

In the late 1980s a company called Gojo introduced a hand-sanitizing product for medical professionals called Purell. Like the traditional products from that company—Gojo has produced cleaning products for mechanics and for factory workers—Purell was seen as an industrial product that was sold exclusively to hospitals, nursing homes, and clinics. Marketers tend to look at "categories," "segments," and "markets." But doctors and nurses who used the product at the hospital started telling their families and friends about it and urging them to use it too. Gojo started getting a flood of phone calls from health professionals and their friends who wanted to use the product at home.

People belong to more than one market, and they are connected to people who are part of other markets. Joe, who's shopping for some new software for his home computer, also has a PC at the office, and his daughter has a PC at college. The computer industry has traditionally viewed the world as divided into three distinct markets: home, business, and educational. But Joe plays a role in all three—and he's not alone.

In the past, a politician could deliver one message to a core group of supporters and a different one to the general public, which is probably impossible to do in a connected world. Today a speech to a domestic audience can be instantly viewed by a global audience. The Internet and communication technologies further blur the lines among different categories.

What does this mean to you? You never know how people in one market category are linked to people in other categories. Messages that you try to direct to one group of people can easily find their way to other people. As a result, stories about bad service experienced at your low-end segment, for example, can move to your high-end customers.

. . .

People love to talk, but who they talk *with* is not random. It's determined by the social networks they are part of. Getting a sense of how these networks operate was the first step in understanding how to stimulate the flow of buzz—the subject of chapters to follow.

A song went around from fiddler to
fiddler and each one added something
and took something away.
—Charles Frazier, *Cold Mountain*

How Buzz Spreads

10 **Now that you understand the** structure of social networks—the highway system, if you will—it's time to examine how buzz—the traffic—spreads through the system. To do this, I'll examine the buzz about one product, the novel *Cold Mountain*, which became a surprise blockbuster bestseller. It's impossible, of course, to expose all the buzz about such a book, since millions of comments related to it have leaped from brain to brain. But analyzing *Cold Mountain* is a good starting point for discussing how buzz spreads.

I should make one point before we start. Buzz is not water and it doesn't flow like water. Yet it is very tempting (and I too give in to the temptation from time to time) to use water as a metaphor to describe the process. When the French sociologist Gabriel Tarde described how fashion spread in France at the turn of the last century, he used the metaphor of a water tower. Fashion, he believed, originated in the highest social class and flowed downward through a "waterfall of imitation": Upper-class women adopted the new fashion first, middle-class women observed them and started adopting the new fashion, and so on. Others who have studied this over the years have used terms such as "trickle-down" and the "two-step flow" model to describe the process. These concepts are not necessarily wrong—in fact, I believe that they describe important components of the process—but these terms immediately suggest that the source is in some way more important than the receiving end. Adopting this view, you assume that a woman who has a new dress is superior to the one who doesn't. A journalist who writes about a new computer is above the reader who isn't yet aware of the new gadget. A publisher of a book is somehow more important than the bookstore, which is somehow above the reader. The water metaphor also assumes that information flows in only one direction, ignoring the fact that there's often a dialogue between people who spread the word about a product and those who are on the receiving end of the information.

While I recognize that some hierarchy always exists in the way information spreads, there is not as much as some people think. If I were forced to use a water metaphor, I would say that buzz is more like underground water. It may trickle any which way: down, sideways, or even up. But I'd rather stick to the concept expressed throughout the book: the importance of networks.

There are 6.6 billion people all around the planet forming a gigantic social network. At some point somewhere in this network, an idea is cooked up in the brain of one person, or sometimes a few people—a node or a small cluster of them. And from there the spread begins.

Where Did It All Start?

Charles Frazier first heard the story that would become the backbone of his book *Cold Mountain* from his father in the late eighties. Frazier's father, a retired high school principal in Franklin, North Carolina, was researching their family history at the time. He told his son about a great-great-uncle, a Confederate soldier by the name of W. P. Inman, who deserted from the army while recovering from his battle wounds. "It's like someone saying, 'Here's a brief outline for a book; what do you think?'" Frazier told the *Washington Post* years later. Frazier couldn't find much more about that great-great-uncle, but the idea was planted in his mind. Over the next seven or so years he developed this very thin outline into a 449-page novel.

At what point does an idea leave the brain of its creator and start traveling in the networks? In the case of Frazier, this would probably have taken a long time if it weren't for his wife, Katherine, who threatened to smuggle part of the manuscript to Kaye Gibbons, a bestselling local author whom the Fraziers knew through their children. Frazier proved willing to part with a hundred or so pages, and Gibbons was impressed with his work. She referred him to Leigh Feldman, a literary agent in New York City who works with Liz Darhansoff, Gibbons's agent. Feldman remembers receiving three outstanding chapters. "I wrote him and said that I loved it," she recalls. Months later she received a large part of the manuscript.

Feldman showed the manuscript to several editors in book publishing houses. She also showed it to a friend, Elisabeth Schmitz, who was the head of subsidiary rights at Grove/Atlantic, a midsized independent publisher. Schmitz's job at Grove was to deal with foreign and domestic rights. She had never edited a book before, but she fell in love with *Cold Mountain*.

Love, passion, and energy are not concepts you typically find in business analysis, but these forces started to form behind *Cold Mountain*. "I walked into my boss's office—Morgan Entrekin—and said, 'This is the most incredible thing I've read since I've come to work for you,' " Elisabeth Schmitz remembers. " 'And I know you have a Christmas party tonight, and I know you usually go and stay up all night, but you have to read this tonight.' " Entrekin read the manuscript that night. He called Schmitz first thing in the morning and asked, "What do we have to do to get it?" A few days later Grove/Atlantic owned the world rights to the novel.

Only so much buzz can be generated in an industry at any particular point in time, and everyone knows that. Therefore, when left alone, most new products and ideas encounter objection or indifference in their industries. There is no buzz. The industry raises its head, mutters to itself, and gets back to its usual business. At first *Cold Mountain* was no exception. "Nobody even gave it two thoughts. It was a first literary southern novel," says Feldman. It would take significant efforts to change that.

How the First People Outside the Industry Heard about It

We'll jump about eighteen months ahead, to around the time when the book was actually published. The first printing of the book was 26,000 copies. As soon as it was published, it started to sell well. "It went on the bestseller list within about six weeks, and it was not from big media attention. It was from word of mouth and old-fashioned bookselling," says Entrekin, the president of Grove/Atlantic.

Mike Jordan, a professor of social psychology at Francis Marion University (near Florence, South Carolina), first read about the book in a prepublication review in the *Charlotte Observer*. He was fascinated by the review and asked the people at his local store, Books-A-million, to give him a call when the book became available. Once he and his wife read the book, they were so excited that they bought three more copies and gave them to their parents and a good friend. In addition to telling people about the book, Jordan posted a review on Amazon.com, participated in a panel discussion about the book that aired on the local-access television station, and, although he is not a literature professor, gave *Cold Mountain* as one of the options for a graduate-student project. Six students chose the book, and "all but one of them loved it and then passed it on and talked about it with other people," he says. Seeing the activities of a network hub such as Jordan, you start to realize how powerful individual hubs can be in promoting a product they like.

Researchers who study communication refer to what happened in Jordan's case as an example of the "two-step flow" model: Information flows from mass media to network hubs and from the hubs to the rest of the population. I talked to several hubs who learned about the book in this way. Lynne Jenkins first read about the novel in *Southern Living*. "It sounded like something I'd like because my family came from that area," she says. Like Jordan, Jenkins went to a bookstore right away, but they didn't have the book in stock yet. When she finally found it, she skimmed it at the store and decided she liked Frazier's style. "He used a lot of the old-fashioned terms like I remember my grandmother used. Definitely regional lingo and slang for different things in the kitchen, different types of herbs . . ." Jenkins bought the book and loved it. She estimates that she told ten people about it. She also gave the book to a relative who lives in the area where the action takes place. She too posted a review on Amazon.com.

Buzz Spreads in All Directions

While the two-step flow model obviously describes one aspect of how buzz spreads, buzz refuses to follow neat patterns. The word about products doesn't disseminate only from the media to opinion leaders and from them to the rest of us. Jo Alice Canterbury, for example, a reader from the San Francisco Bay Area, heard about *Cold Mountain* from a friend, not from the media. She went on to tell at least fifty people about the book. First she recommended it to her husband. This was an important side current within families—a lot of women felt that *Cold Mountain* was a book that they could pass on to their husbands. She also remembers telling family and friends in New Orleans, Arkansas, Texas, Colorado, and Washington. A flight attendant who crossed the Pacific three times a month, Canterbury took advantage of dozens of opportunities to tell passengers about the book.

Some readers heard about *Cold Mountain* from friends who aren't network hubs—just folks who tell a friend or two about a book. Others heard about it from clerks at the bookstore. And in a case of "reverse flow," some clerks got excited about the book only after hearing early readers' reactions. This reverse flow happens at another level of the distribution channel as well. Patricia Kelly, a sales representative for Publishers Group West (PGW, the company that distributed *Cold Mountain* to bookstores), said that she became intrigued about the book after talking with several independent bookstore owners who had already gotten advance readers' galleys from the publisher.

A lot of information about the book was spread over the Internet. When I counted them in 1999, there were more than nine hundred reviews of *Cold Mountain* on Amazon.com. It's no longer one review in the *New York Times* that gets everyone talking. And the media's glowing reviews don't immediately translate into an enthusiastic reaction among today's skeptical customers. Another reader said he simply found *Cold Mountain* at a bookstore without talking to anyone: "I was killing time waiting for a train and picked it up off a front display table in the train station bookstore. I judge books by the quality of the writing, period. I'd never heard of Frazier—how could I have?—but I could immediately tell that the prose was gifted. I almost never buy novels in hardback, but I was so taken in by the first couple of pages that I bought it. There is no marketing substitute for good writing."

The last point is a key one, and one that's not always taken into consideration in studying buzz. The flow of information about a product cannot be separated from the quality of the product itself. Over the course of reading 449 pages, something happens between a reader and a book that determines whether the reader will pass the word on, to how many others, and how enthusiastically. As I argue in the next chapter, "contagious attributes" built into the product, including the extent to which expectations are met or exceeded, are the biggest factors in determining how much buzz a product gets.

What Made the Word Spread

Of course, I could end the discussion right here and explain buzz by focusing on the quality of the book itself. But we have all

seen excellent books that did not become bestsellers. The quality of the writing in a book can only partially explain buzz. What
was it, then, that made people talk about this book out of all the
books they could talk about?

The first observation is that it didn't happen by itself. A
tremendous amount of energy was put behind this book. First,
the comments about *Cold Mountain* were charged with energy.
The people at Grove/Atlantic and PGW deeply believed in this
book and warmly recommended it. Kim Wylie, a senior VP at
PGW, was one of the people "infected" by *Cold Mountain* early on.
She became one of the biggest forces pushing the book, telling
everyone around her about it, including buyers at Barnes & Noble and other accounts she manages. Everyone at PGW started
talking about it as more and more sales reps read the book.
These salespeople in turn spread the word to a network of independent bookstores, who backed the book by giving it special
attention: telling customers about it, featuring it in their news-
letters, displaying it in a prominent place at the store.

Beyond just passion, energy includes the time and money put
behind a product. Entrekin and Schmitz spent hours walking
through the stacks at a Barnes & Noble with a pad and pen, writing down about 150 names of writers around the country who
they felt would be interested in reading *Cold Mountain*. "We
weren't necessarily asking them to give us a quote that we would
use. It was more just 'Here's a great book, we want to share it
with you,' " says Entrekin. Some of these authors in turn started
talking about the book within their networks.

Grove/Atlantic also fueled the book's success by putting
more of their time and money behind it every step of the way.
For example, the first run of galleys was five hundred. When
they noticed that the reaction to the advance copies was outstanding, they immediately printed an additional one thousand
copies. And as these copies started to generate even greater

buzz, they printed another two and a half to three thousand more. Altogether they sent out in excess of four thousand advance copies to bookstore owners, buyers, and anyone who could help spread the word. Of course, every publisher sends out galleys, but the number that Grove sent out was particularly high at the time, especially for a literary novel. Because these copies were produced in small print runs, the unit cost was relatively high (about $8 to $10 per copy), a cost Grove willingly absorbed.

Everyone involved in selling the book, including its author, put time and effort into promoting it. Months before publication, Entrekin took Frazier to meet some bookstore owners, buyers, and clerks. As soon as the publisher noticed that interest in the book was not limited to the Southeast region, Entrekin extended Frazier's tour to other parts of the country. Reaching out to retailers and readers in this way sparked thousands of conversations that allowed news of the book to spread.

Such energy can be contagious. Grove demonstrated so much enthusiasm for and confidence in the book that the rest of the industry responded. Grove even sent galleys to sales reps of competing publishing houses, feeling that they would take an interest in a book of such quality. "People are supportive of a good piece of work even if it's not coming from their company. Everybody in book publishing loves reading a good book," Entrekin says.

At a certain point the book's popularity exploded. A first-time author who creates a serious literary novel that gets on the bestseller list—we all love a success story like this. A lot of goodwill surrounded the book. "Everyone in the publishing industry said, 'Go! Go! Go! Go!'" Leigh Feldman remembers. Carl Lennertz of Random House, who published a weekly newsletter for independent bookstores, featured the book enthusiastically.

Larry Kirshbaum, the CEO of Warner Books, became an unofficial spokesperson for *Cold Mountain*.

Entrekin is quick to emphasize the importance of the quality of the book itself in the buzz that it created. "You couldn't just try to do this for any kind of book. It has to be a special book," he says. "What you're trying to do is get the book in a position where it can make its own fate." Nobody can say for sure what would have happened to *Cold Mountain* if Entrekin, Schmitz, and their colleagues hadn't marshaled behind the title. But we know what happened when they did. The book sold 1.6 million copies of the hardcover edition alone, an astounding number.

Credibility

Buzz travels most smoothly through channels built on trust. Customers of many independent bookstores have learned to trust the clerks behind the counter. One customer in Danville, California, for example, told me how much she trusts Michael Barnard, the owner of Rakestraw, a local bookstore. "Many times he'll recommend a book, and I don't even have to read the cover," she said. When Barnard recommended *Cold Mountain*, that was all she needed to know.

Mike Barnard first heard about *Cold Mountain* from Patricia Kelly of Publishers Group West. "She said that there was one book on the spring list that I really had to pay attention to," he remembers. She gave him the galleys, and he read it. Kelly enjoys tremendous credibility among her clients. In 1999 she was named "Publishers Weekly Rep of the Year." And in an article profiling her, one store owner said, "If she tells you that this book is something she really likes, you know she's not making that up."

I heard almost exactly the same remarks about Morgan

Entrekin. Entrekin was telling people that this was going to be one of the best books he would ever publish, "and he doesn't throw that around freely," one of them commented. About a month before publication, Grove/Atlantic had a dinner for leading booksellers in the San Francisco Bay Area to promote the book. It was the first time that Barnard met Entrekin, and he was impressed—by the way the publisher read, by his enthusiasm, by his commitment to a title that had none of the hallmarks of a book destined to become a bestseller.

People who spread the word effectively are not necessarily loud, and you won't always see them gesticulating furiously. They are people whom we trust. Most of them understand that trust can be fragile. They enjoy their credibility, and when they back a product, they know that they're putting their reputation on the line. "I would not do this for a book that I was not as enthusiastic about, because I just couldn't afford to," Entrekin explains.

This is an important point. Some people make the mistake of getting excited about everything. Every little product from their company is the best thing since sliced bread. Every upgrade is a significant addition to the human race. Enthusiasm is great. It's important. But undiscerning enthusiasm leads to loss of credibility. Pick your battles. Pick the products you're proud to put yourself behind wholeheartedly.

There is another important point about credibility. No matter how much credibility one has, the best buzz comes from third parties, not from the company putting out the product itself. Paradoxically, your competitors often are the ones who signal to the industry whether what you're doing is worth talking about. In high tech, a new product that is not recognized by its competitors (by their reacting to it) is usually dismissed in the industry. In the case of *Cold Mountain*, recognition came from other publishers, who bought the rights to publish the book in additional languages or formats. When Grove/Atlantic sold paperback rights prior to hardcover publication to Vintage, a Random House imprint, for $300,000, that sent a clear message to people in the publishing industry. Such an amount for a first novel by an unknown author made people in the industry talk.

How Buzz Became Buying

Let's assume you have not read *Cold Mountain*. Suppose you meet a friend at a party—let's call him Alex—and you start talking about books. And suppose Alex mentions *Cold Mountain*, saying, "Oh, you ought to read this book." Let's examine what happens as a result of this molecule of buzz.

During the first few moments of conversation, Alex's comments will go through some initial tests in your brain. One is the relevance test: Are you in the market for a book like *Cold Mountain*? This will greatly affect your level of interest. Typically, people are much more receptive to hearing about products they think they might want to buy. If you are interested, you're likely to ask a question about the book, such as "What's it about?" Alex might tell you that it takes place during the Civil War. You may get turned off, pointing out that you don't usually read books about the Civil War era. Alex would then quickly point out that it's not a typical war book. The conversation that develops shows what makes buzz so powerful. Unlike mass media, word of mouth allows you and Alex to exchange information so that you can make sure you understand each other.

Credibility is the next test that Alex's comment will have to pass. How much credibility he has with you depends on your mutual history, his reputation, and your overall impression of him. For example, if he has recommended ten books to you in the past and you loved every single one of them, you will be likely to trust his recommendation.

What will happen next? Any number of things could happen. A waiter may pass by with a plate of mini sausage rolls, or someone may join you and you'll move to a different topic, or maybe the party will be over and it will be time to go home. My point is that a comment is just a comment. Millions of other things in a customer's life will distract him or her from information about a product. This is the environment in which Alex's comment will live in your brain—surrounded by constant distractions.

Although it is possible that you'll go to the bookstore first thing the next morning and buy the book, it is also possible that you'll store the comment for future reference or that you'll let it evaporate from your memory altogether.

Of course, your decision is influenced not only by Alex but by others in your social network. Your behavior depends to a large extent on your adoption threshold, in addition to Alex's credibility, the energy of his comment, and whether you are in the market or not, and on how many people in your network have already bought and read the book. Once enough people in your network have read *Cold Mountain* to surpass your threshold point, you will probably follow their lead.

Let us assume that you bought the book and read it. Whether or not you will pass on comments to other people depends to a large extent on how you judge the book. This is the beauty of the word-of-mouth phenomenon. In an ideal world, every node in the network who decides to try a product ultimately performs his or her own quality-control test and, based on the results, decides whether to pass the word further. As a marketer, you can't force customers to say anything positive about your product, just as you can't order people to love you. Even if they say the words, they won't mean them. Buzz is authentic because it is un-coerced.

Forces That Block Buzz from Spreading

Based on the model I've described so far, it may seem as if a marketer of a top-quality product has little work to do, as the product will take off on its own. In reality, there are several forces that are working against the marketer. We have already talked about both experience-based and secondhand detractors. Other factors include irrational behavior, noise, competition, forgetting, misinformation, inertia, and crowding effects. In simple words: Not everything we do makes sense, we're distracted by competing messages, we forget what our friends told us just a week ago (and sometimes even faster), we distort what we hear, we like to stick to "the good old way" of doing things, and at some point, certain people refuse to try a product because everyone else is already doing it.

This last point has not gotten too much attention in the academic literature. We not only imitate others, we also dis-imitate. Some people define themselves by doing things that others don't, and the moment they detect that "the wrong people" are wearing/reading/using your product, they're gone.

A few years ago, a research team at Stanford sold LiveStrong yellow wristbands to students who lived in one dorm on campus. A week later they started selling these wristbands in a neighboring dorm, which had a reputation as a geek dorm with a stronger academic focus. What happened once the geeks started wearing the wristbands? A week later, the research team measured a 32 percent drop in students wearing the bands at the first dorm. "People in the original dorm abandoned the wristband to avoid other students thinking they were similar to the geeks," explained Dr. Jonah Berger, who ran this study as a Ph.D. student at Stanford.

This is especially true in product categories such as clothes, music, and hairstyles, which are seen as symbolic of identity. Based on research that Dr. Berger conducted with Dr. Chip Heath from Stanford, they concluded that in these categories people want to imitate members of their in-group, but when they notice that outsiders are starting to use the product too, they will abandon it. This, of course, presents a significant challenge to brands in these categories that have to play a delicate game of providing limited edition products to certain groups.

How Risk Affects Buzz

Suppose that you're a cardiologist who is considering a new device for use in heart surgery. A lot more is at stake when you make this decision than when a consumer buys *Cold Mountain*. The worst that can happen if you choose a bad book is that you will be bored and lose a few dollars. By choosing the wrong medical device, you could kill one of your patients.

The increased risk affects how buzz spreads. In risky situations people turn to megahubs for help. As a reader, you may not care that much about what a prestigious critic writing for the *New York Times Book Review* thinks about *Cold Mountain*. As a cardiologist, you care a lot about what the top professor in the country's best medical center says about the device you're going to use on Thursday in Operating Room 3.

The higher the monetary or psychological risks involved in the consumer's decision to buy, the more the classic adoption patterns apply. Scholars who study the diffusion of innovations have traditionally classified the population into five adoption categories: innovators, early adopters, early majority, late majority, and laggards. At first a few innovators who are willing to take risks will adopt something new. This group is usually considered to be about 2.5 percent of the population. They will be followed by the early adopters, a group that consists of about 13.5 percent of the population. Then the first mainstream group, the early majority (34 percent) will start to adopt the innovation, followed by the late majority (34 percent). Finally the laggards (16 percent) will adopt the innovation. This model has its roots in a classic study by Ryan and Gross, who examined how an innovation was adopted among farmers in Iowa. Since 1962 it has been described extensively by Everett Rogers in the five editions of his classic work *Diffusion of Innovations*. In the early 1990s, Geoffrey Moore brought the model to the attention of technology marketers by arguing that there is a chasm between the early adopters (who are interested in the technology) and the early majority, a mainstream group that is more pragmatic about technology.

This model was designed to describe actual adoption rather than just buzz about an innovation. Buzz spreads in a similar way, but there are differences worth pointing out. Since the risk in hearing about an innovation is immaterial, buzz obviously spreads at a faster rate than actual adoption.

Web companies like Google, Facebook, and YouTube reduce the risk of adopting their product to almost zero. The services are free, so the monetary risk is nil. Ease of use is key—it usually takes seconds to get started—so the risk of wasting time is minimal. This means that even someone who might normally wait for others to try a product first is willing to jump right in. Of course, even with this risk minimized, not everyone adopts. Why? It goes back to the forces that block buzz, such as inertia, noise, and crowding effects.

Industry Buzz
versus Customer Buzz

A common mistake companies make is to pay attention to what is being said in industry circles and to assume that they are getting all the buzz they need. They are not. Industry buzz and customer buzz are two different things. Both are important. Industry buzz tends to focus on the future. A rumor you hear over lunch with an industry analyst may prove to be a fact in six months. Customer buzz, on the other hand, centers on the present: Comments read on the Internet or heard on the street can tell you what people think about your product today.

Why are the two types of buzz different? The first reason is the level of involvement. Although customers can become highly involved with certain kinds of products, they usually don't reach the level of involvement of industry networks, where everyone has a lot at stake: money, career, ego, dreams. The second difference is geographical concentration. While customers are often spread all over the world, industries tend to cluster. Silicon Valley, Detroit, and Hollywood are well-known examples, but clustering is much more universal. "Clusters are a striking feature of virtually every national, regional, state, and even metropolitan economy, especially in more economically advanced nations," says Michael Porter of Harvard Business School.

All this explains why industry buzz can be so frenetic. Breakfast at Buck's in Woodside is a good place to hear the industry buzz in Silicon Valley. There at the restaurant you can actually hear the humming buzz of dozens of men and women all talking at the same time about different aspects of the same industry. Tell someone at one table that Microsoft intends to buy Company X, and within minutes you can be sure most of the restaurant will know. Give it another thirty minutes and the word will spread by cell phones, blogs, and e-mail to the rest of the valley, where some seven thousand technology companies are concentrated in a fifty-mile corridor. But what excites the crowd at Buck's may be met with a yawn by actual customers.

If your product gets a lot of talk within your industry, that's good. But if at a certain point this industry buzz doesn't become customer buzz, you may have a problem. Ultimately customers are the people who have to recommend your product to their friends.

Understanding How Buzz Spreads

It's crucial to understand that buzz about a product never spreads as simply as the two-step flow model would indicate—from company to media and megahubs and then to the public. Yet the two-step model has been blithely accepted by countless companies over the years. It's easy to see why. It's tempting to think about the communication process between a company and potential customers as a linear one. Just send a press release to the media influencers, meet them at a cocktail party, and they'll do the work for you. Another version of this model assumes that the distribution channel is king: Just fax the latest news to the company's distributors, and the distributors will rush to tell the dealers, who in turn will communicate the news (enthusiastically, of course) to their customers. But real networks are not linear or predictable. For example, a megahub may sit down next to a customer at the airport who tells him how lousy your service is. Customer A reads a blog in which Customer B warmly endorses your company. The fact is, dealers often hear about new products from customers, not the other way around. The trickle-down effect looks nice and neat on paper, but networks aren't organizational charts.

Why is this important to marketers? Because there are two

traps companies can fall into. The first is thinking that creating buzz is all about network hubs. If you focus exclusively on the two-step flow model, you can leap to the dangerous conclusion that direct communication with your customers is not important. The second potential trap lies in a narrow interpretation of the term "network hubs." Almost all companies try to go after network hubs. But there's a big difference between going after an elite group of forty influencers and going after a broad, less visible population of four thousand of them. Numbers make a big difference in getting the word out.

The spread of buzz is complex. People don't rely on any one source of information, whether it be their friends, the media, or manufacturers. They use all of the above. The way all these different sources interact is still unclear. But the fact that such sources of information may be a bit of a puzzle shouldn't stop us from using what we *do* know to stimulate talk.

This thing is amazing! You can't trick it. *

—A customer about the game 20Q

Contagious
Products

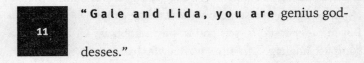

11

"Gale and Lida, you are genius god-

desses."

These are the first words in one of many fan letters

sent to Gale Epstein and Lida Orzeck, the owners of

Hanky Panky of New York City. This letter, from a woman

we'll call Jane, goes on to describe how her thong-wearing

girlfriends tell her it makes them feel fabulous and sexy

all day long. But every time Jane tried one, she got so an-

noyed by it that she ended up removing it after an hour,

going commando and carrying it in her bag all day, or even throwing it away. That was until she tried the Hanky Panky thong, which she calls a miracle.

Some products have what it takes to create good buzz—genuine long-term buzz—that leads to sales. The 4811 thong from Hanky Panky is such a contagious product. In another letter, a "grateful husband" reports that Hanky Panky has become a regular topic among all of his wife's friends, coworkers, and acquaintances. "I can't remember a conversation where Hanky Panky has not come up," the man says, thanking Hanky Panky for the company's dedication to the comfort and style of its customers and for "making my wife feel incredible."

In a way, Gale Epstein and Lida Orzeck are the Steve Wozniak and Steve Jobs of thongs. In the late seventies people started hearing about personal computing. It was something we all could do. It was something that many people wanted to do. But in order to do it, you had to buy a hobbyist kit and learn a complex language—in other words, you had to pull here, stretch there. You had to suffer a little bit. At least, you did until the two Steves came along and dramatically simplified computing through their Apple and later Macintosh products. Everybody was talking about it.

This is exactly what Hanky Panky did. Thongs have existed for many years; some women have been wearing them since the beginning, and many more women have wanted to wear them, especially as panty lines became more visible as tighter pants came into fashion. But to wear thongs you had to suffer a little bit. That was until Hanky Panky created what up to the introduction of the 4811 would be considered an oxymoron: comfortable thongs.

Everything about the 4811 invited women to try it. The promise of comfort. The packaging: a miniature roll that can be thrown in a candy basket next to the cash register at a boutique. The price: upscale thongs can cost $80, and this one was around $15.

In fact, Hanky Panky's founders were following in the footsteps of many other successful entrepreneurs, including George Eastman, the founder of Kodak. Cameras were invented in the 1820s, but they were just too complicated to operate. It took more than fifty years before Eastman reduced their operation to a three-step process: pull the cord, advance the key, and press the button. He also understood that to appeal to mass markets, he needed to offer a simple development process. So the Kodak camera came loaded with film for a hundred exposures, and when the roll was done, the customer just mailed the whole camera to the company for development. Eastman demystified the process for thousands of people who knew about photography but had previously perceived it as a complex process for only professional photographers and serious hobbyists. Eastman also understood the importance of communicating the simplicity of the innovation. To write the product manual, he initially hired a New York advertising man, but he ended up crafting the copy himself (in less than five hours), because the advertising executive, according to Eastman, "utterly ignored" the simplicity of the camera. The simplicity was conveyed through a brilliant slogan: "You press the button—we do the rest." By the mid-1890s, just a few years after its introduction, 100,000 Kodak cameras had been sold and the *Chicago Tribune* informed its readers that "the craze is spreading fearfully."

What does all this have to do with marketing? A lot. People who focus on the promotional aspect of marketing get nervous at this point, but good marketing starts with a focus on the first "P"— product. You can create some buzz for a product that is not contagious, but products that possess a tendency to propagate themselves will go that much further. And the best buzz comes not from clever PR or advertising but rather from attributes inherent in the product or service itself.

And it doesn't just happen. Behind every contagious product there's a stubborn and strong-minded person who refuses to compromise. Steve Jobs did it for the Mac and the iPod. George Eastman did it for the Kodak camera. And Jeff Hawkins did it for the PalmPilot.

Hawkins knew exactly what he was looking for when he created the Palm. He wanted a slim, fast, easy-to-use device that would knock everyone's socks off. But during the development, a lot of well-meaning people came up with solutions to other issues that would make the Palm thicker or slower or less elegant. Hawkins didn't have a problem being the bad guy who says no. "He was really anal about a lot of stuff, and I think a lot of people got frustrated with him in these meetings," said Karl Townsend, who was involved with the company at that stage. But without this passion and exacting approach, Hawkins would have lost sight of his vision. "With all the other products I had worked on, people didn't have the same passion that Jeff had, and the product then becomes a huge gigantic compromise," Townsend said in the book *Piloting Palm*.

The same thing took place with Hanky Panky's 4811. It's difficult to make a comfortable thong, and Gale Epstein obsessed over every small detail. "That wasn't something that just happened," says Lida Orzeck, Hanky Panky's CEO. Epstein fussed over the fabric for months. She was concerned about how some of the possible materials draped over the body. She was looking for something light that would lie flat on the body. (Anything that wrinkles shows through clothes.) She insisted on 100 percent cotton in certain areas and different material in others. The lace she chose for the thong's edge was especially soft; the downside was that this made it difficult to put into the sewing machines (lace sometimes shrinks in width when it's dyed). She wasn't happy with any material for the hip band until she found one with the perfect elasticity—not too tight, not too loose. This fabric's unique properties also allowed her to develop the "one size fits most" sizing that appeals to many customers.

Tools that dramatically simplify your life are just one kind of contagious product. Some products become contagious by evoking a strong emotional reaction that makes us talk. As soon as I walked out of the theater after seeing *Psycho*, I couldn't stop talking about the movie. Neither could my teenage friends. Why? Because we were scared. This is exactly what happened with *The Blair Witch Project*. The movie was marketed in a clever way, but buzz was clearly driven by the fear that the movie evoked among viewers. This was especially true in the first few weeks after the release, when some people still believed that what they were seeing on the screen was actual footage taken by three students who disappeared in the forest.

Fear, of course, is an emotion that evokes positive buzz for just a few products, such as horror films. For most products and services it is usually the feeling of excitement and delight—the "Wow" effect. Look, for example, at 20Q, a toy that claims it can guess what you're thinking about in twenty questions. The surprising thing is that it often does. "This thing is amazing! You can't trick it," one twenty-something told me. So when it guesses that you thought of a cotton swab, you say "Wow," and you turn to your friend and you both try to come up with something harder. "We would come up with things like 'sea urchin' and it would get it," that student remembers. It's not surprising that when BzzAgent, the word-of-mouth consumer panel, ran a campaign to promote 20Q, 69 percent of agents reported at least one word-of-mouth incident. At the time this was nearly 40 percent above the average level of the firm's previous campaigns.

Sometimes the feeling of delight is achieved by exceeding expectations. Let's return to the case of the PalmPilot. When this product was introduced, people in the high-tech industry didn't expect much from personal digital assistants (PDAs), a category that after a long history of failures was essentially considered dead. The PalmPilot team didn't try to change these low expectations.

"It wasn't some big company coming out saying, 'We've invented this thing and it's awesome and you'd better like it,'" says Ed Colligan, now president and CEO of Palm. This humble attitude, coupled with a superb product, created true excitement among people. "When I saw the PalmPilot, there was one of those 'Aha' moments," says Andy Reinhardt, a *BusinessWeek* reporter who was news editor for *PC World* at the time. "It was fantastic! After all the other failures in handhelds, Palm had really gotten it right."

Colligan sounds almost apologetic when he explains Palm's positive buzz. "The product just works, you know? I know that's really simple, but there were just a lot of fundamental flaws about everything else that was done." The initial experience a customer has with a product is critical to buzz. "We're so used to having terrible experiences that when we have a good, easy experience, we tell our friends," says Patricia Seybold, the president of the Patricia Seybold Group and author of the bestselling book *Customers.com*.

Visual Buzz

Another type of contagious product is the one that creates visual buzz. Imagine that it's the year 1888. You walk in the park on a Saturday morning and suddenly notice a man who's holding a box to his waist, pointing it at his wife and two children, and asking them to smile. You're terribly curious to find out what he's doing. A small group of people gathers nearby, and you overhear that the box he's holding is called a Kodak camera. It's almost as if the camera were using this man's family just to show itself off in public. In the following weeks some of the people who observe the man in the park will buy their own Kodak cameras, and they in turn will be seen pointing it in public.

Although in a more subtle way, the 4811 thong also benefits from some visual buzz. It works much like the push-up bra or teeth-whitening spread. In these cases we start to observe changes in other people without necessarily discussing them. But we do take note of these things—fewer panty lines show, women's breasts seem bigger, and people in general have whiter teeth. At this point a question starts percolating in our minds. We may not even be fully aware of it, nor do we know what particular brand is involved, but we recognize that something is different and wonder why.

What happens next depends on cultural norms and personality. Some people will discuss it only with their most intimate friends or with their partner. Others will look for information in the media or on the Web. Many will have no problem discussing the topic with friends and coworkers—sometimes with a live demo. Lida Orzeck once walked her dog in Central Park and got into a conversation with a young woman. When the young lady heard that Orzeck is the CEO of Hanky Panky, she dropped her pants to show her that she's a loyal customer. Women—at least some women—do talk about the most intimate things. "They love to share their best-kept secrets," says Gale Epstein. And while Central Park might seem an odd place for a live demo, a good product can make it happen.

The percolating stage exists not only for intimate products. Think of the first time you saw an iPod or the LiveStrong yellow bracelet. You probably didn't jump on the first person you saw with the new item, but you made a mental note of it. After noticing more and more of these items on the subway or on the street, you finally asked a friend or were attentive to an ad or an article that explained them. A lot of fashion products spread in a similar way. More than half of the respondents who were asked by the market research firm Yankelovich to specify sources of information about new styles said they learn about fashion by observing what others are wearing.

Social learning of this kind plays a major role in buzz among younger customers. Barry Schwartz, the owner of three toy stores in New York State, describes how buzz about Beanie Babies started in his area. Schwartz first saw the toy at a toy fair, and in mid-1994 he displayed some in his stores. A son of one of the store's employees got excited about a pig Beanie Baby. The child took the pig home, and on the following day he got on the bus with the pig stuffed in his shirt pocket. "Where'd ya get the pig?" the other children on the bus wanted to know the moment they noticed it. "That afternoon we might have had thirty-six pieces. They were gone. The following day we had a waiting list. In the first six weeks that we had it, we sold fifteen hundred pieces."

What are the implications for companies? Awareness of this effect at the design stage is key: If you design a new digital camera to look like all other cameras, for example, you are forgoing an opportunity to stimulate discussion. If you design it to look different, you can help the product stir conversation and thus advertise itself.

Color is an effective tool in helping products advertise themselves. Distinctive blue bags in driveways tell people that their neighbors read the *New York Times*. A transparent bag would have not done the trick.

Leaving Traces

Some contagious products self-propagate by leaving traces of themselves behind. This is especially true for products that allow their users to express themselves. In the early days of desktop publishing, the message "I used PhotoShop," or "I used Illustrator," or the more generic "I used my Mac" often came along with the artwork. The same effect helped the spread of the Kodak camera. Not only did the camera capitalize on its observability as an object, its products—photos printed on Kodak paper—were specifically designed to be shown to friends and family.

Another product that has spread this way is Magnetic Poetry. Dave Kapell invented Magnetic Poetry to help him with his own writing—he would cut out words, paste them on magnets, and arrange them on his refrigerator. "When friends would come over, they'd gather around the fridge and play with it and leave these bizarre messages, and eventually people said, 'Hey, you should start selling this,' " Kapell says. He made some kits, took them to craft shows, and found that what happened at his house happened at his customers' houses—people saw the product on their friends' refrigerators, started playing with the magnets, and left their own interesting messages. "For the first couple of years it was all pretty much word of mouth that sold this product," he says. To accelerate the process, Kapell hired sales reps and got into traditional distribution channels, where his product is exposed to many more eyes. But people still tell him that they first encountered it at someone's house. More than 3 million kits have been sold so far.

Some contagious products reward you if you talk about them. Suppose you're in a hotel and you've run out of ways to amuse yourself. Walking through the gym, you find a room with a Ping-Pong table, but you don't have anyone to play with. A Ping-Pong table is almost useless if you don't have a partner, so you go around the hotel and spread the word about the availability of the table. You do it not because you're such a good person (which you are), but because by spreading the word you increase your chances of achieving your goal: playing. This need for partnership is the basic building block of the network effects I described in Chapter 7. Telephone, fax, and e-mail, like most communication tools, are examples of products that increase in value the more people use them.

One interesting part of this network effect is how it gains momentum. MySpace and Facebook are services that you don't really enjoy on your own, so you start inviting your friends to join. Once they do, you start using it more often and in more ways. As the service becomes a way of life, the few who have not joined stand out—and begin to annoy you. It's like having to fax everything to the one uncle who doesn't have e-mail. A student who refuses to be on Facebook is missing out on a lot of information that her friends need to e-mail her separately. Jason Feffer, former vice president of operations at MySpace, remembers talking to users of MySpace who would tell him how their friends kept begging them to join until they did it. "I kinda had to go on it," they would tell him.

· · ·

Researchers theorize that there may be a preexisting structure in our minds that determines what messages we will accept and spread. People are more open to ideas that match their existing set of beliefs, and because of that, ideas that fit their preexisting beliefs will spread faster. One reason for the intense buzz about the PalmPilot was that it was compatible with expectations that many people had. "We have all the lists made out in our head," one customer said, explaining why he bought the PalmPilot. "[I had] in my brain a mental list of kinds of things that I would like an information organizer to do, and then when I saw it, it was just 'click.' " This customer went on to tell dozens of other people about the PalmPilot.

Your product also needs to be compatible with the way potential users already do things. Several previously developed devices ignored that. But the Palm team understood that the first people likely to adopt a PDA used a PC and already had a way of keeping track of their contacts and schedules. Compatibility therefore became a top priority. While other devices allowed you to back up, the PalmPilot was designed as a PC device—as an extension of your personal computer. Pressing one button synchronized the data on the Palm and your computer.

Compatibility often is a matter of cultural traditions and of what is socially acceptable in a particular community. To improve the health of people in Los Molinos, a small village in Peru, the Peruvian government attempted to educate women in the village about general sanitation principles. Government workers encouraged villagers to start boiling their drinking water. Most villagers, however, despite the two-year campaign, refused to adopt the practice, which was found to conflict with their basic belief system about food and drink. Traditionally for these peasants, boiled water was closely associated with illness. Everett Rogers, who describes this example in *Diffusion of Innovations*, makes the point that "the compatibility of an innovation, as perceived by members of a social system, is positively related to its rate of adoption."

Keep in mind that the beliefs of a society are a moving target. One recent example: bottled water. What everybody craved a few years ago now has many detractors who say that the used bottles are an ecological disaster. And in some cities bottled water has even been banned for purchase with public funds.

Products that dramatically simplify our lives, products that are visible, evoke emotions, make people say "Wow!" This is the stuff that makes people talk. We often refer to this as "organic" or "natural" word of mouth, even though making a buzzable product is often well planned.

It is rare to see a product that is contagious in several dimensions. The iPhone is probably the best recent example, because it is visually attractive, easy to use, and evokes a kind of "Wow" reaction. But even products that score high on only one dimension can generate significant talk. And if you have such a product, you don't want to stop there. You want to take it to the next level, which brings us to the next chapter.

**Looking back, I think they were pretty
simple ideas, but I also guess that
good ideas are always simple.**

—Linda Pezzano, about the launch of Trivial
Pursuit and Pictionary

Accelerating
Natural Contagion

12 **Linda Pezzano was really after**

the Scrabble account. Instead she was as-

signed to do the PR for some game nobody had heard of—

Trivial Pursuit, a new release by Scrabble's maker,

Selchow & Righter. Pezzano knew that she'd need to set-

tle for this unproven new game for the time being—and

she also realized she'd need to act fast. It was November,

and Toy Fair 1983 was fast approaching, and although she

had no experience in the toy business, she knew Toy Fair

was important—probably the best place to introduce an unknown game.

Scrabble was a product that stores ordered on a regular basis, and Pezzano realized that buyers didn't have a real reason to visit Selchow & Righter's exhibit at Toy Fair. Nobody was going to stop by the booth to ask if there are any new letters in the alphabet or if the number of points for Z had changed. How, she wondered, could she build some buzz for Trivial Pursuit among buyers before they even came to New York? How could she make sure none of them skipped Selchow & Righter's booth?

Pezzano and her staff created a series of teaser mailings that were sent to several hundred key buyers in the toy industry a few weeks before the trade show. The first mailing was sent in a small envelope, hand-addressed, with a real stamp and no return address. It contained a little card with the Trivial Pursuit logo and a random card from the game.

Imagine that you're a buyer at a toy store and you receive a card with questions such as "What's the largest city between Ireland and Canada?" and "What sport did John Wayne play at the University of Southern California?" It's likely to get your attention, and you may even mention it to your coworkers. Three or four days later, a second random card arrives: "What was Elvis Presley's middle name?" "How many sides does a nonagon have?" "What was Al Capone's nickname?" Now you're really curious as to what all this is about, especially since you still have no clue who's sending you these cards. When the third card comes (finally identifying the sender), I can see you getting up from your chair and stopping the first person you see: "Hey, Susan, guess what word was intentionally omitted from the screenplay of *The Godfather*?" or "Who invented peanut butter?"

Buyers started calling up Selchow & Righter before Toy Fair. Some even complained that others got cards and they didn't. A simple and inexpensive idea created significant buzz. Selchow &

Righter's showroom at Toy Fair was mobbed, and the company wrote up an unusually high number of orders for Trivial Pursuit.

Another part of the promotion was the radio initiative. "In New York there was a guy on the radio who loved to ask trivia questions," Pezzano recalled. "So I thought he was a natural guy to do a promotion with. And then I thought, 'Well, there must be guys like that in every market.'" Pezzano had a student intern call radio stations around the country to find their local "trivia maven." It didn't take long before radio stations started to broadcast trivia questions from the game. More than a hundred stations were running the promotion, and each one of them was giving away copies of the game to listeners who answered trivia questions correctly. This simple tactic created a double effect: The radio personalities broadcast information to thousands of people, and people who won the game began bombarding those around them with questions like "What woman was *Time*'s Man of the Year for 1952?" "What was World War I known as before World War II?" and "What does the J&B stand for on the scotch?"

Pezzano also distributed sample cards in popular spring-break hangouts, organized Trivial Pursuit parties in bars, and mailed games to celebrities like Gregory Peck and Frank Sinatra who were mentioned in the questions. This helped to start buzz (and trivia parties) in Hollywood.

What would have happened without those mystery envelopes? Without the radio promotions? Without the samples for students? Without the celebrity mailings?

It's impossible to tell for sure. I suspect that Trivial Pursuit would still have gotten buzz. It's a great game, and people love to talk about a great experience. I do believe, however, that word about the game would have spread at a much slower rate. Essentially what Linda Pezzano did was accelerate the buzz about the product. During 1984, 20 million games were sold with almost no advertising.

Energy

Chris Byrne was in his twenties when he was hired by Pezzano. It was in 1985, right after the successful launch of Trivial Pursuit, and Pezzano was facing a new challenge. She interviewed Byrne on a Saturday and hired him on the spot. More than twenty years later, Byrne still gets totally animated when he talks about Pezzano's energy, creativity, and sense of humor. (She passed away in 1999.)

The new challenge was to market a game that was invented by a guy from Seattle named Rob Angel. Angel had had some initial success selling the product from a table he set up at Nordstrom in Seattle. The name of the game was Pictionary.

One thing Pezzano learned from her experience with Trivial Pursuit was the value of engaging people in playing. She started parties at her apartment and invited journalists and other people likely to spread the word. Byrne remembers that everyone hated the caviar pie she used to serve but loved Pictionary.

The successful PR effort for Pictionary was bolstered by a grassroots campaign with the same objective: engagement. It was simple. It was straightforward. It worked. When I interviewed Linda Pezzano in 1998, she sounded a bit apologetic about the success of her campaigns. "Looking back," she said, "I think they were pretty simple ideas, but I also guess that good ideas are always simple."

The simple idea in this case was to create a "Pick Pack," which consisted of a pad, five Pictionary cards, a short instruction sheet, and a golf pencil, all wrapped in cellophane. It was enough to give people a taste of what Pictionary was all about.

"Linda was sort of the creative genius, but she sent us to hit the bricks," Chris Byrne says. "Us" meant employees such as Chris and Amy Freedland, who would fly to different cities and stand in a mall all day and play with people. Pezzano also hired actors to dress up as artists and sit with easels and flip charts in parks, shopping centers, and other gathering places. These guys too started engaging people in playing and giving out the sample packs.

What would have happened without the efforts of Linda Pezzano and her team? Without the parties for journalists? Without the massive samplings? Without the games that were handed to TV show producers? Without the artists who sat and played with people?

Again, it's impossible to tell for sure. I suspect that Pictionary would still have gotten buzz. But would it have sold a million copies by the summer of 1987? Perhaps not.

Could Pezzano do it with every game? No. She didn't have a Midas touch, and her predictions weren't always correct. For example, she was convinced that a game called the Quest for the Philosopher's Stone would be a tremendous success. It wasn't. But when her energy, creativity, and common sense met the right product, the results were incredible. She understood this basic fact: If a game (or any product) is contagious in some way, you should have as many people as possible try it as early as possible.

Two things are needed to create buzz successfully. The first one, as discussed in the last chapter, is to have a contagious product. But having such a product alone is not enough. Companies that get good buzz also accelerate natural contagion. Instead of relying on Customer A to tell B, who will tell C, who will tell D (you start to sense how slow word of mouth can be), smart marketers know that word of mouth almost always needs help.

Every new product starts with no one knowing about it except a few insiders. There's an enormous gap between the few people in the know and the rest of the world. To spread the word, the creators of the product or service start reaching out and planting the news in other areas of the networks. This is a critical time in the life of a product; a company needs at least one person who is obsessed with spreading the word. It sounds obvious, but many new products fail because there is no obsessed person in place at the right time. Someone like Linda Pezzano.

Or someone like Ted Sartoian.

On the night of March 12, 1973, employees of a young company called Federal Express gathered near their new facility in Memphis, Tennessee, waiting for the company's Falcon airplanes to arrive from eleven cities, loaded with packages that needed to be sorted. A night that began with a lot of anticipation ended in bitter disappointment. When the airplanes arrived and the doors were opened, the employees found only six packages—including one sent by Fred Smith, the founder of the company. "People hadn't heard of us," one employee told Robert A. Sigafoos, who described the scene in his book about FedEx, *Absolutely, Positively Overnight!* The company learned that it needed to cover a wider network of cities to make its service more attractive—and that it needed to get more aggressive in getting out the word about its service.

Ted Sartoian was one of those who made it happen. Previously a salesperson for UPS, he was hired by Federal Express in September 1973 as the head of the sales force. Business was still pretty bad when he joined; the company had nowhere near the income needed to support a fleet of airplanes like the one it was building. Sartoian remembered shipping about three hundred packages a night out of Chicago. More than twenty-five years later, he couldn't help but get indignant at this low number. "Three hundred packages out of Chicago—that's just sick!" he almost shouted over the phone when I interviewed him in 1999.

Sartoian's approach was to lead a team of eight or nine people at a time into each city and stay there for a few weeks, conducting a sales blitz. "We'd get a bunch of people together and we'd take them to a city like Chicago," he remembered. "We'd sit down the night before or a day before and cut the city up into parts, and each person would have a territory, and you would go around and you would canvass. And you would canvass hard, get as many people as you could. And by canvassing I mean even door-to-door selling. It was very difficult." People of course didn't know what Federal Express was and had to be convinced of the concept. Sartoian and his people would sometimes ship a sample package from a potential customer for free. They would go back the next day with the name of the customer who had signed for the package thousands of miles away to prove that it got there. "That was a great selling tool," Sartoian says, and it helped Federal Express leapfrog into new cities, new industries, new networks. "We'd go in there and sales-blitz that city for four, five weeks with eight or nine guys, and all of a sudden now we're getting *thousands* of packages a day instead of three hundred."

Sartoian wasn't the first to conduct a sales blitz, but originality is not the point here. It's the importance of finding links into a variety of different networks to generate enough momentum for the word to spread. Without these links it is conceivable that, in time, almost every office in America would have been exposed to the brand after receiving a FedEx letter. But this is merely an academic hypothesis. In real life, with competitors and cash-flow issues, companies need to get off the ground quickly. To get buzz going, you can't wait for *natural contagion*; you need a heroic push.

To me, this seems like "conversational spam," and as a tactic it could backfire.

—a blogger about BzzAgent

The Envelope
and the Line

13 **Waiting for a movie to** start, some moviegoers in a London cinema witnessed a dramatic sequence of events in 2003. The theater manager, a slim guy in his twenties, walked in and turned to the audience.

"Sorry to interrupt your evening, ladies and gentlemen, but is there a Sue McNaughton in the house?" he asked.

No one responded, and he asked again: "Ms. McNaughton?"

A young woman in the third row got up, hesitant. "I'm Sue McNaughton."

The manager looked tense. "Would you come this way, please?"

The woman refused to join the manager before she knew why she was being asked to leave the theater. He whispered something in her ear. She was obviously in shock.

"That can't be right!" she said. "You're wrong. I spoke to him an hour ago—he said he was getting on his motorbike. You've made a mistake. It must have been somebody else."

The sound of a two-way police radio echoed in the theater lobby. Obviously something bad had happened. Something very bad.

"Please come this way," the manager said again, trying to be gentle and assertive at the same time. "The police are here. They need to speak to you."

The woman joined the manager, shaking her head in disbelief. They left the theater.

After a moment the manager came back into the theater and announced: "Ladies and gentlemen, what you have just witnessed was a fictional scene. However, the story behind it is all too true. Last year seventy-one motorcyclists were killed on London's roads, and seventy-one families received the news that their loved ones would not be coming home. As more and more people take to the road on mopeds and motorbikes, we urge you to wear visible clothing, keep your lights on, and ride defensively. If you are not a motorcycle rider, please encourage your loved ones and friends who are to be careful. Please watch the following screen commercial, and remember, beware of the driver who didn't see you." The lights in the theater were dimmed and a short safety commercial produced for Transport for London was shown.

People in London certainly talked about this campaign. But

they also had questions. "Is it ethical for advertisers, even those with an important purpose, to use such tactics? How should we judge Transport for London's shock theatre?" John Wigram wrote in the *Financial Times*. "It is, ostensibly, a real-life drama being played out in real time, with no emotional safety net for the audience. There's the real possibility that some people will be reminded of past trauma, others offended."

Justin Foxton from CommentUK, who ran the campaign, indeed witnessed a wide range of reactions from people in the theater. Some people went tearing out of the cinema and screamed at the actors. Some people shook the actors' hands. "Some people applauded it," he says, "because they could see the merits in the message. Other people were outraged by it."

Transport for London pushed the envelope with its campaign. But did it go too far?

Many of the examples discussed so far in this book are pretty straightforward. Foxton's company also runs many campaigns that don't raise any ethical issues. In one promotion for a brand of ice cream, Foxton had teams of handsome male singers in tuxedos stand by the ice cream freezer at supermarkets across the U.K. and sing to passing shoppers an a cappella version of the song "Only You." It made people smile; it made people talk; it sold lots of ice cream.

But the Transport for London campaign was a very different story. It made people think that the accident and pain were real. Did the organization cross the line?

These types of questions are not going to go away. Here's why. Everyone in marketing is always trying to get attention, and edgy tactics tend to get noticed. There's a lot to be said for "pushing the envelope" and "thinking outside the box," but it's also possible to cross the line of what's considered acceptable by the community. The problem is that "community" consists of many individuals who have different ideas of what's acceptable and what's not.

Let's look at another example. In 2004 the TV program *60 Minutes* described an undercover marketing campaign conducted for a company called Essential Reality, which was introducing a cool new glove that allows video gamers to interact with their computer. Instead of using a joystick, a player can fly a jet or fire a weapon onscreen by moving his fingers. According to *60 Minutes*, Essential Reality hired an agency that put together a team of young people who were asked to sit in public places and play computer games using the new device, the P-5 Glove. The objective wasn't to sell it, just to start some buzz.

The *60 Minutes* production team got a hidden camera and taped two of these undercover agents, Theo and Kumani, sitting at a Starbucks using the P-5 Glove while playing a video game. It didn't take long before they were approached by some curious bystanders. Theo and Kumani told them about the glove, invited them to try it, and offered to e-mail information about the product, never revealing that they were actually paid to market the P-5.

Essential Reality created some buzz. But did it cross the line?

At the end of the segment on *60 Minutes*, a couple of the bystanders who took the bite were interviewed. Did they mind that the game players did not reveal they were being paid? The reactions were mixed. One man said that he didn't care. Another man didn't like it. "It just seemed to be a nice friendly encounter, kind of restores your faith in your fellow New Yorker, and then to find out that it was all fake, I don't know . . . I don't like the ring of it," he said.

I don't like the ring of it either. In this case I think that the answer is simpler than in the case of Transport for London: Yes, the company crossed the line. Determining whether Transport for London's campaign crossed the line is more difficult. One can argue that it wasn't really "undercover" because the actors revealed their true identity immediately after their little drama. On the other hand, the campaign played with people's emotions; chances are pretty high that someone in the audience may have actually lost a loved one in a road accident. But it was all done for an important cause—to save lives. That's why it presents such a moral dilemma.

What was wrong with the P-5 Glove campaign? In my opinion, the problem was that people didn't know that they were being marketed to and therefore couldn't put up any defense mechanisms. If men in tuxedos serenade you while holding trays of ice cream, you know that the ice cream company is trying to charm you into buying its product. Many will argue that this is manipulative too—and a lot of advertising is—but because you know "this is marketing," you can defend yourself. Not so with undercover marketing. Malcolm Gladwell argued in that 60 *Minutes* program that there's an element of deception in undercover marketing that isn't present in conventional advertising, which is governed by a known set of rules. "A line is crossed, I think, when you go outside of those normal boundaries and start to deceive people in ways where they are totally unwitting to what's going on," Gladwell said.

Awareness that you are being marketed to is a defense mechanism that I believe customers have a right to. Taking it away is like pulling the rug from under their feet.

I was more than a bit naive when I first wrote *The Anatomy of Buzz*. While I discussed issues like trust and honesty, when the thought of including a short section on ethical issues crossed my mind, I dismissed it. I simply didn't think it was a significant enough issue. I was wrong.

I was happy to see that when the Word of Mouth Marketing

Association was formed in 2004, one of the first things its organizers did was develop a code of ethics. (It was that code of ethics that convinced me to join the advisory board.) This document is a good place to start when you're thinking up your own word-of-mouth strategies (see www.womma.org). In essence, the code concerns several issues: establishing honesty of relationships (if you use any "ambassadors" or "agents," they should disclose their relationships with your company or agency); fostering honesty of opinion (your agents should be free to express their honest and authentic opinion about the product); upholding honesty of identity (no undercover marketing); taking responsibility (you should be proactive in educating your employees and advocates about ethics); and respecting the rules of any media you use (blogs, discussion forums, etc.). The case of the P-5 Glove, as presented on *60 Minutes*, clearly violates three of these principles: honesty of relationships, honesty of opinion, and honesty of identity.

Does undercover or stealth marketing sell products? I don't know. Undercover marketing is . . . undercover. Newspapers and magazines love to write about the sneaky marketers who are selling tons of unnecessary stuff to innocent consumers through devious methods. I suspect that the power of stealth marketing is exaggerated. Consider the P-5 Glove. If undercover marketing was the almighty tool that some people portray it to be, lots of people should have run out and bought this gadget and the P-5 should have become an overnight smash hit. It didn't.

I don't really think that the question marketers should be asking is whether undercover marketing is effective. Companies should stay away from deceptive tactics, not because they don't work or for fear of a backlash once the public finds out about them. They should avoid misleading practices because they are dishonest. Moreover, in some countries undercover marketing is illegal.

Panels

In several of the cases described earlier, I mentioned word-of-mouth panels such as Tremor and BzzAgent. Philips spread the word about its Sonicare toothbrush by sending it to Bzz-Agents. Procter & Gamble sent out the Clairol Herbal Essences conversation piece to Tremor teen connectors.

These panels raise some questions and concerns as well: Are agents disclosing their affiliation with the company to their friends? How can a company make sure that agents are not hiding the affiliation? Are the agents free to say whatever they think?

BzzAgent requires its members to disclose their affiliation with the company. When an agent submits a report, she has to acknowledge that her conversational partner was aware of her affiliation with BzzAgent. If the company determines that a particular agent is not adhering to its policy, it requires this person to complete a disclosure-related online training session before she's invited to participate in any future campaigns. Tremor's approach is different. "We believe companies have an ethical responsibility to be transparent," Tremor CEO Steve Knox says, but he sees disclosure as a specific tactic that is required only in cases where people are compensated, which is not the case for Tremor (or BzzAgent, for that matter). Knox highlights the importance of the consumer's independence. "We believe that the consumer needs to be free to say whatever it is they want to say. Always. One hundred percent of the time. No exceptions to that."

There are also special questions that relate to the participation of teenagers in these panels. Bob Ahuja, a professor of marketing at Xavier University in Cincinnati, ran four focus groups with boys and girls aged thirteen to sixteen and found that, at least in this small sample, these teenagers saw no ethical dilemma in not revealing one's status as a panel participant.

I believe that marketers who get involved in word-of-mouth marketing have an obligation to educate both young and old participants about the need for transparency. We need to explain to and remind people that true word-of-mouth marketing is not about tricking and deceiving people. It's about openly inviting people to try a product that you like. What makes word of mouth so powerful is that people are expressing their honest opinions. In fact, research conducted by Dr. Walter Carl from Northeastern University suggests that agents who disclose their affiliation with the company are no less effective than the ones who don't.

I think that it makes a lot of sense for companies to deal with their customers directly rather than hire others to do so. Rubbing elbows with consumers is invaluable, because it gives you important insights. I get excited about the way NOLS deals with its students or Lego with its customers (described later in the book). Of course, there's more than one way to spread the word, and some companies prefer to use a third party or a sampling network in addition to other initiatives, because such outside parties are likely connected to clusters not currently represented in the user base.

Rewards, if given at all, should stay small. If you introduce significant financial rewards or selling into the system, your word-of-mouth campaign can start to look more like a multilevel marketing scheme, which can put a strain on your panelists' relationships.

Should I Give Incentives for Referrals?

One decision you may face once you decide to launch a tell-a-friend promotion is whether or not to include an incentive in your offer. This raises not only an ethical question but one of appropriateness.

People have a wide range of attitudes on this issue. Here's how Scott Cook, the founder and chairman of Intuit, described back in 1999 the experience his company has had with these types of promotions: "We've tried various artificial stimulants to word of mouth, like financial incentives to recommenders. None have worked. Some produced isolated, but surprising, negative reaction: 'I don't sell my friends for a bit of cash . . .' " So before you start any such promotion, it's worth checking how your customers feel about it. This can be done through focus groups, interviews, or informal conversations.

But incentives can work. Most people love getting something for free, and there are ways to reduce any uncomfortable feelings associated with a referral. One way is to give a small gift to both the person who referred and his or her friend. In other cases you can let the customer decide. Some companies offer a menu of things a person can choose from, including a charitable donation. Another way is to take the sting out of the situation through a game. If you refer somebody, you get a game card which could lead to one of several prizes. Of course, all promotions and incentive programs should be reviewed by your legal department.

Several organizations have dealt with the ethics of word-of-mouth marketing, and I encourage you to read their points of view. Commercial Alert (www.commercialalert.org) is a nonprofit organization that sent a petition on buzz marketing to the Federal Trade Commission. You can find both the petition and the FTC's response on Commercial Alert's Web site, or you can go to the FTC's Web site, www.ftc.gov. The National Institute on Media and the Family (www.mediafamily.org) has written about word of mouth as it relates to children.

As new technologies develop and as new concepts in word-of-mouth marketing evolve, more challenges will emerge. So it's wise to keep track of best practices, regulations, and standards.

The basics—honesty, truthfulness, transparency—will not change with technology or fashion.

In addition to the ethical issues, you should also consider how certain tactics are perceived in the marketplace. If you're considering a tactic that you and 60 percent of your customers feel is perfectly ethical, does it make sense to go ahead? Perhaps, but keep in mind what the other 40 percent of your audience will think.

In 2005, Creative Commons, a nonprofit organization that advocates better copyright laws, wanted to use BzzAgent to promote its ideas by helping its supporters rally around the cause more effectively. It discovered very quickly, however, that some in the community of supporters thought this was a bad idea, as reflected in the quote from the blogger Suw Charman: "To me, this seems like 'conversational spam,' and as a tactic it could backfire." Dave Balter of BzzAgent responded by suggesting that Charman was lying about the facts, which fueled additional opposition from bloggers (Balter apologized). The campaign was discontinued just days after it was announced.

Unfortunately, there are plenty of examples of campaigns that clearly crossed the line. Just one example: In early 2007 briefcases with blinking lights were placed in multiple locations around ten cities in the United States. In Boston people feared that the suspicious packages were bombs and called the police. This caused the suspension of subway service and closure of highways and bridges. In fact the campaign was designed to promote a cartoon on Turner Broadcasting.

Some fans of the program who recognized the characters depicted on the suitcases loved this promotion, which illustrates again that the line is different for everyone. But that's exactly why it's so important to consider it, and to think not only of how your biggest fans will react but how the community in general will react.

. . .

When you're trying to build buzz, it's important to push the envelope and think outside the box. And when you look for original ideas and new ways to reach people, you can't police your thoughts—you need to brainstorm and let your mind explore all possibilities. But after the brainstorming, you have to change your attitude dramatically. This is best done the morning after, over some strong coffee, in the bright light of day. Think again about your wild new ideas. Ask other people what they think. Ask your customers. Ask people in the community: Are we crossing the line?

Simple counts are not sufficient. There
is valuable information in the extent to
which the conversations are taking
place across heterogeneous
communities.

—from an article in *Marketing Science*

Active
Seeding

In 2001 Miramax hired the market-

14

ing expert Marc Schiller to build buzz for a

movie called *On the Line*, starring 'N Sync's Lance Bass

and Joey Fatone. When Miramax approached Schiller, his

small New York agency, Electric Artists, already had a big

success story under its belt: Christina Aguilera. To create

buzz for Aguilera, Schiller and his team identified about

2,900 young people whom they believed were responsible

for music buzz on the Internet. They approached this

group for several months before Aguilera's first record came out. When it was released, the record opened at number one.

Schiller and his team wanted to repeat their success with *On the Line*. They identified the core group of enthusiasts they believed would talk about the movie and started a dialogue with these folks. "The word of mouth that we saw coming back to my team was off the radar," Schiller remembers. "We'd never seen anything like this—the passion was there. The word of mouth was there."

Everything looked rosy. Then the movie bombed.

"I shut the company down for two weeks," Schiller remembers. "I had to figure out what went wrong here."

How did a movie that got such positive initial response fail so miserably at the box office? To try to understand one possible explanation for this case, we should look at a study done by David Godes and Dina Mayzlin, who examined how buzz about TV shows relates to their success. Godes and Mayzlin obtained two sets of data. One was the Nielsen ratings of forty-one TV shows that premiered in the United States during the 1999–2000 season. The other set of data consisted of comments posted on 169 newsgroups about these TV shows. So, for example, they knew that *Judging Amy*, which premiered on CBS on September 19, 1999, was watched in 13.4 million homes, and they also knew that the words "Judging Amy" appeared 189 times in the subject lines of different postings during the period that they covered.

Their analysis revealed that once they controlled for the previous week's ratings, the volume of the discussion was not the best predictor of a show's success. "Simple counts are not sufficient," they wrote. Volume didn't matter as much as another measure: dispersion. This number measures the concentration of posts across different newsgroups. That is, dispersion is greater if the posts are evenly distributed across many different groups as opposed to being concentrated in a few groups. In other words, the fact that *Law and Order: Special Victims Unit* had posts in four different newsgroups in the week following its premiere was more important than the fact that it had a total volume of 201 posts in the same week.

Is it possible that this is what happened with *On the Line?* Looking back, Marc Schiller thinks that this is exactly what happened. "Word of mouth can become very insular," he says. Yes, a core group got excited about it. Excitement and passion are important when it comes to buzz, but the *scope* of that excitement and the passion may be at least as important.

Schiller didn't have access at the time to Godes and Mayzlin's paper, but his intuition told him that this is what went wrong. He reopened the agency after a couple of weeks. And he started to pay more attention to what he calls "breadth in the word of mouth."

What can marketers learn from this? One lesson is that measuring the dispersion of word of mouth can serve as a predictor of future success. Understanding that the buzz, as loud as it may have been, came from only one group of people could have given Schiller a hint that this would not be another Christina Aguilera. Perhaps the movie simply wasn't good enough.

It's also possible that the movie never got the chance it deserved, which brings me to the second lesson: There are things you can do to make sure buzz starts in multiple social clusters. While news about your product may spread effectively in some clusters, it may leap over to other clusters very slowly, if at all. Very few products spread like wildfire. Most products need help, and that's where seeding enters the picture.

What Is Seeding?

To accelerate the rate at which the word about a product spreads, smart companies seed their products at strategic points in many different clusters with something known as seed units. A seed unit is an actual product or a representative sampling from the product that you are trying to promote (a book, a computer, a software package), which you place in the hands of seed customers. The logistics vary: The seed unit can be offered at full price, at a discount, on a loan basis, or for free, as is often done with seeding on the Internet. You can use sampling programs, touring programs, or demo programs, but the principle is always the same: You give people in multiple clusters direct experience with the product in order to stimulate simultaneous discussion in multiple networks and accelerate the regular adoption process. Instead of waiting for the natural (but sometimes painfully slow) transfer of information from one cluster to the next, you take the initiative and ensure that this transfer occurs.

A good seeding campaign goes beyond mailing sample products to a small group of press contacts and the industry elite. Seeding a book should consist of more than sending proofs to a few dozen key buyers; the scale should be much greater. You may recall that *Cold Mountain*, for example, was sent to more than four thousand buyers, readers, authors, reviewers, and other influential people. Numbers make a difference. One of the most successful book launches in recent history was the introduction of *The Purpose-Driven Life*, by Rick Warren. Four hundred thousand people participated in the initial launch of this book through churches and religious groups. People received the book (some churches gave it for free, others sold it at a discount), agreed to read one chapter each day for forty days, and participated in small discussion groups that met once a week. How was Warren able to put this together? Over the years he had built great relationships with pastors who'd read another one of his books (*The Purpose-Driven Church*), visited his Web site, and used various resources that he made available to them. When Warren invited those pastors to participate in his Forty Days of Purpose initiative, twelve hundred agreed, according to Greg Stielstra, who was senior marketing director at Zondervan and described the campaign in his book *PyroMarketing*.

Starting in October 2002, four hundred thousand people all over the country talked about *The Purpose-Driven Life*. It was discussed in twelve hundred churches every Sunday for six weeks, and it was analyzed in the small discussion groups.

Talk about a contagious product! A survey conducted some time after the book release revealed that 83 percent of those who bought the book were actively recommending it. Even more important, nearly 47 percent bought additional copies and gave them away as gifts. How many copies? Stielstra reports that 73 percent of those who gave it as a gift bought one to three copies, and 7 percent reported that they gave away more than ten copies each. *The Purpose-Driven Life* sold 20 million copies in its first two years.

What do you think would have happened if Rick Warren had started his efforts with *twelve* churches rather than with *twelve hundred* churches? It's impossible to tell for sure. With such strong inherent contagion, I suspect that the book would still have been a success. But I am sure that starting on such a large scale made a huge difference.

Tom Peters also attributes part of the success of his first book to an extensive seeding campaign. In 1980 Peters and his coauthor, Bob Waterman, put together a 125-page summary of what later became the classic management book *In Search of Excellence*. They gave it to just a few executives they knew, but very quickly these individuals started discussing what they had read with others. As word about the coming book started to spread, demand soared, and the authors decided to seed the market with 15,000 copies of this preliminary report. Their publisher was worried that Peters and Waterman were giving away too many. Edward Burlingame, who commissioned the book for Harper & Row, said that the company expected to sell around 60,000 copies in the first year, so the 15,000 copies represented 25 percent of that amount. But Peters believes that these copies were important in generating word of mouth and sales. "Within days of the book's launching, supportive reviews appeared, and the network of 15,000 (plus at least an equal number of photocopied knockoffs) hurried to buy the real thing, often in bulk for their subordinates," Peters recalls in *Thriving on Chaos. In Search of Excellence* sold 1.5 million copies in hardcover alone.

Because information can get stuck in clusters, seeding in many places is key. One of the most talked-about products in the mid-1990s was Windows 95, and seeding played an important role in that buzz. Microsoft sent out 450,000 copies before the product was actually released. By doing so, the company placed a copy of its new software at just one or two degrees of separation from any PC user. With 85 million PC owners around the world at the time and 450,000 advance copies of Windows 95 out, it is safe to assume that if a PC user didn't directly know someone who had an advance copy, at least he or she knew *of* someone who did.

How Much Seeding Is Enough?

Here's a little riddle: Which of the following two viral campaigns reached more people? The first campaign was for P&G's detergent Tide Coldwater; the other campaign surrounded Oxygen network's benefit for victims of Hurricane Katrina. The virality of each campaign can be measured by multiplying the likelihood that a person will forward the message by the average number of people they tell. The best-case scenario is when this number is over 1.0 and the buzz is self-perpetuating. But this high a number is rare. The Katrina relief campaign from Oxygen got a very high rating, 0.769. The Tide campaign only got 0.041. Clearly the Katrina campaign was more viral. But the question is, which campaign reached more people?

The answer is the Tide campaign, because there was much more seeding at the onset. It began by exposing itself to 960,954 people. The Oxygen campaign was launched to only 7,064. So although it was more viral, it reached fewer people. Viral reach depends not only on how viral your idea is, but also on your starting point.

Duncan Watts, Jonah Peretti, and Michael Frumin, who reported these numbers, make the point that it is "extremely difficult, and perhaps impossible, to consistently create media that will spread virally from a small seed to millions of people." The alternative available to large companies is to start with massive seeding. That way, "the contagious process may require several steps to burn itself out, during which time a quite respectable number of additional people may have been reached." This is exactly what Microsoft did with the introduction of Windows 95. This is how *The Purpose-Driven Life* was launched. This is what Tom Peters and Bob Waterman did with the introduction of *In Search of Excellence*.

The seeding that took place in these cases was intense; most companies will find it difficult to create that kind of interest in their product. Still, seeding can be effective even if it's not executed on a grand scale. How much seeding is enough? "There's no magic formula," says Matthew Stradiotto, the cofounder of Matchstick, the Toronto-based word-of-mouth agency, which has executed many seeding campaigns since 2001. In one of its early campaigns for a shoe company, it saw excellent results after giving a pair of shoes to each of twenty-five hand-picked women in several cities. Today Matchstick reaches out to at least one hundred people in each large city for each of its seeding efforts, and it tries to go higher when budgets allow. Its reach is much higher with online campaigns. BzzAgent, which is less selective in choosing who gets a seed unit, executes much larger campaigns, as illustrated by the Sonicare campaign, which was given to 33,000 people in North America. People in the industry mention 1 percent of the audience as a desirable percentage, but obviously there is a wide range in seeding efforts.

One potential pitfall in seeding is redundancy. Seeding twenty units of your product in a large organization can mean different things, depending on the distribution of those units. If the twenty units are scattered in twenty different departments, you are probably making good use of these seed units. If all twenty units are clustered in one department, then you've spent a lot of money that could have been used more effectively. (Of course, if the visibility of that particular department is especially high, it may justify such concentrated seeding.)

Pay Attention to Dead Networks

Seeding should be an ongoing effort. No matter how much care you provide, some seeds won't germinate, and as a result their corresponding networks will be inactive. I call those networks "dead networks." A dead network may indicate low activity, or it can suggest that a competing brand is successfully spreading in that network. To identify dead networks, you should use all the traditional sources of information used in marketing intelligence: sales data, marketing research, and your own observations. But instead of focusing on traditional measurements such as brand awareness and media exposure, concentrate on answering a single question: To what extent are people talking about my brand in a particular network?

Anecdotal data are very important in identifying dead networks. A sales rep can come back from a sporting event and report that biking fans in Seattle don't know about the new helmet you introduced to the market. Dead network. You come across a discussion on the Net that suggests that Ph.D. students prefer a product from a competitor of yours and don't even mention your product. Dead network. At one point, for example, our company noticed that medical librarians hardly ever discussed EndNote in their online discussion groups. There were lively discussions about EndNote among medical researchers and biology students, but the network of medical librarians was dead as far as EndNote was concerned. This was especially alarming since each one of these librarians was part of a local network that influenced what students and researchers were buying. We decided to distribute hundreds of seed units to medical libraries around the country. As a result, medical librarians started teaching courses on how to use EndNote, recommending the software enthusiastically to library patrons.

Our natural tendency as marketers is to pay attention to the networks that are "happening" and ignore those that are dead. In fact, the more successful a company is, the more likely it is to be flooded by messages from its existing networks, thereby failing to notice and seed the inactive ones. We pay attention to the networks that stimulate us, and it's hard to look beyond them. But you can expand your audience and your product sales far more rapidly by seeding inactive networks than by focusing all your efforts on active ones.

The Four Rules of a
Successful Seeding Campaign

Successful seeding is an active process. It goes well beyond the *Field of Dreams* cliché "If you build it, they will come." Rather than waiting passively for people to come to you, you must go out and plant seeds all around the forest. Here are a few guidelines.

1. **Look beyond the usual suspects.** Although seeding traditional channels is important, successful seeding efforts go beyond your normal channels, whether these are the media, the retailer, the dealership, or the department store. Think broadly. In the same way that you identify Zip Codes in which you don't have enough customers, you should be able to identify social circles, industry segments, or academic disciplines in which people aren't yet talking about your company, product, or service.

2. **Put the product in their hands.** Most often the seed has to be the product itself. In some cases, such as the sneak preview of *In Search of Excellence*, people may get excited just by getting a sample, but in general people need the entire experience to get truly engaged.

3. **Reduce the price barrier.** In some cases your analysis will show that you can afford to distribute these units for free; at other times a discount is the best you can do. But don't underestimate the price barrier for an unknown product: Make the product free to a seed customer if possible, or at least at as low in price as is feasible.

4. **Listen for silence.** When you hear silence from dead networks, your natural tendency will be to ignore them. Successful seeding requires spotting dead networks and reviving them.

Story

15

When you tell your customer something positive about your product—for instance, that your product is made from the most durable material in the world—there's always a little voice inside his head quietly evaluating your statement: "How can he say that it's the most durable material in the world? What is he talking about?" Even if this little voice doesn't object to the new information, it may be thinking about something else: "I need to be at the dentist in half an hour" or "My in box!!!"

The author Stephen Denning argues that the way to deal with that little voice is to engage it in a story. When you entertain that part of the brain, you give the little menace something to do besides argue. It starts imagining things and building its own story around the one you're telling.

So let *me* tell *you* a story. Blake Mycoskie is a young man who went to Argentina a couple of years ago to relax, learn the tango, and play polo. He really needed some time off after starting several businesses and losing in the reality show travel competition *The Amazing Race* by a very slim margin. In Argentina, Mycoskie noticed that a lot of the polo players were wearing *alpargatas*, simple canvas slip-on shoes that Argentine farmers have been wearing for many years. Toward the end of his trip, Mycoskie did some volunteer work, and in a poor area outside Buenos Aires he came across impoverished kids who were running around barefoot. He learned that this was a real problem in Argentina and many developing countries—lots of kids don't have shoes. The next day, back at the farm where he was staying, he told his new idea to a friend: He would redesign the *alpargatas* by making them more luxurious and durable. And for every pair he sold, he would give away another pair to a child in a developing area.

Notice how fast this story can be told: This guy goes to Argentina and sees cool shoes. He also sees kids with no shoes. He puts two and two together and starts a company that will make cool shoes and donate a pair for every pair it sells.

But a good story, a good *business* story, needs more than that. Too often I hear people talk about storytelling in business as if it's something you create out of thin air. A good business story— a story that people will repeat and that will help your sales— should be anchored in fact. For Toms Shoes' story to be repeated, it needed facts. Details. Credibility.

Here's how that story unfolded. After Mycoskie had the idea, he stayed in Argentina, meeting with shoe and fabric makers until he found someone who would make the shoes for him. He named the company Toms Shoes ("Tom" as in "tomorrow"). Several weeks later he returned to the United States with three duffel bags filled with 250 pairs. He made a cold call to American Rag, a trendy store in Los Angeles, and sold them almost half of his inventory. Placement in American Rag started some buzz in L.A. and got the attention of Booth Moore, a fashion critic. The article that Moore ran in the *Los Angeles Times* was short and sweet, with a big picture of the shoe. Mycoskie had 140 pairs left in inventory the morning the article ran. Within twenty-four hours he had about 2,200 orders. He hired three interns, gave them the keys to his apartment, and instructed them to call or e-mail all the people who placed those orders to let them know that there would be a delay. He himself got on the first plane back to Argentina to make more shoes. In the next six months the company sold about 10,000 pairs of shoes.

In October 2006, Mycoskie and a group of volunteers went to Argentina and gave away the first 10,000 pairs. They didn't just hand the shoes to kids—they actually put each pair on a child's feet. A short video of the shoe drop was posted on YouTube (a link is available at www.tomsshoes.com). Now the story starts to be more real. More authentic. It's not just a story, it's something that is happening.

The lesson here? When they hear a story like this, these little voices inside the customers' heads may still ask a question from time to time, but by now they're too engaged in the story to offer much of an argument.

Where Do You Find Your Story?

Here's the story that explains how I became interested in the phenomenon of word of mouth:

It was 1988, and our small California-based company was still a few months away from releasing the first version of End-Note when we received an order in the mail. From Princeton, New Jersey. I remember all five of us standing around that purchase order, staring at it and trying to figure out how someone on the other side of the continent had learned of us. We hadn't advertised our product. In fact, only a handful of people in California knew EndNote existed.

So one of us called the customer who had placed the order. How had he heard of EndNote? Apparently one of the few people who'd attended a sneak preview of our product in Berkeley, California, several days earlier had been so excited about End-Note that he posted an enthusiastic message on an electronic bulletin board used by academics. One of those academics had just become our first customer.

My own story may not be as exciting as the Toms Shoes story, but it does illustrate the power of word of mouth.

Of course, right after that happened, we all went back to work. Nobody said, "Look at the importance of word of mouth," or "Isn't the Internet amazing?" I don't think these thoughts even crossed my mind. Nor did it even register as a story; it was just something that happened. But when I started working on the book that would ultimately become *The Anatomy of Buzz*, I somehow unearthed this little incident and put it down on paper. Though I could probably compose ten pages about this incident, in writing it down I threw away facts that were not relevant to the main point.

Is this story true? Yes. More than that, it is truthful because over the next ten years I saw this kind of thing happen thousands of times. And this *is* how I became interested in word-of-mouth marketing.

Remember, facts alone don't do the trick when it comes to storytelling. I can tell you, for example, that between 40 percent and 60 percent of our customers heard about EndNote from another person. But that statement falls flat. It's not a narrative. Research shows that stories are more persuasive than abstract statements or statistics, and they are certainly easier to remember than facts.

Luigi Pirandello, the Italian playwright, once wrote, "A fact is like a sack which won't stand up when it is empty. In order that it may stand up, one has to put into it the reason and sentiment which have caused it to exist." The way to engage people is to tell a story. But again, in the context of business, a story has to persuade, not just to engage. So you need the sack *and* you need its content. You need the story of how Mycoskie came up with the idea for Toms Shoes when he saw kids running barefoot, *and* you need to know that he gave away the 10,000 shoes in Argentina.

A lot of good business stories concern the genesis of a company. Blake Mycoskie saw barefoot kids. Brian Maxwell, the founder of PowerBar, was running a marathon when he recognized the need for an energy bar. Songwriter Dave Kapell was suffering from writer's block when he decided to put some interesting words on pieces of paper and rearrange them; the fact that any little wind or a sneeze would send all the pieces of paper flying across the room is how Magnetic Poetry was born. Every serious Nike fan knows the story of how Nike founder Bill Bowerman poured liquid urethane into his wife's waffle iron to experiment with a new sole for the sneaker. These factoids from a company's history are a form of cultural capital within a brand community, pieces of history that are traded among fans to show how serious they are.

You don't have to be a giant company to have a great story. Not far from my house there's a butcher shop, Schaub's, that sells a marinated sirloin called Fred's Steak. On the counter you can find a little story written by the owner of the store, David Schaub, that begins: "Who is Fred? And what did he do to those steaks?" The story goes that one day about forty years ago, a butcher named Fred came up with a black marinating mix that didn't look too good but gave the meat a taste that was simply out of this world. Word spread about Fred's marinated sirloins and people would come from out of town for them. Fred closed his market in Los Gatos in 1979, but customers would still stop him on the street to find out where they could get those steaks. When David Schaub opened *his* store in 1988, he convinced Fred to part with the recipe. The story ends: "Fred passed away in 1996, but his steaks live on. So if you enjoy them as much as I do, let me know; Fred was my dad."

The story is printed on little sheets of paper stacked on the counter at Schaub's. Hardly a suspense novel, but a good conversation starter with your friends as you stand by the barbecue waiting for the sizzling steaks to be ready.

Ask your customers to tell their stories too. On the Coca-Cola Web site you can find dozens of stories from fans about how the drink touched their lives. One woman tells a story about eating dinner with her boyfriend at a restaurant in New Orleans. She ordered a bottle of Coke (as always—she's a big fan), and as soon as she started drinking, she detected something sparkling at the bottom. As she was trying to figure out what it was, she noticed that her boyfriend was kneeling down. He said, "I know you love Coke so much, but will you consider marrying me? I promise you'll have Coke every day if you say yes." She did.

. . .

Toms Shoes is a very young company with a story that is still being shaped. The company has twenty-two employees now, and someone recently asked Mycoskie about a business plan and mission statement, but he sticks to the simple idea that got him so far: For every pair of shoes you buy from Toms Shoes, this company will donate a pair of shoes to a child in need. If for some reason the company suddenly stops putting shoes on kids' feet in developing countries, the story will collapse. But for now, it's doing it. In November 2007, Mycoskie and sixty volunteers delivered 50,000 shoes to children in South Africa.

Toms Shoes is surrounded by a lot of support and goodwill. Through his connections in the entertainment business (Mycoskie had previously started a reality cable channel which never got off the ground), he got several celebrities to wear the shoes, which has helped jump-start the brand's growth. He also had help from the band Hanson, which invites its audience to take a one-mile walk before each concert to raise awareness about children who don't have shoes. Hanson has done over sixty of these walks so far, telling its fans about Toms Shoes and selling the shoes at the show.

About three months after the launch of the company, Mycoskie was at JFK Airport getting ready to check in. He had just come from the gym, so he was wearing running shoes. Waiting at the gate, he noticed a teenage girl wearing red Toms shoes. It was the first time he had seen someone wearing the shoes who wasn't a friend or a family member. He decided to see what she would say, so he turned to her.

"Excuse me. Those are really cool shoes. What are they?" Mycoskie asked.

"Oh, well, they're Toms," the teenager said.

"Oh, that's cool, thanks," Mycoskie said. He was about to turn away, but the girl grabbed him by his shoulder. She had to tell him the story.

What amazed Mycoskie most was how accurately she told it. His trip to Argentina, how he saw the kids, how he hired the interns, everything! At one point Mycoskie couldn't hold back anymore and told her who he was. "Oh my gosh, I've seen you on the YouTube videos!" she said. "Your hair is shorter now."

Mycoskie is sure that this has happened thousands of times as people notice their friends wearing the shoes. He calls them Sole Ambassadors. "They're the ones who are responsible for our growth," he says.

"I wish I could give you some great topical or tactical way we're doing this, but the truth is it's just a great story and people feel good telling it," Mycoskie told me. Sounds pretty simple, but there are so many brands that don't have a story—or don't know they have one. You need to find that great story and put it out there.

Give Us Something to Talk About

16

One day in 1974 a tall man named Mechai Viravaidya stood onstage in front of two thousand teachers in Bangkok and delivered a lecture. It was a hot day, and ceiling fans were whirring overhead trying to dissipate the heat. Viravaidya, the son of a Scottish mother and a Thai father, both medical doctors, was delivering a lecture about family planning.

Lectures on family planning can be surprisingly dull, and as Viravaidya was listing the different methods for birth control, he noticed he was getting a lot of blank looks. He was peppering his talk with colorful metaphors as he tried to get people interested in the pill or the intrauterine device, but people were self-conscious and some looked plain bored. The atmosphere in the large auditorium was somber, and Mechai Viravaidya doesn't like things so sedate.

To appreciate the outrageous nature of the events that followed, one must understand how conservative Thailand was back in 1974. Condoms could only be prescribed by a doctor. Talking about sex was simply not done. Even the staff of the government agency that was supposed to educate the public about family planning seemed to be mortified by talk about sex.

So when Mechai Viravaidya pulled a condom out of his pocket, the atmosphere changed. There was some laughter, giggles, smiles. "I knew I was on to something, so I said, 'Let's open it up. A lot of you have maybe heard about the condom but have never seen it or touched it,' " Viravaidya remembers. He tore its packaging and started talking about alternative uses of the condom. Dangling the rubber in front of the giggling audience, he explained that it could be used to carry water, it could cover a barrel of a gun, and you could tie your hair with it. Then he remembered how as a child he once found some condoms at his father's clinic and blew them up. "It can also be used as a balloon," he cheerfully explained to his audience. As he started blowing into his new toy, the laughter got louder and louder. "It was like magic," he says. "One minute they were sitting there looking stiff and self-conscious, and the next they were roaring with laughter."

In his work for the government, Viravaidya had met too many farmers' families with seven or ten children and very little food to share. He strongly believed that the way to deal with poverty in Thailand was to reduce the population growth. Now, standing onstage with a condom-turned-balloon, he felt that he was really starting to get people's attention, and he decided to make the most out of the situation. He asked his staff to distribute sample condoms that they brought along. Some in the audience had no problem taking the condoms that were handed to them. Others were more reluctant, but Viravaidya didn't let them off the hook. "It's just a piece of rubber," he explained. "The condom is really clean if your mind isn't dirty. If you have a dirty mind, please don't take one."

Viravaidya encouraged people to tear the packages open, feel the rubber, and blow up their condoms too. In the carnival atmosphere that followed, he invited "those with the cleanest minds" to join him onstage for a condom-blowing contest. With some help from his staff, dozens of teachers ended up onstage, and Mechai Viravaidya announced, "On the count of three, I want all of you to start blowing up your condoms. The one to blow up the largest condom in one minute will win a year's supply." All hell broke loose when the contest started. Viravaidya, like a football reporter, gave a blow-by-blow account of the contestants' progress. Two thousand people were laughing uncontrollably.

The impact on word of mouth that day wasn't ever measured, but it's not hard to imagine that many of these teachers told their colleagues, families, and friends about their experience.

People love to talk about the unexpected—things that are different and surprising. And we're more likely to talk when we participate in an experience. In the thirty-odd years since that lecture, Mechai Viravaidya has kept both those points in mind when promoting condoms, first as a way to battle poverty and later as a way to fight AIDS. He took the idea of condom-blowing contests to the street, organizing spontaneous contests in markets and on street corners. He set up a program called Cops and Rubbers, in which policemen in Thailand handed out condoms on the streets. And the list of his buzzworthy activities goes on and on.

Take the restaurant that Viravaidya's organization opened in Bangkok, called Cabbages and Condoms. In addition to tasting delicious Thai cuisine, you can enjoy looking at the beautiful lampshades, clothing items, table settings, and other decorations, all made out of condoms. At the end of the meal, along with your coffee, you don't get a mint, but . . . You guessed it. Last year the restaurant brought in about $1.5 million in profit, which Viravaidya's Population and Community Development Association (PDA) uses to improve the lives of the poor and to promote its message.

When I referred to his practices as shocking, Viravaidya insisted that his objective is never to shock people but to surprise them. Shocking may lead to resistance, and his surprises have purpose; his goal is never to shock for the sake of shock.

Outside observers have taken his contribution to health in Thailand seriously. When PDA was awarded the 2007 Gates Award for Global Health by the Melinda and Bill Gates Foundation, Dr. Nils Daulaire, the president and CEO of the Global Health Council, said, "The world needs more leaders like Mechai, who are willing to tackle taboo subjects like sex and HIV/AIDS directly in order to save lives." Dr. Allan Rosenfield, the dean of the School of Public Health at Columbia University, and Dr. Malcolm Potts, a professor at the UC Berkeley School of Public Health, commented that "his open, fearless, commonsense approach to problems that other leaders all too often avoid has made him a model for other countries, both rich and poor."

Mechai Viravaidya is not only a master in creating buzz but also a skillful strategist. To secure the support of religious leaders, he worked with scholars who studied Buddhist scriptures to find support for family planning. Armed with the quote "Many births cause suffering," he got the blessing of Buddhist monks. To make the condom widely available, PDA built a network of over 10,000 village distributors. To get access to teachers, he worked with the teachers' union; his organization trained 320,000 rural schoolteachers within five years. In the period since PDA started its work, the annual population growth rate dropped from 3.3 percent in the mid-1970s to 0.8 percent in 2002.

Mechai Viravaidya has constantly given people something to talk about. In fact, his name has become so closely associated with the condom that in Thailand, a condom is called a Mechai (which he doesn't mind at all).

The Biggest Enemy of Buzz

In the past few years I participated in several automotive industry events. The problem with those events was simple: they were boring. They gave people nothing to talk about and served to remind me that the biggest enemy of buzz is routine.

These failures stood in stark contrast to a BMW driving event that I attended a few years ago in Berkeley, California. Afterward I told everyone about BMW's traction-stability presentation, a demonstration that no ad could re-create. To demonstrate the car's stability on a slippery road, the organizers first laid a huge sheet of plastic on the ground and poured buckets of water on it to create the effect of a puddle on the road. They asked for a volunteer and instructed him to sit in the driver's seat. A driving instructor sat next to him to make sure events wouldn't get out of control. The volunteer was told to drive on the dry ground to develop some speed, then cross the sheet of plastic. In order for us to appreciate the usefulness of the new system, they were first going to demonstrate what happens when the system is turned off. "Everyone take three steps back," the instructor said, and the crowd laughed nervously.

"Put the pedal to the metal!" the instructor shouted. "Ready, set, go!" The volunteer floored it. The car spun twice on the sheet before he was able to drive off it. No one who was there will ever forget that sight. Then they asked him to do the same thing again but with the traction-stability system on. Deep inside, I suspect everyone wanted to see the awesome spinning again, but instead the car slowed down automatically and passed the slippery area without even varying in direction. This is the kind of demonstration people tell their friends about. It gave us something to talk about.

Horses Go to the Movies

As with everything else, some publicity stunts are good, others are bad. The best reinforce the spirit of the product. My favorite was the 1974 stunt to launch Mel Brooks's Western spoof *Blazing Saddles*. At the premiere of the comedy, Warner Brothers invited some very special guests. "Any picture by Mel Brooks calls for something outrageous, so for his picture *Blazing Saddles* I invited horses to a special showing of the picture," Marty Weiser said in an interview taped in 1987, a year before he died. Weiser, who worked for Warner Brothers for over fifty years, was the man behind many ideas that generated a lot of talk over the years. Weiser and his staff at Warner Brothers rented a drive-in theater in Los Angeles, placed a small ad in the *Los Angeles Times*, and put up flyers near stables in the area advertising a free showing of the movie to horses and their owners. Then they waited and prayed that someone would show up. The media loved the idea; at the designated time the parking lot was full of TV crews and journalists. But no horses. Just when Weiser was beginning to lose hope, a police motorcycle drove in, escorting a parade of horses. About 250 of them—and their owners—showed up to watch the comedy and have some oats and "horse d'oeuvres" at the "horsepitality bar."

Another favorite of mine involved a man who understood the value of shock: Alfred Hitchcock. Imagine walking along the Thames River in London one morning and noticing a floating body. When you get a little closer, you realize that the body is that of Hitchcock himself! While shooting the movie *Frenzy* in the early 1970s, he created a dummy of himself and tossed it into the Thames. Those who saw the "corpse" in person and many who saw a picture of it in newspapers naturally told friends and family members, which was exactly what Hitchcock wanted them to do.

When Tina Brown put a picture of Demi Moore nude and pregnant on the cover of *Vanity Fair*, a lot of people talked. But it was the uniqueness of the shot that created the buzz. If you simply repeat what *Vanity Fair* did with another actress, don't expect much. The key to staying at the top of your game is always to top your last stunt. Always push the envelope—without crossing the line.

Your Hook and Your Product

In an earlier chapter I talked about listening to your customers in order to find conversation hooks. There are all kinds of hooks (and not all are found by listening). A publicity stunt is another kind of conversation hook. And the closer your conversation hook is to your product, the better.

Sometimes the product itself is the hook. The iPhone is an

obvious example of a product so unique that it becomes the focus of conversation. But often you have to introduce a hook that will give people something concrete to talk about. In the case of Brita, the hook was two bags of tea.

Moss Kadey, who introduced Brita to North America, believes that those two tea bags got thousands of conversations going. Brita included two bags of tea and something it called the tea-test card with every pitcher it sold. The card encouraged people to prepare two cups of tea, one using regular tap water and the other using water filtered by their new Brita. "The visual difference between the two teas, especially in areas where the water is fairly hard, is quite staggering," Kadey says. The cup made with tap water would be cloudy and murky, while the cup of tea made with the filtered water was perfectly translucent, with no unpleasant deposits.

People were invited to write their comments on the tea-test card and send it to Brita. Tens of thousands of customers did. While the actual amount of word of mouth was not measured by the company, Kadey is convinced of the hook's impact. "There is no doubt that it created word of mouth," he says. "It's the type of thing that you wanted to show someone else: 'Look at the difference between the teas. This is what we're drinking!' " Kadey continued the practice of adding tea bags to new boxes of Brita filters until he sold the company to Clorox in 1995.

When you think about it, the tea test basically translates the benefit of the product as it pertains to one sense, taste, to another sense, sight. So one way to think of a conversation hook is to look for ways to expand the sensory experience. Since it may be hard to taste the difference between water that has been filtered and unfiltered water, the tea test provides a visual proof of the filter's effect.

Like the Herbal Essences hair-coloring booklet and the NOLS veggie bus, the tea-test card is an effective hook because it starts a conversation that relates to the product and its benefits.

Contrast these examples to a publicity stunt done simply to get attention without somehow showcasing the essence of a brand. Such stunts may have some value in creating awareness, but they won't cause people to recommend the product. Linda Pezzano stressed this point. In all her campaigns for Trivial Pursuit and Pictionary, the product was always king. "You need to find ways of doing things that relate to the product so that you're reinforcing the concept and the message behind the product," she said.

You should also distinguish between word of mouth that is created because of true excitement about your product and word of mouth that is created because of a new communication medium you use. The first company to use podcasting, Second Life, blogging, or another new medium in its marketing is likely to be talked about. This can certainly position the company as one that's on the cutting edge of technology, but don't mistake this for word of mouth that focuses on the product.

People

Can a top executive be a conversation hook? Is it good for business if everyone talks about your CEO? It may seem obvious that investors, employees, and customers are attracted to a company led by someone with high visibility. In fact, at least when it comes to media buzz, researchers from Duke and Harvard found that 20 percent of chief executives generate 80 percent of media coverage. But interestingly enough, there was no statistically significant difference in average shareholder returns between companies with a celebrity CEO and other companies.

Still, while at the macro level there is no correlation between celebrity and profitability, there are cases when a company can greatly benefit from people's interest in its visible employees. Consider the case of a celebrity chef who opens his own restaurant. It's easy to see how he can benefit from talk not only about the food but also about the person behind it. Similarly, artists, actors, and authors are so close to what they produce that talking about them isn't very different from talking about their products.

The question is, how close is the conversation hook to the product benefit? Consider the following comment: "That is one powerful machine. Thank you for your 5 years and 5,127 prototypes, James Dyson."

The woman who wrote this on her blog is talking about her vacuum cleaner, and she's wrapping in the story of James Dyson, the inventor of the machine. Dyson promoted his machine by telling his own story. He's an industrial engineer who got frustrated with conventional vacuum cleaners that lost suction. Determined to create a better model, he built one, but it didn't work. So he built another one, and *that* didn't work. After five years and 5,127 prototypes, he finally got it right.

A few years ago Dyson got a medal from Queen Elizabeth II for his achievements in industry. He stood in a long line of people who were honored that day. When it was time for him to get the medal, the announcer gave his name. As he bowed in front of Her Majesty so that she could put the medal around his neck, she asked, "And what do you do exactly, Mr. Dyson?"

He told her he was the manufacturer of the Dyson vacuum cleaner.

"Oh really?" she said. "We've got dozens of them about the palace."

I love this story. I can see James Dyson with his head down in front of the Queen. I can picture the Queen walking around the palace in the morning while dozens of maids with yellow vacuum cleaners vacuum the carpet. Notice, however, that this story (which Dyson tells in his autobiography) still has a product focus: The Dyson vacuum cleaner is so good that the staff uses dozens of them at Buckingham Palace.

When you think of experts in the area of vacuum cleaning, Queen Elizabeth II is not the first name that comes to mind. But when it comes to buzz, mentioning her name still makes sense. Celebrities get our attention. They give us something to talk about.

The Power of Gossip

- "What's the deal with Carmela and Tony? Is their relationship this bad?"
- "Notice how Carmela scowled at Tony all during the barbecue, but smiled whenever others might have seen her."
- "I think Charmaine slept with Tony before Tony and Carmela were married."

These snippets from actual online conversations may sound like simple gossip. In fact, they are part of the early buzz about one of the most talked-about television programs in recent years: *The Sopranos*.

Fictional characters are natural conversational hooks. Any talk about Tony and Carmela Soprano is talk about *The Sopranos*, and the creators of the program brilliantly used the power of gossip. First they realized that we all have met enough boring people in our lives, so we don't usually bother telling others about them. We do, however, talk about colorful and unusual people, and we certainly find those on *The Sopranos*. Like Tony Soprano, a mobster on Prozac. Or Livia, Tony's mother. "Oh my god! am I sick of that old bag!" one viewer wrote in an online forum. Interesting characters aren't necessarily lovable. In fact, we all know that annoying people often trigger the most interesting conversations.

The *Sopranos* characters are also very relevant. They feel so real and authentic that we start thinking of them like people we know. In a way, they become an extension of our social network. As we meet them week after week and learn about their daily struggles, we become more involved with their lives and the issues they have to deal with: relationships, midlife crises, power struggles, worries about social status. Tony and Carmela have to choose a college for their daughter, convince Tony's mother to move to a nursing home, and deal with a problematic soccer coach. How much this relevance drives buzz becomes evident when you read discussions about *The Sopranos* in online forums. Many conversations are about relationships, about who did what to whom and what they should do next.

To stimulate talk even further, David Chase, the show's creator, used an ancient method—shock treatment. When people we know are involved in outrageous things, we have to relieve the tension somehow, so we talk. If you peeked at a *Sopranos* fan list the day after Tony's sister shot her fiancé, you would have seen just that. The cries of shock and disbelief were amazing. "I can't believe Janice capped Ritchie!!!!!" one fan posted shortly after he saw the program. Another reported, "I was watching the show with about seven Soprano addicts, and when Janice shot Richie there was some serious 'Holy S—!' being screamed." In 2007 Chase managed to shock everyone yet again, with a most controversial ending. Reading some blog posts in the days that followed the concluding episode, you could see that some viewers loved it. Many hated it. But he certainly gave people something to talk about.

This kind of shock—and even outright public disapproval— can also sometimes work as a way to promote buzz about real people in the entertainment industry. But this kind of buzz is industry-specific. While a celebrity who's misbehaving can benefit from the additional visibility, the same is rarely true in other industries. Yes, it can lead to awareness, but except for rare cases, I don't see how it can positively affect the bottom line.

Mismatched Hooks

There's also a category of hooks that are so far from the product's core, so absurd, so much fun, that they work. In the spring of 2007, Intuit invited its users to rap about taxes. Rapper Vanilla Ice introduced the contest on YouTube and people submitted their raps. Taxes and rap? A mismatch.

For years the makers of Duck brand duct tape have been running a prom-night competition in which kids make their dresses and tuxedos out of duct tape (to check it out, go to www.stuck-atprom.com). A tux out of duct tape? A mismatch.

In 2006, White Castle, a U.S. hamburger chain, announced a special event for Valentine's Day. To participate you needed to make a reservation. When you arrived, a hostess led you to your reserved seat and lit candles for you and your companion. If you've ever been to a White Castle, you know that it's not exactly a romantic place. White Castle and Valentine's Day? A mismatch.

People like to talk about the counterintuitive, the absurd—horses that go to the movies, people rapping about their taxes, a car shaped like a hot dog. Ironically, the more boring your product is, the easier it is to come up with a mismatch that people will talk about.

These are the exceptions, though. Usually you want to focus on your core message and let the excitement come from the product itself and the way you communicate these benefits. How do you do it? Perhaps it's best to listen to Viravaidya's advice: "Don't be dull. Don't stand up there and preach," he says. "Make it fun, make it interesting, make it culturally relevant, and let people participate."

Let people participate—an idea that takes us right to the next chapter.

The Power
of Participation

17 **Anders Søborg built a candy** machine made completely of Legos. You insert a coin, make a selection among three different types of candy. Next a spiral starts turning, pushing the candy forward, just as in a regular candy machine. The lid opens and you take your (real) candy. It's neat.

Anders is proud of that candy machine and the scanner, pinball machine, brick sorter, and all the other stuff he built with Lego's robot kit, Mindstorms. His projects are posted on his Web site, some with movies that demonstrate how they work.

Think of yourself in preschool. You're sitting with the rest of the kids and drawing a picture of a house. You make a door and two windows, and the windows have curtains (those came out really great). You color the roof bright red without going outside the lines. Now you add a chimney and some smoke coming out of it. You add some clouds in the sky and a bright yellow sun in the middle. This picture is beautiful. You're done.

What do you do next? You show it to your teacher or to the other kids. You show it to your mom. This is what we do: We create. We share.

Next time you're at a computer, search for the phrase "check out what I did." You'll discover more than 150,000 people who can't wait to talk about what they've created.

Lego benefits greatly from our instinct to share what we create. Anytime someone like Anders finishes a project, he or she posts a picture or a video to show how it works and invites others to check it out. One Mindstorms robot that knows how to solve the Rubik's Cube got over 1.4 million views on YouTube as of May 2008. Anders's movies on YouTube get more modest views, in the thousands. Together with others, though, it all adds up to millions of views of Lego-related stuff on YouTube. There are over 50,000 videos related to Lego on YouTube. About 2,000 of them relate to Mindstorms.

Online buzz is just part of the story. People who build Mindstorms robots also show the projects to those around them. Anders Søborg likes to solicit project ideas from nontechnical people, so he asks his friends and family what they'd like him to build next. "They come up with a lot of crazy ideas that would be impossible, but some of them are really interesting," he says. The idea for the candy machine came from his girlfriend. There was a birthday party coming up in the family, and she thought it would be really cool for the kids at the party to have a candy machine. Anders pulled up his sleeves. He carefully studied how a candy machine worked. For a couple of months he spent weekends building the machine, and he finished in time for the birthday party. On the day of the party the kids had a blast. Everybody was talking about it, and about the drinking fountain that Anders built, also out of Legos.

The kids at the party insisted that the cover of the candy machine be open the whole time so they could see how it worked. They also constantly looked for ways to outsmart the machine, sticking round objects into the slot to see how Anders's sensors would deal with them. And what a joy it was when they figured it out and the first free candy rolled out! "We ran out of candy pretty fast," he says.

Outsmarting the Candy Machine

Not long after Lego introduced its Mindstorms platform in 1998, a Stanford graduate student named Kekoa Proudfoot managed to reverse-engineer the RCX brick, the brain of any robot built with Mindstorms. He posted his findings online, which enabled several other people to develop tools for Mindstorms, including an open-source operating system.

Lego faced a dilemma. Should the company fight it or embrace it? "Of course our lawyers didn't like it," says Søren Lund, the director of Mindstorms at Lego. But the product development team reacted differently. "We were so proud somebody would hack it!" Lund says. "I mean, if it was a boring product, why would you hack it? It must be because there's something to this product that you like to work with." Lego's first official standpoint was neutral. The company didn't endorse it but also didn't try to stop the hacking. But after a few months of internal debate, Lego chose to go all the way: Its software license now has a "right to hack" section that allows users to modify the code.

This opened yet another level of creativity and another level of show-and-tell. The candy machine would have taken longer to build without hacking, Anders Søborg says. In his pinball machine you can record your name and score. This is something that would not have been possible to create with Lego's standard software (or, more accurately, firmware). Several other projects, including a small robot that knows its way around Anders's apartment in Esbjerg, Denmark, would have not been possible at all without hacking. The bottom line is this: With the right to hack, you can do more stuff with Mindstorms, which means that there's more you can show your friends and there's more to discuss with other enthusiasts.

There's friendly competition among Mindstorms enthusiasts. Your status goes up if you're the first one to come up with a solution. Anders gets an ongoing flow of e-mails with questions, and when he needs help he contacts another expert user or posts a question on an online forum.

The interaction and the sharing keep people involved and lead to more projects being created, which leads to more outsiders learning about Mindstorms, which led to Mindstorms becoming Lego's all-time bestselling product.

The Power of Participation

The *Oxford English Dictionary* was created in the nineteenth century with the help of volunteers who contributed thousands of words on little slips of paper. In the past few years we've seen this kind of participation soar with the advent of initiatives such as Linux, Mozilla Firefox, and Wikipedia (where I first learned about the making of the *Oxford English Dictionary*).

How do these projects build buzz? I'm sure that each one of the people who contributed to the *Oxford English Dictionary* told some friends and family about his or her contribution. Participation creates involvement and a sense of ownership, which in turn leads to talk. If you can create this type of participation, you will create buzz.

In 2004, Lego, which was already getting a lot of grassroots buzz because of its openness, decided to kick it up a notch. As Lego's development team started working on the next version of Mindstorms, they decided to involve a few users at a much deeper level. Combing through forums, blogs, and community sites, they looked for those users who were most referred to and linked to by other users. "We really used the Google approach," says Lund. His team gathered a short list of about twenty people and then narrowed it down further, to four enthusiasts who became part of the development process of the Mindstorms NXT. Under strict confidentiality, these hobbyists helped outline the specs for the motors, sensors, and firmware of Mindstorms' new version.

In a second wave of this project, Lego added eleven other users who gave their input, and in an effort to finish the project, the company recruited one hundred additional Mindstorms enthusiasts to test the pre-release kits. This sort of participation can stimulate word of mouth in two ways. First, the folks who are involved develop a great sense of ownership and pride, and once they are allowed to talk, they will buzz about the new product. In May 2006, about three months before the official launch, Lund gave the 115 users the green light to post online photos and videos of the new robots they created with Mindstorms NXT. This created waves of buzz among enthusiasts.

This type of customer participation creates word of mouth in another, more significant way—it can improve the customer experience. "Empowered involvement creates advocacy," says the social psychologist Paul Marsden, "but more importantly, it gets the companies doing things that people want." Søren Lund emphasizes the passion of these volunteer cocreators. When they believe in a new feature or idea, they become very singleminded. "They keep bugging you because they want something changed," he says. Indeed, Lego revisited and changed several things because of the persistence of these customers. "They keep pushing barriers. They keep pushing to make things better," Lund adds.

The Limits of No Limits

Sometimes it makes sense to put absolutely no limits on creativity, as in the case of Lego Mindstorms. Other times you'll get more talk if you do set some boundaries. To examine this idea, let's look at a totally different example. The only thing that it has in common with the Mindstorms "right to hack" story is the fact that in both cases people are motivated to talk because they've created something.

CareerBuilder knew it had an asset in those chimps that have been used for several years in their TV commercials. The commercials feature a hardworking guy who's trying to get his job done. Trouble is, he's working with a bunch of chimpanzees who are joking around, doing stupid tricks, and ignoring the fact that sales are going down. The line at the end: "A better job awaits."

The advertising agency Cramer-Krasselt wanted to extend the chimps' popularity to the online world. Now, think of the possibilities! Think of a video contest on YouTube. People could wear monkey suits at the office. Maybe someone would take his own chimp in to work. Perhaps people would create animated films. The possibilities were endless.

Of course, that presents a dilemma: Just how many people will participate in such a video? A thousand? Five thousand? Let's look at the alternative that CareerBuilder chose.

Shortly after Super Bowl 2006, CareerBuilder started inviting people to send a "Monk-e-Mail," which basically means that you can use a chimp as your spokesperson to send a message to your friend. And you can be creative. You can choose which chimp you want to represent you and choose his headgear, clothes, what he holds in his hand, his glasses, the place in the background, and, most important, what the chimp says.

Although you have a wide range of options (well over 100,000 combinations, even before you determine what the chimp will say), you do everything within very clear guidelines. In other words, it's not overwhelming. The Monk-e-Mails became an overnight success, spreading like wildfire. As of January 2008, over 120 million Monk-e-Mails had been sent, and they continue to be sent.

Most people want the easy, simple stuff. They don't have time to come up with something out of nothing. So make it easy for them to be creative.

Consider this: People have four ways to instruct the monkey what to say. You can use text-to-speech (the monkey will say whatever you type) or a prerecorded message (including the unforgettable song "You Wear Way Too Much Cologne"), call a special phone number to record your message, or use your microphone to record it.

Which option is used most often? Most people, by far, use either the text-to-speech interface or one of the prerecorded messages. They create something that is unique enough and press the send button. Very few users record their own message.

Advertisers who approach Oddcast, the company behind the campaign, sometimes want to add more and more options to their viral campaign. "It's too much," Adi Sideman, the CEO of

Oddcast, tells them. he urges them to keep it simple and warns that if they don't, users might lose interest.

Remember the Bob Dylan video I discussed in Chapter 1? What's so brilliant about this video is its simplicity. You type words onto ten cards. That's it. You can be extremely creative with very little work or risk.

So is that all it takes? Just make your campaign simple and you'll go viral? Of course not. "Viral marketing campaigns are much like Hollywood movies," says Sideman. "The taste of the consumer is a mystery." It's not always apparent what is going to be successful, and the creative concept is key. In the case of the CareerBuilder campaign, there's another secret ingredient—the chimps. People love monkeys and apes, and in general Sideman has noticed that people have much less of a problem participating in campaigns where the avatar is an animal.

I'm not trying to set a rule in stone here. Rather, I want to highlight the trade-off. Jackie Huba and Ben McConnell point out that about one percent of visitors create content in sites such as Wikipedia and that, similarly, only a small percentage of your audience will create content related to your product. In other words, if you give people full freedom, very few will participate. But the involvement of these few (and therefore the buzz they create) will be high. On the other hand, if you set some boundaries but still allow people to be creative, you're likely to have more participants but possibly with lower involvement. Whatever you do, inviting people to participate, to be part of the experience, is a way to stimulate excitement, and therefore more talk.

Voting

Some participation can be created through pretty simple devices, such as engagement polls, explains Piers Hogarth-Scott, the cofounder of Yooster, a word-of-mouth marketing and research company. You engage people by asking them to help a company make a decision. You close the loop by letting them know what the results were and how their opinions have affected the brand or product. When people see the results of their vote in the marketplace, you create the "I did that" effect, which builds a sense of engagement, empowerment, and advocacy.

Dr. Paul Marsden and Martin Oetting argue that marketers can greatly benefit from letting consumers call the shots when it comes to marketing and innovation. "Don't just listen to them through classic market research, but actually empower consumers to cast deciding votes on what gets done," they write. Marsden and Oetting give a few guidelines on how to accomplish this. You set up a simple poll and you let people vote online, by SMS, by telephone, or on interactive TV. The topic of the vote can be anything: which fashion model to use in your next ad, what background music to use in a commercial, what packaging to use for your next product, what's the best poster, merchandise, logo, or tagline. They note that you should keep options to a minimum and keep the voting hassle-free and simple. When the votes are in, act on them and let participants know the results. In past years consumers voted for a billboard campaign for Vanilla Coke, picked the name of a new crayon for Crayola, and chose the logo for the teen movie *Win a Date with Tad Hamilton!* Even the Tate Museum in London invited visitors to help label exhibits.

Marsden has been explaining the power of participation (and other aspects of word-of-mouth marketing) through the Hawthorne effect, a classic study that was done in a Western

Electric production plant in the town of Hawthorne, near Chicago, in the 1930s. Researchers from Harvard Business School were looking for ways to increase productivity in the workplace. They tested several methods by inviting small groups of employees to try various new working conditions before anyone else. The Harvard team found that working in brighter lighting conditions resulted in higher productivity. But when the researchers studied the effect of softer lighting, they were surprised to find that this too improved productivity. Shorter working hours boosted productivity, but then so did longer working hours. The conclusion was that the increase in productivity had nothing to do with what was being tested. It was all about the special attention that was given to participants. By involving the participants and inviting them to give feedback, the researchers created a sense of involvement and ownership that resulted in goodwill, which in turn led to enhanced productivity. Marsden argues that this is exactly what is happening in a lot of these promotions. The very fact that you give people a say gives them a sense of ownership that creates more goodwill and advocacy.

The One Topic That We Never Get Tired Of

Toward the end of our meeting in his office in San Mateo, California, Jia Shen started talking about his shoes. They looked like regular sneakers to me, but when he turned them over I could see that they had wheels. They are called heelies. I had never seen them before on a grown-up—and had never even realized that heelies are made in adult sizes. After the meeting, as we were walking toward the exit, Jia suddenly shot forward like a human roadrunner and stopped on a dime before smashing into the glass door. He's obviously multitalented; the guy has a degree in computer science from Johns Hopkins University.

Jia Shen creates widgets—tiny apps for users of MySpace, Facebook, and the like. And he knows his customers really well. One reason he has heelies is that he spends lots of time in shopping malls and likes to get places quickly. He also reads *Seventeen* and *CosmoGirl*. He has a bowl cut, speaks fast, and can tell you what color is in this year. Most of the users of RockYou, the company he cofounded with Lance Tokuda, are teenage girls.

There's one topic we never get tired of talking about, and if you keep it in mind when you invite people to participate, you will get some talk. The topic? Ourselves.

When I say talking, I don't only mean talking with words. We tell the world about ourselves in many other ways, of course. One of the ways in which Jia's teenage customers express themselves is through accessories. Shen and Tokuda understood that no girl wants to go to school on the first day in jeans and a white T-shirt. Everybody wants to look a bit unique. They understand the importance of self-expression. And not only in the schoolyard but also on MySpace.

Their first widget was called SlideShow. Essentially, it allows you to spice up your MySpace profile by creating a cool slideshow about yourself. "In our first month we got 100,000 users. In the first two and a half months we got 1 million users," Shen says. There was no advertising or PR beyond six initial postings on MySpace.

This is not about cocreation. This is about me and how I look when people visit my profile on MySpace. The viral effect is simple. A girl—let's call her Jessica—downloads the widget. Amber, a friend who visits Jessica's MySpace page every day to see what's new, notices the new slideshow and how awesome it looks. Amber downloads it too, and all her friends are exposed to it in hours. The RockYou Web site now gets half a million visits every day. This is a great way to introduce people to other widgets and see what grows virally.

Another successful Facebook app is Likeness. Likeness involves different quizzes that enable you to find out how similar you are to your friends. For example, in the pet peeves quiz, you rate the things that annoy you most: stubbornness? penny-pinching? rudeness? bad driving? Once you've arranged the ten things you hate most in order, you can see how similar you are to your friends—but you have to invite them to play, or else there will be no way to compare your results. Self-expression plus network effect created one of the top applications on Facebook.

Surrogate Participation

The next time you go to YouTube, take a look at a video called "Gmail: Behind the Scenes (Final Cut)." Since August 28, 2007, when it was uploaded, it has been viewed more than 5 million times. It's about sixty short clips that were stitched together, running a bit over two minutes. The star of the video is the M-velope, which is Gmail's icon and represents an e-mail message. The video tells the real "under the hood" story of what happens when you press that Send button in Gmail. If you thought that you activate some complex communication protocol between servers around the world, think again. Here, as energetic music plays in the background, you learn that your message is actually delivered by a guy sky-diving, who hands the envelope to someone surfing, who passes the envelope to someone on an inflatable inner tube in the water, who hands it to a class of kids in India, who pass it to . . . you get the idea. All the action I've described happens in less than ten seconds.

This video wasn't created by Google but by Gmail users who

were invited by the company to participate in a collaborative video project. People were asked to film themselves passing the M-velope from the left side of the screen to the right side of the screen and upload it to YouTube.

What's viral about this campaign? Participation and co-creation can explain part of it, of course. If you submit a video, you're going to involve your friends in the process or at least tell them that you're going to be a star. If your video is highlighted on Gmail's site, you'll e-mail all of your friends, and of course when your clip is in the final, you'll tell the whole world about it. The comment that opens this chapter, "Snappy is famous," is from a woman from Singapore who sent in a video of her crab, Snappy, crossing the screen holding the M-velope. When Snappy got in, she told everyone about it.

This effect certainly increases the virality of the campaign. But with 1,100 videos submitted, it can't really explain the 5 million views. At least 2 million people came from different Gmail sites. Massive seeding coupled with some viral effect leads to success.

But I think that something else is at work here. I use Gmail and I love it. Why? Because it really makes my life easier. Personally, I probably wouldn't participate in something like this, but as a user, I was thrilled to see all these fellow users creating this. Maybe this can be called surrogate participation. I suspect that many Gmail users forwarded the video to friends because they felt like I do.

Depth

You always want to maximize user involvement. The more time people spend with your product, the more likely they are to talk about it. Hacking the Mindstorms system opened more possibilities to users, which meant they had more things to do and more to talk about. And although you can create a Monk-e-Mail in seconds, there's enough variation there for you to spend an hour playing with those chimps.

A few months ago I downloaded to my computer a virtual sunflower offered by a new organic food chain called Sunflower Market. The company will not release numbers about how many people downloaded it, so I don't know how viral it really was, but I can talk about my own experience with it.

Essentially you download a pot that features the company's logo. I stared at the dirt in the pot, trying to identify a sign of life. Nothing. I set up the water and the fertilizer levels to "high" and waited. Nothing happened. The following day I noticed a little green thing in the middle of the pot. Even though I'm aware that I had nothing to do with this, I was happy.

During the time this thing grew on my desktop, I observed a couple of things. First, eight weeks is a long time. It meant that I had plenty of opportunities to talk about the sunflower. The second observation is that I usually talked about changes. The time I saw the first leaf, when I noticed the bud, the first day I observed some yellow petals showing through the green, and, of course, the day the beautiful flower opened in full bloom. Our brains are programmed to notice change, and this is also the stuff that is worth mentioning. If you want to design a successful widget like this one, if you want to stimulate talk, you should aim for two things: to try to stretch the user experience over time, and to include frequent changes.

(By the way, when the flower was in full bloom I went to Scotland for a week without my laptop. I left detailed watering instructions for my son for the real tomatoes I was growing in the backyard, but I totally forgot that the sunflower might also need water. Big mistake. When I got back, it was a shadow of its old self, and despite massive injections of water it really never recovered. Of course, I told everybody about this too.)

Remember *The Purpose-Driven Life*? In the first few pages of the book, Rick Warren urges the reader to read only one chapter a day. The book consists of forty brief chapters, and Warren encourages the reader not to rush through them but to stop after each one and think. What happens as a side effect? A person who has a spiritual experience spread over forty days has more opportunities to speak about that experience than someone who rushes through a book in a weekend.

Uneven Distribution

18

The children emerging from the first screening of the movie *The Wizard* on a winter night in 1989 had just come out of a time machine. They had journeyed somewhere none of their friends had been: four months into the future. Four months doesn't sound like much when it comes to time travel, but for these kids this experience was more meaningful than a trip to the year 3000.

It wasn't the movie itself that excited them so much.

I've certainly seen more exciting films. *The Wizard* tells the story of a boy named Corey, who takes his younger brother, Jimmy, on a cross-country trip to California to enter a video game championship. What excited the audience so much was what was shown toward the *end* of the movie. With only three contestants left in the championship (little Jimmy among them), the announcer let the contestants—and the audience—know that for the final, tie-breaking match, they would have to play a video game no one had ever played before.

For months rumors about the next version of Nintendo's Super Mario Brothers were circling the playgrounds. And now the children in the movie theater had a sneak preview of it right there on the screen. "Ladies and gentlemen, we have three contestants . . . one . . . two . . . three," the master of ceremonies announced dramatically. "So I give you Super Mario Brothers Threeee!"

"The excitement in the theaters was far greater for Super Mario Brothers 3 than for the movie itself," David Sheff wrote in *Game Over*, his book about the history of Nintendo. For about five minutes, kids were able to see the upcoming game in action. New challenges. New tricks. It's not difficult to imagine what these children did first thing after they got home. They did what any reasonable person would do after being in a time machine—they called all their friends and told them what they knew. "Mario can fly now, and they have these whistles that take you to any level you want!" In the following days each one of them tried to tell as many other kids about it as he or she could. As more and more children went to see the movie, kids were increasingly geared up for the release. When Super Mario Brothers 3 hit the stores, it outsold any video game in history up to that point and grossed more than $500 million.

The anticipation for the game was already there, but Nintendo understood that buzz needs to be fueled. Without new information, comments about a product become empty and dull, and customers eventually move on to other, more exciting topics. The company used the sneak preview concept routinely in other ways to keep interest up. Nintendo employed hundreds of game counselors, assigned to help players who called with questions and problems. Once the counselor resolved the issue, he or she used the opportunity to get the customer excited about the next version ("Oh, by the way, wait till you see what we're working on now"). "In a sense they made kids feel that they were part of this insider club," says Sheff. "They were getting inside information about something that was incredibly relevant to them and their friends."

The psychological principle behind the sneak preview idea is simple. When we tell others something new, we feel that we're in the know, and we're typically rewarded by their reaction. One Tremor member summed it up succinctly: "It's cool to know about stuff before other people."

When you think about it, buzz starts with an uneven distribution of information. You're not going to send an e-mail to your friends telling them that McDonald's sells hamburgers. Why? Because you know that they know it. No need for buzz. We consider buzzing only when we suspect that other people don't know what we know. Sometimes you can stimulate buzz by assuring a small group of people that they are the only people who have a piece of information.

One campaign used this concept deliberately and on a very wide scale: the 1995 launch of the BMW Z3 Roadster. The BMW Z3 Roadster was a contagious product. Early owners of the car told me that they couldn't go anywhere without being bombarded with questions. One of them, Fred Kern, said that at one point he was so tired of answering the same questions about the car over and over again that he considered putting a sign on it:

> Yes, it's the car from the movie.
>
> $28,750, but the leather was more—about $32,000.
>
> About four months.

The people at BMW understood very well that they had a buzz machine on their hands, and they wanted to get extra mileage out of it. "We knew that if we brought it to market in a traditional launch, it would do very well," says Jim McDowell, a former VP of marketing for the company. But they also saw this as an opportunity to position the Z3 as the icon of roadsters and to draw attention to the BMW brand. Managers at BMW were talking about this as "leveraging the buzz." And about getting the car on "people's conversational agenda."

The first, and probably the most memorable, element in the campaign was placing the car in the James Bond movie *Golden-Eye*. (This is the movie that Fred Kern was referring to). As with the case of Nintendo and the movie *The Wizard*, the movie *Golden-Eye*, which was going to be released a few months before the car, provided a perfect sneak preview. Because this was a truly special-looking vehicle, BMW didn't have to point it out too aggressively. In fact, the Z3 was shown only very briefly in the movie. The character Q, the head of R&D who develops all the neat gadgets for Bond, presents the new car to him early on; later Bond is shown driving it out in the country. That's it.

Once *GoldenEye* was ready but before it was released to the public, BMW ran private screenings of the movie. While any kid who wanted to could go and see Super Mario 3 by buying tickets to the movie *The Wizard*, this was invitation-only. Each dealer invited between two hundred and four hundred of his best customers, and some combined it with receptions before or after the show. A dealership in Concord, California, for example, had a party at the Blackhawk Automotive Museum, where the new roadster was displayed next to one of Bond's older cars. Overall, about 40,000 customers participated in these prescreenings. The following day at the office, on the golf course, or over lunch, those who attended were likely to tell their friends about what they had seen—the new James Bond movie *and* the new BMW.

The buzz about the new car was further fueled by a special press event in New York's Central Park. More than two hundred media representatives showed up. A huge box that looked as if it came from a scene in the movie was set onstage. Supporting characters from the movie also appeared onstage and explained how the car worked, but nobody was able to open the box, not even Q. Finally Helmut Panke, the chairman and CEO of BMW Holding Corporation, came to the rescue by entering the secret code that exploded the crate and unveiled the car. Simultaneously, in drove Bond himself (Pierce Brosnan at the time) in another Z3. "Photographers were trampling on top of each other," remembered Jeff Salmon of Dick Clark Communications, which organized the event. People rushed to take pictures of the car onstage, and of Brosnan. After the initial excitement, the journalists got the chance to interview the actors and the BMW management team as well as drive the Z3 around Central Park.

When the movie was released to the public, the car drew a lot of attention, so much so that one cartoon showed Bond leaning against the car while three paparazzi taking pictures are trying to figure out who's the star, the new 007 or the new Z3. For old Bond fans there was an additional news element here: The BMW replaced Bond's signature car, the Aston-Martin he'd driven in many of the previous movies.

Not every customer who bought the car was swayed by these marketing activities and the extensive media coverage that followed. The car provided its own buzz. Some customers I talked to saw the James Bond movie after they already owned the car. Still, in an informal survey among six BMW dealers around the country, the most influential marketing efforts were the sneak preview and the car's placement in the Bond movie. "It was one of the most successful product launches I've been involved in in twenty-five years in the car business," one dealer said. Another emphasized that the movie launch helped the car hold its full sticker price (of around $30,000) for a very long time. More than nine thousand orders for the roadster were prebooked, about four thousand more than the company projected.

Other Types of Uneven Distribution

In his book *Influence: The Psychology of Persuasion*, the psychologist Robert Cialdini tells how he never had any desire to visit a Mormon temple in the city of Mesa, Arizona, where he lives, until one day he read about a special inner sanctum of the temple that only faithful members of the church can enter. The article said that this section would be open to non-Mormons for a few days. His instinctive reaction was to go, and to call a friend to ask if he wanted to join him.

In the examples of Nintendo and BMW, people talked because they knew that they had some exclusive information. In the case of Robert Cialdini, he talked because he had sudden access to something that is usually scarce.

We value anything that is scarce: rare baseball cards, places with restricted access, and information that is not widely available, also known as a secret. Anytime you tell a customer a secret, anytime you take a customer behind the scenes, you create a special feeling.

Marketers love the game of holding information close to the chest in order to build buzz. It's not always the best strategy, though. Every year marketers keep the information about their upcoming Super Bowl commercials under a veil of secrecy. The idea is that people are dying to know what these commercials are, so once the information is released, they will talk about it like crazy. In 2007 several Super Bowl advertisers, including Doritos, Chevrolet, and Nationwide, went against conventional wisdom and promoted their ads on the Web before the game. Jim Nail from Cymfony ran a study to see which strategy got more buzz. He found that an aggressive promotion strategy before the game was actually the most effective way to generate postgame consumer discussion. So playing things close to your chest is not always the best strategy. My sense is that it can fuel buzz when there is a lot of anticipation for the product, as in the case of Super Mario 3 or Halo 3. But for that to work, there has to be a strong underlying interest in the product to begin with. No matter how mysterious you are about the new clothes hanger your company is designing, you're not likely to make many customers curious. Also, there's a limit to how much you can play this game, because customers can tire of it.

But even for older products, secrets—or any sort of special insider information—can sometimes create buzz. In-N-Out Burger, a West Coast–based chain, has a secret menu with items that are not on the official menu. If you tell the cashier that you want a 4×4, you'll get four patties. If you say "animal style," they'll add grilled onions, extra spread, and pickle. Initially this was a true secret, which spread exclusively by word of mouth. Secrets don't live forever, though, and a few years ago the company posted the secret menu on its Web site. It's now called "The Not-So-Secret Menu."

This same concept has a long history in the software and entertainment industries, where it is known as an Easter egg (or, when it comes to music, a hidden track). You hide something in your content and don't publicize it. In this case, you don't choose a group of privileged people who will be in the know. Instead you plant a secret somewhere; whoever discovers it gains exclusive knowledge that they are motivated to share with their friends.

The important point to remember is that people talk about the stuff that they suspect others don't know. In other words, when a person suggests that what he's telling you isn't general knowledge, then you might just be tempted to tell more people about it. Marketers tend to shout at the top of their lungs. But sometimes a well-planned whisper will reach more ears.

More of a Café than a Subway Station

19

■ "I beat my friend at Roshambull last week."

■ "I met Cheryl, a lead Fiskateer. She is just about the
sweetest person ever."

■ "The Thorn Tree is easily the best travel forum out
there. If there's a better one, I haven't found it!"

Three comments from three real people, all

involving brands. Even if you don't recognize the brands

yet, trust me, the brands are there.

What do these three comments have in common?

They result not from product experience but from human

interaction. If you can somehow tie the interaction to your brand, you can get some buzz.

Let me start with a simple example. Suppose you have a gym called Jimmy's Gym, and you throw a big party for all your clients. You put out drinks and food and arrange activities and live music. A hundred and fifty people show up. It's a great party. People mingle and dance.

What do you think will happen the following day? At least some of these people will tell their friends about the social interactions they experienced at the party:

> "I met this guy at Jimmy's Gym last night."
>
> "You won't believe who I saw at this party at Jimmy's."
>
> "I was at Jimmy's Gym and this woman told me that if you drink green tea . . ."

The level of buzz and its content depend on the party. If it's a smash party, with lots of mingling, you can be assured that there's going to be lots of buzz. If the party was boring, there will be less buzz. But people always tell others about these kinds of interactions. The same is true whether it's an interaction that takes place in person or online. And if you're smart about it, you can use these social situations to stimulate talk about products and services.

Smack Talk

In 2007, Red Bull introduced a game called Roshambull on Facebook. The game is essentially rock, paper, scissors (also known as Roshambo) with a "Red Bull flavor." The first thing that you need after you get the game is someone to play with, so you challenge your friends. But this network effect is just the beginning.

As you win, you may feel an urge to brag to other friends about it. When you lose, your cubicle neighbors may hear about it too. The software also helps you with this reporting. When you win, it will broadcast to your friends that you "destroyed the competition." Right now, my Facebook friends can read on my Mini-Feed that "Emanuel is worse than global warming."

Red Bull caters to an audience with a certain style of social interaction: tongue-in-cheek banter, lots of bragging, and real competitiveness. Roshambull fits well in this context. There's a feature that allows you to talk smack when you compete and even one where you can see live smack talk from other matches.

Reading the live feed, you can see that some of it is indeed used to break the opponent's spirit ("Bring it on, punk!"). But another part is simply chatting: "I totally could have gone today, but i didn't get this until now! how about tuesday?"

Last time I checked, 334,234 people had downloaded this application. A guy named David Stein was in first place, with 1,444,548 points. Roshambull was one of the first applications to be released when Facebook opened its architecture, so part of the appeal of the game came from its novelty. But months after its release, people keep playing, challenging each other, and interacting under the wings of Red Bull.

Scissors

The second comment at the beginning of this chapter was about meeting a woman named Cheryl who's a lead "Fiskateer." What is that all about?

People love to talk about people, and this comment is a side effect of some interaction created by Fiskars, the scissors company. Fiskars has been around for more than three hundred years. Everybody knows its orange-handled scissors, but it makes a lot of other stuff for scrapbooking. Research showed that the company image was kind of bland. Customers were asked, "If Fiskar was a snack, what would it be?" The answer? A saltine cracker. Pretty dull. This lack of emotional connection was a problem especially in the area of scrapbooking, a field known for the passion of its dedicated "scrappers."

Fiskars hired a company called Brains on Fire to do something about it. When Brains on Fire learned that scrappers have an extremely rich, vibrant community, it decided to build an online community of scrapbook fans who'd use Fiskars products. How did it do that? It started by hiring four women part-time to become "crafting ambassadors," known as the lead Fiskateers. When you join the community, which you can do only through one of the lead Fiskateers, you get a welcome kit that includes a pair of scissors with your Fiskateer number.

I have to admit that when I first heard Virginia Miracle from Brains on Fire talk about this, I thought the whole thing was a little weird. But this thing is working, and it's working because it has a purpose. Participants share layout and project ideas with others and socialize a bit. After all, people who make scrapbooks are creating stories—about their families, friends, and pets; of course the hobby lends itself to conversations. The four crafting ambassadors—Stephanie, May, Cheryl, and Holly—blog frequently, and their postings are clearly read, as is evident from the dozens of comments each posting gets. There's talk about crafting on the blog, but there's also lots of talk about social interaction. Interaction creates talk.

Like Lego Mindstorms enthusiasts, when Fiskateers create, they share. Other hobbyists appreciate good work, and a compliment from a fellow hobbyist may be worth just a bit more than a compliment from a family member.

The quote that began this chapter came from a woman who met Cheryl at a store event put together by Fiskars. During the event there was obviously lots of talk among the Fiskateers; later, participants went on to tell their friends or write about the people they met at the event.

Ten years ago Steve Jurvetson and Tim Draper put it this way in the now-famous article in which they coined the term "viral marketing": "Are you like a subway station with banner ads flying by the commuters who are just trying to get to their destination, or are you like a café where customers mingle and feel like they belong?"

Mingling creates buzz.

Lonely Planet

The third comment that opened this chapter was about Thorn Tree, a travel site. Suppose you're traveling in South America and you're looking for a hotel in Peru. You post a question on Thorn Tree and you get a useful answer. You report your finding to your friends:

> "Where did you find this place?"
> "Thorn Tree."
> "What's Thorn Tree?"
> "It's this Lonely Planet thing."

Thorn Tree was started in 1997 by Lonely Planet, the publishers of the travel books; it's now part of the Lonely Planet Web site. You need advice on dog sledding in Canada? Want to find a travel companion for your next trip to China? Check out Thorn Tree. You can also look for house swaps, advice on visas and passports, and someone to buy your old gear.

The Thorn Tree Web site is brimming with life. People not only ask questions, they flirt, argue, have fun, and tell stories. Above all, people on Thorn Tree seek and give advice. "Do Australians need to obtain a visa prior to entering Slovenia?" "What's considered acceptable clothing for women to wear in Cambodia?" "Can anyone who has done gorilla trekking give me advice?"

Community forums like this can help even when it comes to "boring" categories. Look at accounting, for example. "We're really trying to help users connect so that they can answer each other's questions," says Scott Wilder of Intuit, who oversees the company's small-business community sites. He often notices that advice-giving leads to comments outside of the forum and brings in new participants. A small-business owner comes to one of the company's forums and posts a question. He's delighted to get a quick answer from another user, and he shares his experience with a colleague.

When Your Product Is Social

If you start a club or an association or an online forum, social interaction can play an especially important role in your buzz. Consider MySpace. Social interaction played a huge role in its growth. But here's the interesting thing. Before social interaction could occur, something else was needed. Think about a party with a bunch of strangers in a big hall. Awkward. Now think of the same party with a bunch of strangers, but also with a band in one corner, a juggler in another, a guy sculpting a crocodile out of white chocolate, face painting, and a climbing wall. Now there's something to talk about. Something for the social interaction to grow on.

A similar dynamic took place in the case of MySpace. A lot of the early buzz about MySpace consisted of people referring their friends to check out content on the site. MySpace created the tools, and people uploaded their music, their art, or their picture with their new tattoos or hairstyle and invited the world to check out their profile. Some of them attracted only a handful of visitors; others, like Tila Tequila and William Hung, attracted tens of thousands of new users—or more. (On January 1, 2008, Tila Tequila had 2,590,949 friends on MySpace.)

Many of the people who came to see Tila Tequila or William Hung or the snake man were not interested in expressing themselves, certainly not for the whole world to see. "Self-expression and vanity played a huge role in the viral growth of MySpace, but only for a certain segment of the users," Jason Feffer, a former executive with MySpace, says. What many of these folks wanted was to interact with each other.

At some point there were enough users out there that MySpace became the center of social interaction. Girls told other girls to check out the profiles of cool boys. Boys told other boys to check out the profiles of hot girls. You could view someone's profile without being a member, but if you wanted to look at that person's pictures or leave a comment, you had to join.

This description makes MySpace's growth sound like a two-step process: first came the self-expression, then the social interaction. In reality, things were more interwoven. But there is an important lesson here. Interaction is built on something—content, a common purpose. The Fiskateers talk about their art. People on Thorn Tree talk about travel. Then they interact.

In the case of MySpace, different streams of buzz—self-expression buzz, vanity buzz, social interaction buzz—combined to form one gigantic river. "It was really word of mouth that made the difference between failure and the phenomenal success that MySpace was," Feffer says.

The *Wall Street Journal* and the Lingerie Business

20

Lida Orzeck was on vacation. Sitting in her hotel room at the Georgian in Santa Monica, she wasn't in any hurry to go downstairs to see if the *Wall Street Journal* had finally published an article about her company, Hanky Panky. You may recall from Chapter 11 that Hanky Panky developed quite a following for the 4811 thong, and Orzeck knew that the *Journal* was working on a story about the company. But now she was on vacation, and with the sand and the ocean just across the street, who cared about some *Wall Street Journal* story in the small-business section?

It had been about a year since Wendy Bounds, a *Wall Street Journal* reporter, started poking around the company Orzeck and her good friend Gale Epstein had founded back in 1977. When Bounds first went to visit Hanky Panky's loft in New York City, she said she would need to sell the idea to her editors, and Lida thought to herself, Why are we wasting our time talking to her? It's never going to happen. Since when does the *Wall Street Journal* write about thongs?

Now she knew the story was supposed to appear in the *Journal* because Bounds had been frantically fact-checking over the past few days. But so what? She was on vacation.

And yet, vacation or not, e-mail couldn't wait. And when she checked her messages, she realized that something had happened. Something big. A flood of e-mails from people she'd never spoken to at radio and TV stations and stores and newspapers from all over the country had poured in, all asking about the 4811, the company's flagship thong.

Lida Orzeck rushed downstairs to the lobby, grabbed the *Wall Street Journal*, and there on page one, top of the fold, in color, she saw a picture, front and back, of her thong. The 4811 had hit the front page of the *Wall Street Journal*.

In their loft in New York City, I ask Lida Orzeck and Gale Epstein if the story affected sales. After all, thongs are not the first product that jumps to mind when you think of the typical *Journal* reader.

They are too polite to burst into laughter.

"It totally changed our business," says Orzeck. Before the article came out, Hanky Panky was a small manufacturer selling to a relatively small network of boutiques. Word of mouth played an enormous role in its business. Hanky Panky would come up with new designs and spread the word to boutique owners, who in turn would sell them to their best customers. It was all pretty intimate, and the company was always profitable—"Small but profitable," says Gale Epstein.

The *Wall Street Journal* story changed things dramatically. Men who wouldn't set foot in a lingerie store before walked into little boutiques, some of them clinging to the *Journal* as a reference, and asked for the 4811. Perhaps the fact that the product name was a number and not something like Sexy Nights in Lilac or Dreams of a Hot Summer Night made it easier for men to order. Who knows? In a way, the article legitimized the category. Department stores, which had stayed away from it up until then, were now clamoring for the product.

It didn't take long before Hanky Panky sold its entire inventory and, as is common in these cases, stores got angry because buyers thought the company was selling the hot thongs to the other guys. "It really wasn't like that. They cleaned us out of everything, and then we had to ramp up in a new way, at a whole new level," Orzeck says. Since the article came out in mid-2004, their business has tripled and maybe even quadrupled.

If anyone tells you that mass media no longer matter in this era of "consumer-generated media," tell them about the 4811. It's not always the *Wall Street Journal*. For other demographics, it may be Oprah Winfrey or Stephen Colbert, but don't underestimate the power of mass media.

Wendy Bounds had never heard of Hanky Panky before she ran into Gale Epstein. Somehow, the fact that there was a company out there with a thong that's known only by its number—the 4811—stuck in the *Wall Street Journal* reporter's mind.

It might not have gone any further than this, except for the fact that when Bounds called some retailers and asked them about thongs, they all started talking about the 4811. Sometimes buzz is the best press release.

The boutique owners raved about the product and dropped some names. Cindy Crawford bought the 4811. Actress Julianne Moore bought them in a rainbow of colors. This story was getting interesting.

It was interesting partially because it was unusual and sexy. But Bounds was also intrigued that the company had managed to carve a niche for itself in the cutthroat lingerie industry. And as Bounds started to get to know Hanky Panky, she began to see it as a story of friendship, of two women who had managed to work as partners and friends for almost thirty years.

"The mistake, I think, that people often make is that they come to you with a story that's been told a million times," Bounds says. The 4811 story, though, felt more real. Orzeck and Epstein didn't hold anything back: They shared the good, the bad, and the ugly of thong-making. "They were so accommodating in terms of walking through the nuts and bolts of how they make this product," Bounds remembers. All companies want their product to be featured in the national media, but Bounds says that only a few are willing to open up the way Hanky Panky did. The same no-nonsense open attitude that gained the support of boutique owners now gained them the ear of Wendy Bounds—and then, through her, of the *Wall Street Journal*'s readers.

Street Buzz and Media Buzz

Street buzz not only leads to sales, it gives journalists this warm and fuzzy feeling that your story is for real, that there is true excitement for your product. When you think about it, journalists live by word of mouth. If someone else has written about a particular thing in a particular way already, it's not as interesting.

To examine the relationships between mass media and word of mouth further, we'll switch to a totally different domain. In 1990, in a health clinic in South Africa's Alexandra Township, on the outskirts of Johannesburg, a young physician by the name of Garth Japhet was growing frustrated with his work. He felt that so many of the issues that he was dealing with at the clinic on a daily basis should have not happened in the first place. Children in the poor township died from dehydration, from burn accidents, and from diseases that could have been prevented by immunization. There is no reason, for example, for a child to die from dehydration caused by diarrhea. The simple solution to the problem involves mixing the right amounts of water, salt, and sugar. But in Alexandra Township, parents were unaware of this simple lifesaving remedy. The problem was a lack of information.

So Japhet started writing a column about health in the *Sowetan*, South Africa's largest daily newspaper, to spread the word. But despite the enthusiastic response, he realized that he still wasn't reaching people at the scale he wanted, especially not the poorest and the least educated. He grew to believe that the way to affect the largest number of people was through a prime-time TV drama.

In 1992, Japhet got together with Shereen Usdin, another young physician who experienced similar frustrations with health in South Africa. Usdin too was convinced that the way to touch people was through drama. People talk about soap operas with their friends. If Japhet and Usdin could weave some of their health-related messages into stories, perhaps they could help people educate each other about these issues.

Arvind Singhal, a professor of communication at the University of Texas, El Paso, feels that their naïveté at that early stage was an asset. "Their beginners' mind was an open mind," he says. They focused on the task at hand—educating people—and were not shy about talking to the private sector, government, donor organizations, and anyone else who would help them achieve their ultimate goal.

With the help of partners from the entertainment industry, they developed a TV drama that takes place in a fictional township called Soul City. The setting was a familiar place to both physicians, and one that is loaded with potential for drama: the community clinic.

The first season was a smash hit. It wasn't an educational program that lectured people about how to take care of their kids. It was a drama involving death, love, drinking, and sexual abuse as well as some lighter themes. The health messages were woven in naturally as advice that characters gave each other. The viewer heard the advice the way she would overhear two friends talking.

Did it cause people to spread the word further? After the second season, 56 percent of respondents to a survey reported a discussion they had had with others about various health issues featured in the program. How does the show generate so much talk? First, there's plain gossip. Those folks that you meet every week on the show become your virtual friends, and you talk about their lives, their problems, and the tragedies they face. The show always leaves open issues that one can discuss: Who was right in that argument, the husband or the wife? Should the doctor have called the police or not?

Extensive research is conducted before each season to make sure the program addresses real issues and to learn how people talk and feel about these issues. For one season, for example, preseason research included face-to-face interviews with two thousand people. The result is a program that is authentic and rings true with people—a critical issue for buzz-building.

Another reason that *Soul City* gets so much talk is that the drama is so widely available. To reach a more rural audience, *Soul City* is available as a radio program in nine different languages of different tribes as well as in English and Afrikaans. Printed booklets that reinforce the programs' messages and serve as conversation starters are inserted into high-circulation newspapers or handed out for free.

Contrary to the view that portrays word of mouth as the exclusive result of guerrilla or nontraditional tactics, mass media can generate massive waves of buzz. In the United States, the Keller Fay Group found that on any given day, 55 percent of Americans have at least one conversation related to media and entertainment! And most of these people have more than just one conversation: The average is 2.8.

This may explain in part why marketers are so attracted to product placement. It's not only about the fact that Carrie from *Sex and the City* loves Manolo Blahnik shoes but also about the idea that women mention this to their friends. Paid product placement spending grew 33.7 percent to $2.90 billion in 2007, and is projected to keep growing, according to PQ Media.

Horizontal Buzz Meets Vertical Buzz

Soul City **increased** awareness about the fact that wearing a condom can prevent the spread of HIV/AIDS. It even caused a major increase in condom use among people who watched the program. But could the soap opera change people's bone-deep attitudes? In the fourth season of the program, Japhet and Usdin were tackling a huge challenge, one rooted deeply in local society: domestic violence.

As a practitioner, Shereen Usdin remembered seeing too many bruises, broken bones, multiple miscarriages, and depression caused by domestic violence. Usdin always wanted to do something to change things, and toward the fourth season, *Soul City* partnered with the National Network on Violence Against Women to try to help on this front.

The challenge in dealing with such an issue can be best described as horizontal buzz meets vertical buzz. For every comment against domestic violence that will be passed among peers as a result of the show, there are dozens of comments such as "The man is captain of the ship," which have been passed down from generation to generation—notions that justify domestic violence.

And not only among men. Young girls learn from their mothers how to deal with an abusive husband. During the research in preparation for season four, one word was mentioned repeatedly by women. It was the Zulu word *ukunyamezela*, which means "to endure," and it reflected the way many women in the country thought they were supposed to deal with domestic violence—it's something that they just had to live through.

From pretesting the script for the season, the show's developers learned that the abusive husband character came across as a monster. That wasn't good. It meant that people could easily distance themselves from the character and see domestic violence as a rare problem. The writers toned down the character and moved the violent eruption from the first to the fourth episode, to allow the audience to see the husband as human and start liking him. Patrick Shai, a well-liked star in South Africa, was chosen for the role because of his nice-guy image.

Even during filming it became clear that the program was hitting a nerve. In one of the most violent episodes, Shai's character was supposed to slap his wife across the side of her head and knock her down to the floor. Shai got so agitated by the scene that at one point he shouted "Cut!" and ran out of the studio.

Strong reactions continued during the prescreenings. The word *ukunyamezela*, which was woven into the script, clearly resonated with audiences. People responded immediately when they heard it. Tony Blair, on a visit to South Africa, was also among those who got a preview of the show (which is partially funded by British sources). He was "obviously emotional" about the episode, as reported by Ed O'Loughlin in the *Independent*. O'Loughlin also described Patrick Shai's performance as a wife batterer as "chillingly convincing."

When the domestic violence episode went on the air, a help line number was shown at the end of the show, and four thousand calls were answered the following day. In the next few weeks that pattern would be repeated: The show would air on Wednesday night, and on Thursday the help line would be inundated with calls.

It's not that domestic violence had never been seen before on South African TV, but it typically appeared on foreign TV programs and so the problem could easily be dismissed as something that only happens far away. Now it was happening to *Soul City*'s Matlakala, a beloved character whom people had known since the first season of the show.

Multiple Fronts

Real change hardly ever comes from a TV show alone. Recognizing this, *Soul City* worked on several other fronts to tackle the issue. One problem was that despite a domestic violence act, the police usually ignored complaints or did not take them seriously. The National Network on Violence Against Women ran workshops about the act, and details of the law were woven into the TV program. Special hearings about the topic were organized in the parliament. This, of course, was reflected in the media.

Then something totally unexpected happened. As part of the media advocacy for the cause, Shereen Usdin and Patrick Shai were being interviewed on a radio show when all of a sudden Shai started talking about abusing his wife in real life. "I remember just being completely astounded," Usdin remembers. There she was, sitting in a radio studio and hearing for the first time, along with the rest of the nation, that the man who was part of *Soul City*'s major campaign against domestic violence had actually abused his wife.

Shai talked about his experience on the set that day and explained why he had run out of the studio. He talked about the fact that it made him understand, for the first time in his life, how much pain and fear he was inflicting.

After the initial shock, the *Soul City* team got together with Shai to think about the next step. Did he want to continue with this public confession, and, more important, was his wife willing to be part of it?

Both answers were positive. As life imitated art, the incident added another level to the buzz and reinforced an important point that the show was trying to make—that domestic violence is not the exclusive territory of bullies and that a woman's complaints should not be dismissed just because her husband is seen as Mr. Nice Guy. "And Patrick *is* such a nice guy," says Usdin. "He is such a lovely person and we had all loved working with him."

Shai started talking in public forums about his experience. He said that this performance gave him a rare opportunity to see himself in such a violent state and to understand the fear he'd caused. "It was incredibly empowering for women to hear that acknowledgment," Usdin says. And it was incredibly powerful for abusive men to look at someone who's a huge celebrity in the country and to see his humility and regret.

Did the campaign cause actual change? Usdin says that domestic violence is still rampant in South Africa and a lot more should be done. Still, eight months after the help line was established, 41 percent of respondents in a follow-up survey had heard about it and there was a 10 percent increase in respondents disagreeing with the idea that domestic violence was a private affair.

The political scientist Bernard Cohen once wrote that the press is usually not too successful in telling people what to think, "but it is stunningly successful in telling its readers what to think *about*." In a similar way, *Soul City* was determining not what people would say about domestic violence, and certainly not what they would think about it deep inside. But the campaign certainly ensured that domestic violence would be talked about. Indeed, one out of three respondents to a survey talked about domestic violence when season four was on the air, and those who watched the show frequently talked about the issue significantly more than those with low or no exposure to the program.

Does Madison Avenue Still Matter?

21

A headline in a 2007 *Advertising Age* article pre-

sented an intriguing question: "Want Online

Buzz for Your New Product?" The subtitle provided the

answer: "Better Have an Ad Campaign, Nielsen Finds."

The article went on to say that "the somewhat ironic con-

clusion" of a new Nielsen study is that your best bet for

getting lots of buzz may be a big ad campaign.

Really? If that's the case, you may think, all your troubles are gone. You can close this book and just pour lots of money into advertising. Thanks for stopping by.

But after examining the Nielsen study itself—the study that this article was based on—I suggest that you keep reading.

There are people who believe that advertising is a solution for everything: Advertising builds awareness. Advertising builds sales. Advertising makes people talk. On the other end of the spectrum, there are people who will advise you to stop advertising altogether and rely on buzz alone. After all, in the preceding chapters you read about products that did extremely well with little or no advertising—Trivial Pursuit and *Cold Mountain*, to name a couple.

The truth, as is often the case, is somewhere in the middle. Perhaps the best way to start exploring the complex relationships between advertising and buzz is to answer three questions: Can advertising buy buzz? Can advertising stimulate buzz? Can advertising simulate buzz?

Can Advertising Buy Buzz?

The Nielsen study mentioned in *Advertising Age* looked at hundreds of consumer packaged goods product launches in the United States in 2005 and 2006 and tried to determine which factors contributed to buzz (this study primarily looked at blog buzz). Indeed, among the products studied, advertising budget had the strongest relationship with the level of buzz. But the researchers at Nielsen also said this: "Strong media support can be an important driver of buzz, though buzz in the context of a strong media presence is sometimes no more than the echo that results from making a lot of noise. The formula for generating meaningful buzz is not as simple as spending money."

The breadth of a product's distribution was also found to be a very important factor related to buzz, which illustrates a simple point: If you are never exposed to a product, if it's not available at your local store, you're less likely to hear about it and thus write about it on your blog. In other words, advertising and distribution can really help buzz by increasing the pool of people who know about the product. The researchers also pointed out, however, that a lot of products were advertised but achieved little or no buzz, In fact, this was true for *most* products in the study. A few products, like Coke Zero and Enviga, got a lot of buzz, but most of the products studied, even when advertised, didn't get buzz.

While this study's findings are interesting, it's clear that much more research is needed in this area. After all, this study looked only at consumer packaged goods and online buzz. Still, it clearly demonstrates that things are a bit more complex than just "Want Online Buzz for Your New Product? Better Have an Ad Campaign."

Can Advertising Stimulate Buzz?

A good ad can help get people talking. An ad that is well conceived, well placed, and well timed can contribute to buzz in several ways. First, it can jump-start buzz. After all, information has to come from somewhere. The day your new product is released, very few people know about it. What is the likelihood that someone will tell his friend about your product? Very low. Once you've accumulated some customers, there are more people out there capable of using their experience to talk about the product. How do you get these first customers? In some cases your product is so contagious that you don't need to advertise. In other cases you get enough buzz from seeding, sneak previews, and other buzz tactics. But often you're not that lucky, and you find that while there's good buzz in some clusters, other clusters need encouragement.

One of the first things we did when we released EndNote was to send a press release to various scientific publications. *Science*, the largest scientific journal in the United States, published a short article about the product. This announcement started buzz in certain networks, but only in rare cases does such buzz grow exponentially. That's why we followed up with small ads in *Science* and additional publications to recruit first users in additional networks. These ads generated only one-tenth the leads of the original product announcement. Still, since the editors of *Science* weren't going to repeat the editorial for us every week, we needed some way to follow up our efforts.

Advertising is also a fairly effective way to reach network hubs. Several studies confirm that opinion leaders are more exposed to print advertising than "average" people are. Because they're hungry for information, they read more. By advertising in a magazine like *Car and Driver*, you reach hubs who recommend cars and related products to others. The mirror image of the last point is that an ad can also stimulate people to seek more information about the product from network hubs. "I saw an ad for the new Jeep recently. Is it worth checking out?" a neighbor may ask the local car expert.

Messages that spread among people are constantly distorted, twisted, and diluted. Remember the old telephone game we used to play as kids, and how a phrase like "fish in the water" was transformed into "dishes in the dishwasher"? Buzz can distort your message in a similar way. By broadcasting accurate information, your ads can at least partially take care of that. In 1989, when the apple industry had to deal with public panic that Alar-treated apples could cause cancer, growers published ads stating that a person would have to eat 28,000 pounds of Alar-treated apples every day for seventy years to reach a dangerous level of exposure.

Advertising content shows up in buzz all the time. The Keller Fay Group found that 21 percent of conversations in which a brand was mentioned also included a reference to advertising. It's as if people use advertising to validate their comments ("I read it in an ad"). People refer to other marketing sources as well: point-of-sale displays (8 percent), promotion (7 percent), and direct mail or e-mail (4 percent). But Keller Fay's research found something even more interesting about advertising. It found that in those conversations where advertising was cited, recommendations to buy or try the product went up from 40 percent to 47 percent.

What does all this mean? It means that when your advertising gives your customers something that they can pass along, it may increase buzz and sales. And I'm not talking about fluff like "a tradition of quality and excellence in customer service," but something that a customer can actually tell her friend, like "I saw that Barbara Kingsolver has a new book out," or "Target has Wii games on sale," or "Have you seen that gorgeous necklace from Cartier?"

Advertising as Buzz

Sometimes ads generate buzz because people talk about the advertising itself. "Got milk?" and "Where's the beef?" and "Yo quiero Taco Bell" are some examples of ads that got people talking. It's not a coincidence that all these campaigns are humorous. Nothing spreads faster than a really good joke. I remember being dragged to the TV by my children, who insisted that I see that talking chihuahua—one that speaks Spanish! The dog created waves of buzz as "Yo quiero Taco Bell" became a catchphrase. According to Taco Bell's tracking study, advertising awareness after the campaign was over 50 percent higher than the pre-chihuahua level of awareness for the same season in the previous year. The campaign's objective was to stop the fast-food company's decline in sales. Indeed, not only did the ads help stop the decline, but Taco Bell was able to report an increase in sales as a result of the campaign. Chihuahua T-shirts and other novelty items accelerated the visual buzz on the street, as did the dogs themselves as they popped up in neighborhoods all over the country; the American Kennel Club reported a 72 percent increase in chihuahua sales in 1998.

There's another type of advertising that is priceless in terms of word of mouth: the (rare) phrase that becomes part of everyday language. A recent one is "What happens in Vegas stays in Vegas." The suggestive nature of the slogan prompts people to use it in many situations, and not only ones that relate to selecting a travel destination. "Deal or no deal" and "a Kodak moment" are other expressions that have entered the American vernacular.

The practical implications? If your ad agency can create a commercial that the whole country will talk about, by all means go ahead. But saying that is a little bit like advising writers to write with the Nobel Prize in mind—"It will be good for your career." Everyone in the advertising industry would love to create an ad that gets that kind of buzz, but very few become such megahits. Remember that for every chihuahua or Energizer Bunny, there are thousands of commercials that try to make people talk but fail. In the process of creating these commercials, some ad agencies forget what ads are originally meant to do: Sell a product.

Can Advertising Simulate Buzz?

What about ads that masquerade as word of mouth? This is a tricky topic. An ad can hardly ever enjoy the credibility of buzz, but an ad can gain some credibility when advertisers either successfully mimic a tone used among friends or bring the friends themselves into the advertisements to give testimonials.

Back in 1966, Ernest Dichter, a psychologist who specialized in consumer motivation, noted, "When the consumer feels that the advertiser speaks to him as a friend or as an unbiased authority, creating the atmosphere of word of mouth, the consumer will relax and tend to accept the recommendation."

Dichter's idea still has validity, but the way friends talk to each other may have changed since 1966. Irony, sarcasm, and cynicism are common in conversations about commercial products today. Companies that try to sound friendly by using a chatty, confidential tone often fail to create an authentic atmosphere. On the other hand, those that manage to create ads with a wink and a nod often have a better chance of producing the desired effect. If you want to simulate word of mouth, you shouldn't use phrases like "Perhaps, like true love, we were meant to last forever," or "We believe we have the management teams, the strategies, and the market position to achieve success well into the next century." This "marketing speak" appears in actual ads and doesn't come close to the way real people talk to one another.

An ad, again, will hardly ever enjoy the credibility of a personal recommendation from a trusted friend, but it can get closer by simulating buzz, as in the case of testimonial advertising. The execution is challenging, however. Many ads are so bad that you wonder if they were meant as parody. But occasionally you see some that really do the job, where the testimonials are given by real customers who act and talk like real people.

Many companies also have invited consumers to create their ads. MasterCard, Chipotle, and Converse are just three examples. This certainly is valuable, because, as I discussed earlier, participation leads to talk. But the feeling you get from watching some of these user-generated commercials is not of genuine endorsement but of people "playing advertising." As with agency-created advertising, there are good ones and there are bad ones. And as with agency-created advertising, it is rare to watch a consumer-created commercial that makes you really want the product or truly believe that it is better in some way.

Authenticity is key here. Think of ads that are supposed to show the broad range of "ordinary folks" who use a product. Often these kinds of commercials are victims of the advertisers' endless pursuit of political correctness. The ads feature such conspicuously diverse people that it's hard to believe they were chosen at random: a black man, a white woman, a Latino man, and an Asian woman. Customers see through that. These commercials may still build awareness and even sales, but don't expect them to have nearly the impact of an ad that rings true.

Bringing real customers into an ad is very different from using celebrities. Famous people draw our attention, and we sometimes imitate their behavior. But since we all know that they're being paid for doing an ad, many of us don't believe that their use of the product is authentic. "Anytime you're using a borrowed interest, whether it's from a celebrity or from an idea that is not intrinsic to your product or your company, then you have to be aware there's a good chance that the consumer is going to see this as an overt attempt to sell him something," says John Yost, who advertised brands such as Yahoo! and Saturn.

I don't argue that companies should avoid using celebrities. They definitely draw our attention and can prompt us to imitate their behavior. But their appearance usually doesn't simulate word of mouth the way an authentic testimonial ad from average folks can do.

Can Advertising Kill Buzz?

A lot of customers say that they don't like advertising. A study from Yankelovich in April 2004 found that 65 percent of Americans report they feel constantly bombarded by too much marketing and advertising. This does not necessarily signal the death of advertising, because these people are still exposed to advertising, and there are also those 35 percent who don't feel bombarded. Still, this number clearly indicates an anti-advertising sentiment that many share. Consumers may still like an ad that is relevant, clever, and entertaining, but if it's just another ad, they often ignore it.

Although there are many good reasons to advertise, advertising is a tool that should be used very cautiously, because it can also kill buzz when people feel that someone is shoving the message down their throats. A customer tells her friends about new products she has discovered because it reflects on her as an innovative person. She doesn't want to sound like someone who's repeating a company's propaganda. Nobody does.

So what do you do to be sure your ad doesn't end up killing rather than building buzz?

One word that comes to mind is "honesty." Your ad must be honest, not only factually but also in the sense of being true to the product. "I can't think of an example of a product or a service that really generated a firestorm of positive word of mouth that didn't market from a platform of truth and honesty and directness in its relationships with its consumers," says John Yost. "As a generation, we've been so overly marketed to, and we've been so exposed to hype, that at this point we're pretty savvy customers and don't fall easily for some of these traditional pitches anymore."

The Four Rules about Ads and Buzz

1. **Keep it simple.** The message needs to be simple in order for people to pass it on. Short, straightforward messages based on current beliefs have the best chance of replicating themselves. Use simple language. This sounds obvious, but very often companies use jargon and acronyms that prevent buzz from spreading.

2. **Tell us what's new.** Fluff doesn't travel well in the networks. A typical customer will not recommend a company because it "offers a tradition of excellence, the best value for your money, and a set of powerful features." For your ads' messages to be passed on, they need to be relevant and have news value. No one is going to pass along the comment from a bank's vice president who says that the bank truly cares about its customers. Conversely, a useful comment like "Bank X opens its branches on Saturday morning" has a much greater potential to spread from person to person.

3. **Don't make claims you can't support.** Don't tell customers that you care about them unless you really mean it and can consistently demonstrate superb customer service. I once called a company that boasted about "great customer service" in its catalogue. It also talked about three easy ways to order. I sent the company an e-mail, which it ignored. When I called on the phone, I was put on hold for twelve minutes. The fact that this firm bragged about its customer service made me twice as furious.

4. **Ask your customers to articulate what's special about your product or service.** You may be very proud of the quality of your

product or the level of service you provide, but your pride won't help buzz spread. Your *customers* need to feel the difference. A very simple way to find out if they do is to talk to them. If they can't tell you what's unique about your product, they won't be able to explain it to their friends.

Remember Mechai Viravaidya and his condom-blowing contests? Viravaidya is a big fan of the grassroots approach. He likes having direct contact with people and knows that grassroots efforts are usually less expensive than advertising. But when Viravaidya could afford advertising, he used it. Did he ever!

In 1990 a study estimated that if nothing was done about HIV in Thailand, by the year 2000 up to 4 million Thais could be infected. So the following year, when Viravaidya was appointed minister for tourism, information, and AIDS in the Thai government, he made it mandatory for 488 radio stations and 15 television stations in the country to broadcast a thirty-second spot featuring AIDS education for every hour of broadcast. "We have to use all means—radio, television, soap operas, movies," he said. Banks and insurance companies distributed printed information about the disease. McDonald's restaurants and toll booths on the highway distributed free condoms. Millions of condoms were provided to sex workers by the government.

A massive campaign that worked on multiple fronts caused a dramatic decline in the spread of the disease. Viravaidya's approach is pragmatic. Now that he's returned to his nonprofit organization, he's back to the grassroots. "You either go out to restaurants or you cook at home, and if you don't have money, you cook at home," he explains.

Companies are usually very proud of the fact that their product spread by word of mouth, because it says something about the product's quality. Word of mouth adds an aura of authenticity to a product. But word-of-mouth marketing should not turn into an ideology that excludes advertising. "The awareness of mass media plus the credibility of word of mouth is a really powerful package that leads to trial and purchase," says Piers Hogarth-Scott of Yooster.

The bottom line is this: If it makes sense to advertise, try it and measure the results. If you see that it works, go for it. When used correctly, advertising can help buzz, and very few products can rely on word of mouth alone. Don't fall into the either/or trap.

Buzz in
Distribution Channels

22 **Rock stars have a following.** Political parties have a following. Megachurches

have a following. But retailers? You don't typically think

of them that way.

But then I heard about Dave Nichol. The first person

to tell me about him was Moss Kadey, who had intro-

duced Brita water filters in Canada. He told me that

Nichol had a huge following and that his support had

helped move a phenomenal amount of product in Brita's

early days. So I started reading about Nichol. I talked to some Canadian friends about him. The more I read and heard about Nichol, the more interested I became in a certain type of reseller who seems to bring together buzz and physical distribution.

Nichol started gaining the trust of Canadian consumers with No Name, a successful line of generic products from Loblaw, the Canadian grocery chain that he ran. In the mid-1980s, Loblaw introduced its own blend of coffee, which used arabica coffee beans, which tend to be more aromatic than the bitter robusta bean that was used up to then. President's Blend, as Loblaw called its coffee, was a real success and was followed by a premium product line known as President's Choice, with items such as Memories of Szechwan Peanut Sauce and Dressing. In 1988, Nichol introduced the Decadent Chocolate Chip Cookie, a delicacy with something that was unheard of at the time—40 percent chocolate chips. Forty-seven million packages of that product were sold in the first five years. And perhaps that is how Nichol built his credibility with the Canadian public—one Decadent Chocolate Chip Cookie at a time.

Another building block in this trust was a newsletter he created, the *Insider's Report*, which looked a little more like a comic book than a flyer from a grocery store. Printed on newsprint in black and red with yellow highlights, the newsletter had one feature that is so often forgotten in promotional material—it was interesting. It wasn't simply offering stuff for sale but giving useful information about food. Everything was explained by Nichol (although an extensive team, including Jim White, a food writer with the *Toronto Star*, was behind it). It was essentially the story of a small-town boy who was now searching out restaurants around the world to bring exotic food to Canadians. Nichol was selling—there was no attempt to hide this—but the whole thing read much more like a blog than a brochure or a catalogue. (Trader Joe's, a grocery chain, has a newsletter called the *Fearless*

Flyer, which is similar in tone and style to the *Insider's Report*. Not a coincidence, really, since Nichol bought the newsletter name and format from Trader Joe's.)

One thing that made the newsletter interesting was that it included stories about people rather than just about food. There was always some new tale, such as how Nichol met the guy who created Häagen-Dazs and learned what goes into its strawberry ice cream. Nichol and his team understood that people are interested in people; in just one page of one issue, he made reference to Dorothy Parker, Queen Elizabeth I, and the *Toronto Star* food editor Marion Kane, and he somehow connected them to the store's special Dijon mustard, hot cross buns, and lasagna, respectively. There were also jokes, quirky cartoons, recipes, and anecdotes, all of which turned the *Insider's Report* into something that people started asking for at the store. It was published four times a year and was read, according to Nichol, by about six out of ten Ontario householders, who spent an average of four hours browsing through it.

Recommendation is about trust, and over the years the *Insider's Report* gained the trust of a large segment of the Canadian public. Nichol was so popular at one point that a cartoon in a Canadian newspaper showed an unhappy Canadian talking to his TV set: "Why can't they just let Quebec be distinct, dump the Senate, lower the GST, end the recession, and let Dave Nichol run the country?" Another newspaper published a piece called "The Only Man Who Could Save Canada," pointing out that Nichol was someone who "never disappoints us. Someone who is everywhere. Someone we can trust . . ."

So when the *Insider's Report* carried a long write-up of the Brita water filter, Brita began to fly off the shelves. "He probably could sell anything that he'd put in that [newsletter] if he said it was good," says Kadey.

People are overwhelmed by too much choice. When Sheena

Iyengar was a Ph.D. student at Stanford, she ran an experiment at Draeger's, an upscale grocery store in Menlo Park, California. She set up a table at the store and offered people jam. In some cases she offered a variety of twenty-four different kinds of jam, and in some cases she offered just six kinds of jam. What she found was that 30 percent of those who stopped by the table with the six jams subsequently bought a jar of jam. On the other hand, only 3 percent of those who stopped by the table with the large choice of products ended up buying jam. "What the consumer wants is an edited choice," Dave Nichol said in a 1995 interview. And perhaps this is the best way to describe Nichol's role at Loblaw: an editor.

Remember Michael Barnard, the owner of the bookstore in Danville who helped make *Cold Mountain* a local success? There is a special breed of retailers whom people trust. Barnard is one of them. Nichol was one. So is the respected owner of an art gallery or the owner of a trendy boutique who has a local following among fashion aficionados. Why are they so trusted? Perhaps one can say that they are simply good editors—editors of merchandise, who sift through all the products available out there and prove to us, time after time, that they can find the ones we want.

A brand can be perceived as a good editor too. When Starbucks selects a book such as David Sheff's *Beautiful Boy* for its book program or a game like Cranium to display next to its bags of java, it acts as a hub that enjoys the trust of its followers. Costco and Trader Joe's are two other brands that come to mind in this context.

About twenty years before Nichol sold exotic sauces to Canadians through his *Insider's Report*, a young man named Stewart Brand started a newsletter called the *Whole Earth Catalog*. Brand's audience was different, his values were different, his tactics were different, but Stewart Brand and Dave Nichol have a lot in common—they are both editors who at some point enjoyed tremendous credibility with their audiences.

In 1966, Brand drove around Northern California with his "truck store," supplying communities with what he felt they needed. In 1968 he put together a six-page list that included some books on topics that ranged from how to build a teepee to cybernetics. Later that year he put together an actual catalogue, which he and a small group compiled using an IBM Selectric typewriter and a Polaroid camera.

In a 1971 edition of the catalogue (449 pages!), you can find a book on how to raise goats, a portable shower, looms from Sweden, a welding torch, and tons of other stuff. But there was a significant difference between the *Whole Earth Catalog* and Dave Nichol's *Insider's Report*. The listing of the book on dairy goats is accompanied by a reader review. The musical saw on page 336 was suggested by another reader, and on the opposite page, Tiny Alice from Los Angeles recommends a company in Scotland that makes bagpipes. ("Importing them yourself is about 4 times cheaper than buying one over here," she advised her fellow readers.)

Word of mouth was woven into the *Whole Earth Catalog*. In this way, Stewart Brand's editorial style is much more similar to Jeff Bezos's style—that is, in the customer reviews intermingling with information on Amazon.com—than to Dave Nichol's.

The rise of democratic voting tools has also affected the editorial style of resellers. Anyone who has spent some time on Amazon knows that this goes way beyond just reader reviews: ratings, collaborative filtering, images posted by customers, tags, listmania, videos, and other mechanisms all let you learn about products from other people.

I discussed this in the first edition of this book, but I totally missed the mark on another point. In that edition I questioned the ability of Amazon itself to make a recommendation that will be taken seriously by its audience. Boy, was I wrong!

About a week before my book came out, I got an e-mail one morning from Amazon that apparently was sent to lots of other people. The e-mail suggested that since I'd bought *The Tipping Point* by Malcolm Gladwell (which had been published a few months earlier), I might enjoy reading *The Anatomy of Buzz* by Emanuel Rosen.

Before I finished reading the details, the phone rang. It was Daniel Greenberg, my agent. "Your book is climbing this morning. It was number 274 on Amazon last time I checked. What's going on?" Daniel asked.

I told him about the e-mail I got. In the next few hours we watched my book rise to number 97, then 65, and then 30. Harry Potter was number 8 that afternoon, and when my book passed Harry and landed at number 6, even my kids, who were usually pretty indifferent to my book, said that this was "neat." I obviously vastly underestimated how much people can trust an on-line retailer.

Seeding the Channel

Creating excitement among those in your distribution channel—or anyone who talks to customers, for that matter—can make a huge difference in launching a new product. Remember the teasers that Linda Pezzano sent to toy stores to promote Trivial Pursuit? Here's a similar example.

In early 1991 about five thousand managers, clerks, and buyers at bookstores all across America received a package from the publishing company Knopf. When they took off the gift wrap, they found a special hardcover edition of Josephine Hart's first novel, *Damage*. Enclosed was a note from Sonny Mehta, the president and editor in chief of the publishing house. Knopf picked the right title for this kind of promotion. Hart's dark and passionate novel is the story of a successful British doctor and politician who lives a staid life until he meets Anna, his son's finacée, and falls in love with her. Outrageous stimuli, as we know, get more buzz. It's the type of book that leaves you with the feeling you get after witnessing an accident or seeing a person collapse on the street—you have to tell someone about it. Many of the booksellers who received the book did just that. One bookstore owner whose store got three copies told *Publishers Weekly*, "Everyone read it in one sitting and loved it. We'll sell ten times as many because of that." The book became a *New York Times* bestseller.

As always, numbers make a difference. Knopf didn't send a hundred books. They sent five thousand books. As in the case of *Cold Mountain*, the credibility of the publisher played a role here. "Sonny would not write more than a letter a year, so when Sonny wrote, you knew it was powerful stuff," says Carl Lennertz, a former marketing director at Knopf.

Think People

Forget for a moment the physical flow of products and try to identify *people* in the channel who meet a lot of your potential customers. Maybe they sell your product, maybe they don't. Consider this: John Holden is the manager of Blue Ridge Mountain Sports in Charlottesville, Virginia. If you ask him to recommend an outdoor program, he's probably going to say NOLS. Blue Ridge Mountain Sports doesn't sell NOLS courses, but people who come to outdoor stores are good candidates for the National Outdoor Leadership School, so it makes sense for NOLS to make retailers aware of its program.

NOLS's preferred retail program includes four hundred retailers, all of whom spread the word about the school. They keep catalogues, they refer people to NOLS, and in return NOLS refers students to buy their gear. To increase the number of store employees who have actually experienced a NOLS course, the school periodically allows two or three employees from a store to participate in a course at a discount. Eight employees of John Holden's store in Charlottesville have gone through a NOLS course. He also likes to hire NOLS graduates, and he keeps updated, detailed equipment lists for all NOLS courses.

The symbiotic relationship between the store and NOLS makes so much sense that it may sound trivial. But the fact is, there are lots of outdoor programs out there, and NOLS is the only school that has consistently stayed in touch with Holden over the years. The NOLS folks come to the store to give slide-show presentations; they talk to Holden on a regular basis. In May 2007 the NOLS bus parked in front of the store for a whole day.

A channel's ability to spread buzz differs from one industry to another. Moviegoers, for example, don't usually ask the guy at the box office to recommend a movie, but customers at bookstores do ask store personnel for their recommendations. The same goes for surf shops, where the store clerks (if you can call a dude at a surf shop a clerk) are often part of the same social networks as the store's customers.

Think again about that table at Draeger's with twenty-four different kinds of jam. What would have happened if Mr. Draeger had stood next to the table and told each customer, "They're all great, but I tried this one, and it's just delicious!"

Even within each industry, some stores are more effective in spreading the word than others. In some bookstores you have to look hard for someone to talk to, let alone trust. In others sales-people enjoy tremendous credibility with their customers. These booksellers are no different from any other network hub. When they recommend a book, it becomes a local hit. A similar situa-tion exists in the sporting goods industry. In some stores, espe-cially heavy discounters, you're on your own. On the other end of the spectrum you find stores that specialize in running shoes or mountaineering equipment where a clerk or the owner is an enthusiast, and his recommendations are taken seriously.

Validation

When Margot Fraser decided to market German-made Birkenstock sandals in this country, she first went to the most natural channel: shoe stores. But shoe store owners didn't be-lieve that the product would be accepted by Americans. When Fraser displayed Birkenstocks at a shoe trade show, the reaction was so bad that she decided to leave early, despite the fact that the show organizers were going to penalize her for leaving the booth before closing time. "I picked up my stuff and escaped through the fire exit," she recalls, laughing.

There is a time in the history of many brands when the prod-uct searches for validation. Because it's still unproven, tradi-tional distribution channels often reject it at this stage. This is never an easy time for the entrepreneur, but in a way, it's part of "growing up."

Small alternative channels are often easier to access during this stage. For Fraser, it was health-food stores. A friend told her about a convention of health-food stores that was taking place in San Francisco. Fraser rented a table at the show. "I just talked to people going by: 'You know, you ought to try this.' And that's how it started." Owners of health-food stores were somehow more receptive to the unconventional sandals, and many of them bought Birkenstocks for their own use. When they got back to their stores, they buzzed to their customers about the magic of these sandals. The word about Birkenstocks initially spread through the networks of health-food enthusiasts.

PowerBar went through a similar process when it was initially sold through bike shops. Bicycle shops tend to employ racers, who know a lot about biking and therefore have high credibility with their customers. Perhaps it's supposed to be that way. Before you can sell to a larger consumer base, you get your authenticity from one core group. Adidas got it from soccer players, Nike got it from runners and basketball players. Under Armour got it from American football players.

Of course, if the Wal-Mart or Macy's buyer calls you back, I suggest you take the call. There's no doubt that mass distribution can take your product to a new level. But more often than not, the traditional and especially the large channels will reject you before they see real demand.

In the case of Birkenstocks, the shoe stores eventually entered the fold. After a while the demand created in the alternative channels started to get the attention of shoe stores. "I see people coming out of the health-food store with shoe boxes under their arm," one shoe store owner told Fraser when he called to inquire about the shoes. The few stores that started to carry the product gradually gave it the validation it needed in the traditional channel.

Putting
It Together

23   **Each of the previous chapters** focuses on a certain theme, and so the examples often ignore other elements of the buzz-building strategies of the companies I discuss. This chapter features stories that are a little more in-depth and take you from start to finish of a buzz campaign. It's my hope that these stories will help you develop a buzz program for your own product or service.

A Hotel with a Pillow Menu:
The Benjamin Hotel

It was 1999, and the Benjamin Hotel had just opened. John Moser, the new property manager, was in a panic. He knew that out of the ninety-five people he had hired for the new midtown Manhattan hotel, only five had ever worked for a hotel before. Everyone else had to learn things from scratch—how to make a bed, how to check somebody in, how to open the door. He knew they were all rookies and they were making mistakes. He also knew that the owners of the hotel wanted to run a satisfaction survey, which is routinely done in the industry. "Don't do it right away," he pleaded with his bosses. "Give me a couple of months to get these people warmed up." But the company had made a significant investment in renovating this 1927 building, and management wanted a report as quickly as possible.

The Benjamin, located at Lexington Avenue and Fiftieth Street, is the flagship property of the Denihan Hospitality Group, which owns several other hotels in New York, Washington, D.C., and Chicago. When Moser got the envelope with the survey report, he was afraid to open it. For a while he sat at his desk and imagined all kind of Keystone Kops scenarios that his customers might have endured. But when he finally got the courage, he was pleasantly surprised. The hotel had received excellent scores. The people he had hired had no experience, but they were people who cared. So when they made a mistake, they genuinely apologized and fixed the problem. "I think that the attitude got us to world-class well before we deserved to be there," he says.

Reading the hotel's reviews on TripAdvisor demonstrates how critical each customer touchpoint is in this business. Every encounter is an opportunity to create a positive or a negative impression. Someone named Bumblebee from San Francisco gave the Benjamin one star (out of five) because he said he was disconnected three times when trying to make a reservation. This first encounter was so disappointing that Bumblebee never stayed at the hotel. With an average of 4.5 stars, however, most reviews of the Benjamin are extremely positive, often highlighting exceptional service.

Perhaps the most important word-of-mouth tools in the hospitality industry are your hiring and training practices. When Moser hired his staff, he asked each and every one of them something he called the "spa question." Suppose you're vacuuming in the hallway and a guest asks you where the spa is. What do you do? Some candidates said that they would direct the person to the house phone. Some said that they would tell the person that the spa was on the second floor. The people who said that they would stop what they were doing and take the guest to the spa personally were those who were hired.

I stayed at the Benjamin a few months after it opened, and I remember very friendly staff and first-rate service. One thing that stayed with me about that visit was an envelope that was handed to me after I checked in. It had some business cards with my name, the words "Guest in Residence," and the phone number and fax number in my room. I put them in my jacket pocket and didn't think too much about them, except for noting that the Benjamin had made the choice to spend some money on their guests (these were attractive cards). The following evening I had dinner with a former boss of mine. When he asked where I was staying, I remembered the cards and pulled one out of my pocket. It was word-of-mouth marketing in action.

A few months after my visit, I called to ask about those business cards and realized that I was probably the only one who saw this as "marketing." The Benjamin saw it more as customer service—a way to make guests feel good and to highlight the fact that each room has a fax and a direct line. Since that stay, I've been watching the Benjamin and have been impressed by its ability to keep coming up with buzzworthy additions to its offerings.

The sleep program is one example. When the hotel opened, the managers decided to offer people a variety of pillows by creating the pillow menu. Do you prefer a buckwheat pillow, which conforms to your head and neck, or a hypoallergenic pillow? Or maybe a full-body feather-and-down pillow? There were eleven different pillows on the menu, which resonated with some people. Encouraged by the positive feedback from guests, the Benjamin developed the sleep program further, and today the hotel has a full-time sleep concierge, who can advise you not only on the best choice in pillow but also on sleep-inducing food, "executive" naps, and services such as aromatherapy that can help you fall asleep. The pillow menu itself is evolving too, and if a certain pillow type is not requested often enough, it is dropped from the menu and replaced by another one. As other hotels have adopted the idea, the Benjamin is trying to stay one step ahead. Recently it added a pillow that connects to your iPod.

The Benjamin certainly gives people something to talk about—and journalists something to write about. The sleep concierge and the pillow menu have been written up in numerous publications (twice in the *New York Times*). So was the hotel's pet program, which was featured on the CBS *Early Show* (it offers a choice of beds for your dog as well as a bathrobe and "everything a pampered pet may need to enjoy their travels in high style").

While these items add to the talk value, reading through more than two hundred reviews of the hotel on TripAdvisor makes it clear that people talk mostly about the basics: service, the rooms, location, comfort, cleanliness. But the pillow menu is also mentioned quite frequently. It may be a perfect hook for starting a conversation.

Hotel managers religiously check TripAdvisor and other rating sites for new reviews. When necessary, they respond publicly to explain the hotel's point of view. The customer database contains both contact information and preferences. If you chose the Satin Beauty pillow for your previous stay, they'll offer it to you next time. That's a level of service that people might mention to a friend.

Moser believes that talking directly with customers is still the best way to find out what's working and what's not working. Now that he is chief marketing officer of the Denihan Hospitality Group, he encourages his salespeople to attend the manager's cocktail party on Tuesday nights. It's a great opportunity to hear directly from guests how they feel about their stay and what similar hotels in other cities are doing. "They sometimes will tell you about this great hotel in Dallas that they just stayed in or about this great experience they had in Alaska," he says. And with this attitude of listening and paying attention to details, it's no wonder that the hotel consistently gets guests buzzing about it. "Just got back and was excited to tell everyone about the Benjamin," a guest from North Carolina wrote on TripAdvisor. "A great place to stay in New York and we've tried many. We had our 2 kids with us who loved the pillow menu. (They agreed the water pillow and the jelly neck roll were the best, the magnetic facial one—not so much.)"

The Evolution of Seeding: BCBG and CK in2u

Mavis Fraser had been successfully marketing a line of fragrances under the Calvin Klein brand. In 2001 she faced a new challenge. Everybody knows Calvin Klein, but how could she introduce a fragrance associated with another designer—Max Azria and his BCBG line, which had very low awareness in Canada?

Just around that time, Fraser, who's the director of marketing for the cosmetics company Coty, was approached by Patrick Thoburn and Matthew Stradiotto, who had recently formed their Toronto-based word-of-mouth marketing agency, Matchstick. They didn't have much to show, certainly not in the fragrance category, but Fraser intuitively felt that this agency might be just what BCBG needed. If anyone in Canada would know about BCBG, it had to be the young, fashion-conscious people that Patrick Thoburn claimed he could help her find. Fraser had been in the business since 1978 and knew the importance of word of mouth. She's also the sort of person who's always looking to experiment with something new. Matchstick got the green light.

Thoburn and Stradiotto's methodology was pretty straightforward. They found a product seeder whom Thoburn describes as "aspirational to the target market," a woman who was obviously fashion-conscious and fluent in the language required for the job, fashion talk. Where do you find fashion-forward people? Every big city has its chic neighborhood, and in Toronto it's Yorkville. The young woman went out and started interviewing people "who had the right look and the right vibe," as Fraser puts it. Through the interviews, Matchstick was looking for people who scored high in four dimensions. They were the first to try new products, were active information seekers, demonstrated good knowledge of key brands in the category, and had above-average per-month spending on lifestyle products. If someone was familiar with BCBG or had a special connection to the brand—for instance, if the person owned one of BCBG's fashion items—that was a plus.

Two hundred people in Toronto, Montreal, and Vancouver were recruited in about two weeks; each of them got one hundred samples to give away to their friends. The sample postcards had four bubbles filled with the fragrance, enabling people to wear and share it. Altogether, 20,000 postcards were given away.

Not long after the initial seeding, and before the product was available on the market, Fraser started hearing about people asking for BCBG at stores, some holding the postcard in hand. Just fourteen days after the seeding, in a telephone survey among the hubs, the respondents said they had inspired 496 sales of the product by friends. The brand became one of the top ten fragrances at the Bay, a Canadian department store, and the product launch (which also included traditional advertising) outperformed the U.S. launch. The budget for the buzz campaign was $18,750 Canadian.

Over the next five years Matchstick ran several campaigns for Coty, the agency's methodology evolving as it gained experience and insight. The seeding periods grew somewhat longer. Besides the four criteria initially used to identify the influencers—attitude, behavior, knowledge, and spending—who used two new dimensions, status and connectedness. The budgets grew as well. Referring to the initial budget for the 2001 campaign, Patrick Thoburn comments, "Some of our programs are ten times that size now."

In 2006, at the launch party for a new fragrance, Fraser started talking with the Matchstick guys about a new product that was coming and would require a different approach to launch. Calvin Klein was introducing two new fragrances—CK in2u for her and CK in2u for him—that were supposed to appeal to eighteen- to twenty-four-year-olds. This was new territory for Fraser and for Calvin Klein, whose traditional audience was somewhat older. It was clear to everyone involved that an online strategy was necessary.

In January 2007, Matchstick conducted thirty online and in-person interviews with young people in Toronto, Calgary, and Montreal to determine the characteristics of a typical influencer in this case. Based on what they heard, the marketers determined that a good starting point in searching for influencers would be to look for someone who hosts a cultural blog that gets more than 500 daily visitors or someone who has more than 250 friends on Facebook or MySpace.

For about ten weeks, Matchstick staff combed through social sites and blogs looking for the most connected people. They found about 450 people, who were invited to fill out a survey with questions about their attitude, category knowledge, and behavior. Based on the survey, Matchstick picked 150 influencers, 50 in each city, all of whom received the products as well as 48 samples (24 for him, 24 for her) and a few small gifts.

One such influencer was Lauren White, a blogger from Toronto. She gave away the samples pretty quickly to friends at parties (she goes out four or five times a week). A cashier at a store who commented on her scent got a sample. Lauren's dad got one too. White was also e-mailed a widget to place on her blog and Facebook profile with a link to an interactive branded game. "The objective of the game and the widget were to give these very connected online influencers an added tool that would help them spread the word to all of their friends," Patrick Thoburn explains. Once these friends played the online game, they could also request samples of CK in2u for themselves. Lauren White says her blog gets between two and three thousand hits a day. She has close to eight hundred friends on Facebook.

Krista Dayman, a young mental health worker from Toronto, was another one of these influencers. She loved giving out samples to her friends. When I asked her if there was anything Matchstick could do to improve the program, she said it would be to give more samples, because she ran out of those pretty quickly. Dayman doesn't see herself as a big partier, but she socializes a lot. When the campaign took place, she was on a sports team, she was in the Toronto scooter club, and she met friends once a week to play dodgeball. Dayman has 270 friends on Facebook.

On average, each influencer reported giving samples to thirty-two friends and speaking to seventy-two people about the new fragrance. When asked how many individuals purchased the product at least in part because of their influence, the average answer was 3.8. Friends of the influencers who played the online game and requested their own samples reported talking to an additional 9.9 individuals. Altogether, Matchstick estimates that the campaign generated 86,000 offline conversations, 79,000 online impressions, and about 19,000 sales.

Is this the end of offline seeding for Matchstick? "We haven't abandoned the offline world," Thoburn says. "We think that it's really important that the influencers have a rich offline experience," he adds. After all, a lot of the talking happened in the real world—and passing out samples could *only* happen offline. As in other cases, online technology was used to accelerate the process and significantly increase the campaign reach.

Are Barbers Influential?: Prostate Net

"Jim, have you gotten it checked?"

Jim, an older black gentleman who's waiting to get his hair cut at the Coleman Brothers barbershop on the South Side of Chicago, removes his iPod earphones from his ears.

"What?"

"Have you gotten your prostate checked?"

Jim makes a gesture that makes it clear he doesn't want to hear about it. He puts back his earphones and closes his eyes.

James Coleman, the barber who posed the question, continues to cut the hair of another customer. That customer, also an older man, who's been getting his hair cut here for the past thirty years, assures Coleman that he is getting his prostate checked on a regular basis at the VA hospital.

What does a barber have to do with prostates?

A few years ago a New Jersey man by the name of Virgil Simons was told by his doctor that he had prostate cancer. He knew next to nothing about prostate cancer, and as he started reading about the disease, he found out that as an African-American, he belonged to the group at highest risk for prostate cancer. He learned that African-American men die of the disease at approximately twice the rate of other American men. He also learned that if it is diagnosed early, prostate cancer is highly curable. The trouble is that on average, African-American men don't go to the doctor as frequently as others. So detection of their prostate cancer usually happens later.

Simons, formerly an executive in the textile industry, is the kind of person who can't just sit back when he hears this kind of news—he has to do something about it. So he started an organization called Prostate Net to educate people about the disease and give them the tools to make an intelligent decision regarding their treatment. He put together some brochures, set up a Web site, and established an 800 number that a patient could call to talk to a survivor.

But he still felt that he wasn't reaching a lot of people—that there were a lot of men who, exactly like him a few years earlier, didn't ever think about this disease and didn't really want to think about it, let alone go for a checkup.

Then one day in 2002, Virgil Simons was watching a comedy called *Barbershop* in a movie theater in New Jersey when the idea hit him. Growing up in Chicago, he had seen barbers as people who carried a lot of weight in the community. "If they said something, you believed them," he recalls. So the idea he had in the theater was to spread the word about prostate cancer to black men through their barbers.

When Simons heard that MGM was working on a sequel to *Barbershop*, he called the company. It took him about six months to finally get in front of the studio executives and give a presentation. When he did, he persuaded them to do a co-promotion. Barbers around the country would spread the word about the movie by giving out tickets and putting up posters in their shops. They would also encourage men to get checked for prostate cancer.

At the time, Joe Harrington was working at Rush University Medical Center in Chicago, recruiting people for clinical trials and conducting health-related educational programs among African-American men. When someone told him about the initiative with MGM, he contacted Virgil Simons. The idea of working with barbershops wasn't new to him, but he liked the tie-in with the movie, which he expected would create buzz for the program.

Harrington started contacting barbershops in Chicago. Barbers showed interest, because many of them knew someone who had the disease. But they were less enthusiastic about spending their time going through training without compensation. Barbers work long hours and weekends, and they were not going to spend their one day off talking about prostate cancer. But when Harrington found the budget to pay them for training and created an incentive program, interest shot up.

As Harrington expected, the tie-in with the movie helped give the project visibility. The concept had that special talk value that gets the attention of writers for late-night shows—they love this stuff. Indeed, in his opening monologue one night, Jay Leno referred to the program. Local newspapers, like the *Defender* and the *Chicago Tribune*, wrote about the initiative, and the stream of patients who were sent for screening grew.

The idea was that each barber in Chicago would give a visitor a written pretest, show him a ten-minute video, and then have him fill out the post-test. This proved to be too complicated to manage in the somewhat chaotic barbershop setting. "We weren't able to evaluate it to the extent that we wanted to," says Joe Harrington, "but we know for a fact that most of them have used the video and passed out the information." The objective wasn't to make the barbers into experts, Harrington explains, but to let them expose people to the video and to the brochures, and they did that.

Altogether, Prostate Net ran training sessions for barbers in fifty-seven medical centers across the country. The results were impressive. That first year 10,034 men were screened who never had been before and 442 cases of early-stage prostate cancer were identified, according to Prostate Net. Over five hundred other urological diseases were diagnosed as well.

Do barbers possess special influence? Although I've heard them described as opinion leaders, I don't think that this has been proven. It's clear, however, that barbers have plenty of time to talk to a captive audience and that they talk to a lot of people. This is especially true in African-American communities, where the barbershop is a social center where local events and gossip are discussed.

"The barbershop has always been a source for information where people gather to share and talk," says Rahman Williams, the owner of Maxima Salon in Chicago. "It's always been that way." Craig Atkins, another barber I visited on the South Side of Chicago, says that people are more comfortable talking about health issues at the barbershop. Part of the reason is trust, he added. Another barber, Sam Smith, told me that he also distributes information to female customers discouraging them from wearing flip-flops, which he believes are the culprit for lots of knee and back problems. And he believes that a lot of doctors will not give this simple advice to a patient because it goes against their economic interest. "A woman can walk into his office and she's having knee problems and she's wearing flip-flops, you think he's going to say, Stop wearing the flip-flops?" he asks.

In many cases the success of a word-of-mouth campaign comes down to getting information into the hands of people whom others can trust. Several people I talked to mentioned the mistrust of the medical community among African-Americans, which is rooted in exploitation of black people by some doctors before the Civil War. The Tuskegee Study, in which black men were deliberately denied effective treatment for syphilis, is the most prominent example of this type of exploitation in the twentieth century. When such a belief is out there, it makes sense to reach out to folks through someone they *do* trust. And for many around South Stony Island Avenue in Chicago, that someone is James Coleman, who's been cutting their hair as far back as they can remember.

Tasting Yogurt with Your Friends: The Word Of Mouth Company

Think of the difference between seeing an ad for a new pizza and tasting it at a sampling counter in your local supermarket. In-store sampling awakens your senses. You start smelling the new pizza as you walk into the store. You feel the warmth of the bite-sized piece they hand you, you taste the delicious blend of cheese, tomatoes, and mushrooms . . .

What happens when this type of sampling moves to a social context where you learn how to make the pizza with your friends?

Every month, the Word Of Mouth Company runs dozens of presentations in community centers, at mothers' groups, at sporting associations, and at other social gatherings all around Australia. A typical presentation takes about one hour, during which a presenter in a red apron dedicates about eight minutes to each product she is introducing that session. The presenter might start with a tasting of Chang's gluten-free rice noodles (a great addition to stir-fries or salads), followed by a story about the healing power of a new type of adhesive bandage (they call them "plasters" in Australia). The presenter gives everyone some Brita filtered water and explains the benefits of water filtration and then hands out samples of low-fat yogurt from Vaalia and talks about how it helps your digestive system.

As people touch, feel, taste, see, hear, and smell the different products, they inevitably talk about it with those around them, which the presenter encourages by asking lots of questions: Have you tried this before? Have you seen this on the shelf? What did you think? "It's a very interactive presentation," says cofounder Jo Schultz. When people articulate their opinions, it makes it easier for them to discuss the product later with others outside the group.

The presenters also keep their eyes open for current product advocates. "It's very easy to identify those advocates," explains cofounder Vicki Foster. "You can see that they are absolutely raving fans." These people may receive a new product to take home. Sometimes they are invited to special events and are sent information about upcoming products.

Storytelling is another important part of the presentations. The stories are quick and simple. A woman whose husband had an infection after surgery called the Word Of Mouth Company and told them that SilverHealing from Elastoplast worked so well for his wound that she bought these adhesive plasters for all her friends and family. Not exactly a cliffhanger, but still an anecdote that is easily passed on. "The story has to be easy to repeat," says Foster.

What type of buzz can be created through such an effort? Here's an example. Between February and July 2007, close to 40,000 people in Australia, most of them women, sampled and learned about the health benefits of Vaalia yogurt at presentations organized by the Word Of Mouth Company. In a follow-up survey, 84 percent of participants reported that they had recommended the yogurt to at least one other person. Based on the breakdown of the number of people told (21 percent told one person, 26 percent told two, 14 percent told three, 12 percent told four, 4 percent told five, 3 percent told six, and 4 percent told seven or more), at least 90,000 people heard about Vaalia from friends at the first generation. In addition, 81 percent of the original participants reported that they bought at least one package of the yogurt within three weeks.

Does it always work? A few years ago the company promoted a new wet and dry vacuum cleaner for wooden floors. People got excited about it, but when a few actually bought it and realized that the product didn't live up to expectations, the word of mouth turned negative. And another thing happened: People started calling the Word Of Mouth Company to complain. "That was a real problem for us," Foster remembers. Eventually the problems were resolved, but the folks at the company learned an important lesson about their business: If they want to be invited again to these community groups, they can't disappoint them. Furthermore, they need to deliver a presentation that's both fun and helpful.

Especially helpful. Most participants are women who try to juggle jobs, kids, and a household. What they are looking for are products that will improve their daily lives. "Women love to share solutions with their friends and family, so if you give them one, they'll share it," says Dr. Karen Stenner, a former Princeton professor who is in charge of the company's research efforts. So in addition to sampling and stories, recipes are given out, and ideas and tips for how to make life a bit easier are shared. When it works, the presentations lead to invitations to new events, since many people belong to more than one community group. "We end up generating our own word of mouth within those communities," says Schultz.

There's not much marketing research at the presentation itself, for fear that too much prodding at this stage might distract people from the product experience. Participants fill out a postcard, which is followed up a few weeks later by an online survey. From this survey, the company is trying to learn how much buying and recommendation is going on and who's doing the talking. In the case of Elastoplast's SilverHealing adhesive plasters, Elastoplast was expecting to see most buzz among families with children. They were surprised to learn that the people who talked about it most were older folks, whose skin usually heals slowly.

In 2007 the Word Of Mouth Company started an online forum that lets people (mostly those who have attended presentations) continue the conversation by sharing ideas and recommendations. Its core business is still the offline world, where it runs about four hundred presentations a mouth, seeing approximately 14,000 household shoppers. The system that it has built combines natural storytelling, communicating with customers at the grassroots level, and appealing to all of our senses.

Will People Talk about Chewing Gum?:
Wrigley's Extra Professional

In the summer of 2007, Wrigley introduced two new products in Germany: Wrigley's Extra Professional plus Calcium chewing gum and Wrigley's Extra Professional Forest Fruit mints. The two products had specific benefits that could possibly become the subject of discussion—the calcium gum helps strengthen and clean teeth, and the new mints leave a noticeable clean feeling on the tongue and in the mouth. But can people be motivated to talk about something as mundane as chewing gum or mints?

A visit to the campaign Web site suggests that the answer is yes. Meet Calcium-Girl. She's a beautiful superheroine clad all in gray except for a large golden C on her chest. A consumer's creation, Calcium-Girl symbolizes the power of the new calcium chewing gum. Another customer posted a comic strip that illustrates the benefit of Wrigley's Extra Professional Forest Fruit mints. These are just two out of 2,617 photos and films that were uploaded in praise of Wrigley's Extra. Additionally, there were 4,007 comments on the campaign blog, and participants in this campaign reported that they told more than 120,000 people about the two new products.

Why do people take part in this? "I think it's a lot of fun," explains Christian Basten, Jr., an optometrist from Düsseldorf, who likes the forest fruit flavor. Basten estimates that he gave samples of the forest fruit mints to sixty friends and ten acquaintances (only one of whom didn't like it, he reports). He also handed samples to beer vendors at a beer festival in town.

Martin Oetting from trnd, the word-of-mouth agency that organized the campaign for Wrigley in Germany, believes that the key to explaining the word of mouth created is "empowered involvement." When people get to participate in the marketing process, they generate more talk. Oetting, who's also working on his Ph.D. in marketing on the topic, had previously run an experiment with Wrigley that showed that people who voted for their favorite advertising for a new chewing gum talked about it more than those who just saw the ad.

In the two-flavor campaign, an additional force motivated people to talk: a sense of competition. In mid-July 2007, trnd sent out an invitation to about 50,000 members of its consumer panel to participate in the "EXTRA Championship 2007." Participants could apply to be part of either the Waldfrucht (forest fruit) team or the Calcium team. About 2,500 members were chosen for each team. And if you think this is kids' stuff, you may be surprised to learn that the average age of the Calcium team was thirty-three and the average age of Team Waldfrucht was twenty-seven.

Once you joined a team, you got a campaign button to wear on your clothing or on your bag, a brochure listing the benefits of your gum or mint, and some product samples for yourself plus fifty small samples to give to your friends. Every time you gave a sample or talked to a friend, you were asked to submit a report. Every report received a personal response and was rewarded with points by trnd employees. (The number of points did not depend so much on the number of people you talked to, but rather on the level of detail provided in the report.) The goal of each team was to achieve the highest number of points.

The competition fueled the responses, and the flood of reports coming in during the first few days was overwhelming. It took trnd a few days to beef up its staff so it could achieve its normal response time of twelve hours. At peak times a dozen trnd staffers were responding to the incoming reports.

"It was exciting to see how enthusiastically and seriously the participants took their role as brand ambassadors," Gabriela Froehlich, the brand manager for Wrigley's Extra in Germany, wrote in an e-mail. The project blog was swamped with comments from participants cheering for their teams. The greeting posts alone, which opened the campaign, got 2,114 comments. For the next three months, the two teams' scores were reported on the blog on a regular basis, which stimulated further participation.

Even though the campaign officially ended in October 2007, there were still more than a thousand visits per day on the project's Web site two months later. People obviously got very involved, which supports Wrigley's marketing team's thinking of ways to keep the momentum going in future efforts and perhaps turn such a campaign into an ongoing project.

This campaign was not a spontaneous burst of enthusiasm for a product. And yet people enjoyed participating and talking about these two products, which have clearly found some fervent believers. Before I hung up the phone after talking with Christian Basten (whose team won with 24,299 points; the Calcium team got 22,569 points), he said that I should taste the forest fruit flavor. "Waldfrucht is the best product they ever made," he said.

Putting Word-of-Mouth Marketing on the Agenda: Intuit

You work at a large organization and you're a great believer in the value of word-of-mouth marketing. Great! But how do you build support for the idea within the organization? Here's how it happened at Intuit.

"If you're in a big company and you're thinking about word-of-mouth marketing, one of the things that I strongly recommend is—just like what you would do with your customers—start talking to people," says Kira Wampler, who was the first word-of-mouth marketing manager at the Fortune 1000 company. And this was exactly what she did at Intuit—she started talking to anyone who had ever done anything that could fall under the umbrella of word-of-mouth marketing. "And when you're having that conversation, be sure to ask at the end, Who else should I talk to?" she adds. With about eight thousand employees and significant internal mobility, Intuit (like all large organizations) has its hidden pockets of knowledge, and that's one way to start looking for them.

Within the first week on her new job, Kira realized that when she said "word-of-mouth marketing," different people had different interpretations of the term. Some read it as "blogging," some read it as "buzz marketing." So creating a common language was an important first step.

Involving the company's leadership was the next important factor that Wampler believes helped put word-of-mouth marketing on the map at Intuit. She briefed executives on academic research, industry best practices, and metrics as she gained new insights. The ability to measure business results of word of mouth has been critical in this respect. She also started working early on with the legal, privacy, and finance departments to get them involved in the word-of-mouth marketing programs. Doing so early ensured that there were no surprises down the road.

Intuit is a pretty conservative company when it comes to its marketing spending, and it approached word-of-mouth marketing with caution as well. "We're not a company that will throw around a gazillion dollars and see what happens," Wampler says. All involved agreed to build a testing plan so that they could develop a sense of what kind of results they could expect.

Wampler also started what's known at Intuit as "opening up the window"—taking a look at what's happening out there. She called Dina Mayzlin at Yale, followed Walter Carl's blog at Northeastern, and contacted other researchers doing studies on word of mouth and related topics. She also started talking with colleagues from noncompeting companies to hear what they were doing.

The picture that started to emerge from the internal and external discussions was that Intuit had strong organic word of mouth. The company was very good at listening to its customers through the Net Promoter Score survey, "follow me home" observation sessions, and the Inner Circle feedback forum for its TurboTax products. But Intuit had little experience in amplifying word of mouth.

One thing Wampler did *not* want to do was to build a word-of-mouth marketing department that would simply become another silo within the company. From talking with other companies, she learned that word-of-mouth marketing works best when it's part of the company's DNA—when people across the organization are aware of the discipline and are looking for opportunities to apply their knowledge when appropriate.

To engage people across the company, Intuit launched WoM-Wiki in March 2006. The choice of a Web 2.0 tool was not accidental, explains Scott Wilder from Intuit: "It was a very good way for people to use the technology in order to learn the power of what a wiki could do," he says. It didn't take long before the wiki attracted several dozen Intuit employees from six brands and four divisions of the company. They use it to ask questions, read articles about the topic, and share results of word-of-mouth campaigns or insights gleaned on the topic from conferences or articles.

The word-of-mouth folks at Intuit—who started to refer to themselves as Wommers—began to have monthly meetings. A typical meeting included a guest speaker, a discussion, and the sharing of insights.

Within a few months, hundreds of people at Intuit, based in several different locations and divisions, were trained in word-of-mouth marketing, the basics of writing a blog, and related issues. As a result, pilot projects and experiments around word of mouth began popping up. In some parts of the company, like the accounting division, where Wampler had previously been a brand manager, word-of-mouth marketing plays a much more central role than in others. The main point, however, was not to turn every marketing effort into an exercise in word of mouth, but to make sure that knowledge about the concept is widely available. And this is certainly happening.

There's a lot of sharing across teams. People can bring ideas to the monthly meetings to get feedback. There's also analysis of past campaigns. So, for example, the TurboTax group that launched the rap-about-taxes promo with Vanilla Ice (which I mentioned in Chapter 16) shared insights about the campaign— what worked and what they might have done differently. Another project discussed was a partnership with Meetup, aimed at encouraging small-business meetings in the offline world. The ninety-day goal for that pilot was achieved within seven days, and the final number of groups that met was 3.5 times higher than the original objective.

At this point, anyone at the company can pick up the phone and talk to one of dozens of people who know something about the topic. Word-of-mouth marketing at Intuit is no longer in testing mode. It is now incorporated regularly into marketing plans. "We're doing it!" Wampler says.

The Secret of Finding a Plumber: Angie's List

It all started when Bill Oesterle decided to renovate his house in Columbus, Ohio. He had a couple of bad experiences with contractors and grew more and more frustrated. So he hooked up with Angie Hicks, a former intern of his at a venture capital firm, and together they started Angie's List.

The year was 1995. The list began as a call-in service and a magazine for people seeking home-repair help. When Jenny in Columbus was looking for an electrician, she could call the 800 number and hear the rating of a particular shop in town or get some recommendations. The magazine that came with the service included articles about home repair and maintenance as well as evaluation forms for customers to fill out. Like any other young business, it faced a huge challenge in acquiring new customers. "I would take calls from members during business hours, and then in the evening I would go door to door signing up consumers to join the list," Hicks remembers.

The rating system back then was very basic. You could give either a positive or a negative review to someone and describe the work. In the next few years the service expanded at the rate of one market a year. First Indianapolis, then Cleveland, and then Charlotte, North Carolina.

A big turning-point year for Angie's List came in 1999, and perhaps the most significant thing that was added was depth. The Web site that was created that year enabled members to read much more detailed reports than they would be willing to listen to on the phone. The positive/negative rating left a significant middle ground that wasn't covered, so it was replaced with a school-like grading system of A, B, C, D, and F. The Web made the service more accessible and allowed more people to join and more people to submit reports. Depth gave people more stuff to talk about.

Angie's List is obviously an aggregator of word of mouth, but it also takes advantage of word of mouth *about* the list. People talk a lot about home projects, so word of mouth has been a huge factor in the growth of the company, as people tell each other about the electrician or the plumber they found through the list. The company made sure it kept in touch and updated people even on what was happening in other markets. This paid off, especially when it started operating in a new city. "It's always interesting to see how much carryover we have from city to city," says Hicks. This applies not only to cities in one region but also across the country. Somebody from Indianapolis who has a sister in San Diego might tell her that Angie's List has arrived.

The company uses any and all opportunities to remind you of your friends. During the holiday season, there's an effort to encourage members to give membership as a gift. When you bring in a member, you get a one-pound bag of M&M's. The company also used to send a blank check for seven dollars that you could make out to yourself or your favorite charity, but it discontinued this promotion for lack of interest.

In each new market there's a concentrated local effort to make sure there are enough members and reviews. Having just a couple of reports per category is not really useful, so a lot of work is done to reach a critical mass. The service is now available in about 120 cities and the company employs about four hundred people. Each and every report that goes into the system (currently more than 15,000 a month) is reviewed by an employee to detect any red flags.

When you submit a report, the general public cannot see your name, but you agree that your name can be shared with the company you're reporting on. This is done so the contractor can respond to your review, something that makes sense in this category. Then readers look at the case, read both sides of the story, and decide for themselves. "It gives a greater insight to consumers who are using the list," says Hicks. "Because sometimes you read a report and you say to yourself, 'Yes, I agree with that consumer 100 percent,' and other times you may read the information and say, 'You know what? I think that company makes sense. I think maybe that consumer is a little unreasonable there.'"

I asked Angie Hicks for advice she could give to a plumber on how to get good grades on Angie's List, and I think that her response is relevant to other businesses as well: "One of the biggest things we see is that companies are not responsive. They don't return phone calls. So one of the things I tell people is, make sure you're managing expectations. If you're really booked up, leave a message on your answering machine on what your turnaround is. Always return phone calls, even if it's to say that you can't do the job." Indeed, when I called a couple of roofers from the list last year, I was surprised when one of them called me to apologize because he wouldn't be able to take any new jobs for a while.

All this might sound obvious, and yet so much negative word of mouth originates from companies neglecting to return phone calls or respond to e-mails. And it always comes back to listening and having an open dialogue with your customers. Perhaps the most important piece of advice from Hicks is this: "Make an effort to ask customers along the way if they like how it's going." Problems detected early are easier to fix.

Buzz
Workshop

24 **This chapter leads you through** a
series of questions to keep in mind as you
think about whatever product or service you're trying to
market. It's not a summary of the book, but it should get
the ideas flowing.

Do You Have the Right Product?

People will pass on positive comments—the kind of
buzz you want—*only* if the product or service really does

impress them. There is no point in stimulating buzz unless your product meets the test.

- *Are you offering a good product or service?* Not all products that get positive buzz are of the very highest quality, but your product must work from day one and offer everything that is promised, if not more. Do you underpromise and overdeliver?

- *Does your product enhance the lives of people who use it?* Is it compatible with what people do, fitting readily into their current belief systems or lifestyles?

- *Are there any other opportunities to create a "Wow" effect?* In addition to the product itself, there are many opportunities to impress your customer. Write down all the contact points your customer has with your product and company—inquiry, packaging, delivery, billing, instructions, support, etc. At any of these touchpoints, can you somehow surprise and delight your customer?

- *Is your product visible—and can you help make it more so?* Contagious products are often visible—they draw attention to themselves. Can you do something to make your product, or its users, more noticeable in a positive way?

- *Abstract concepts can be made visible too.* Approximately 55 million people around the world wear a yellow LiveStrong wristband in support of people living with cancer. The abstract idea of fighting cancer was translated into something tangible that stimulates millions of conversations.

- *Are you offering something new?* Buzz reflects excitement. Excitement doesn't build around old ideas, familiar approaches, or "me too" products. Something about your offering must be fresh and different. You can still get buzz for an existing product line (see the Clairol Herbal Essences example in Chapter 6), but you need to find a new angle, a new audience, a new . . . anything!

- *Is your product ready?* If buzz begins now, is it too early? It's a good idea to start before the product is out but not so early that the excitement dies out before the product is available.

Conversation Piece

In October 2005 I learned about a Nike-sponsored marathon in San Francisco to benefit the Leukemia & Lymphoma Society. But I didn't see it on TV. I didn't read about it in the paper. How did I know about it? Because a couple of days after the race, my friend Terry showed me a blue box with the Tiffany logo. Inside there was a silver necklace with a figure of a woman running. The Nike swoosh and the year '05 were engraved on the charm. Terry went on to tell me that she ran a half-marathon and that at the end of the run, men in tuxedos were handing a box to each woman who crossed the finish line. The foundation of this snippet of buzz was the experience (run a marathon) with something to talk about (men in tuxedos at a sporting event) and a gorgeous memento (Tiffany jewelry). Would Terry have told me about the event without the reminder? Probably. Would she have mentioned Nike's involvement? Much less likely. This necklace made sure that the brand was part of the conversation. We tend to appreciate objects that mark our own engagement in an important event—and, more important, we talk about them. Nike's charm was just such a conversation piece. (For less expensive examples of conversation pieces, see the examples of Herbal Essences, LiveStrong, the Benjamin Hotel, and the Brita tea test in this book.)

Do You Have the Right Approach?

Generating buzz calls for a different attitude and a different approach to the promotion of your product.

- *Are you operating in a spirit of truth, honesty, and directness?* Openness and candor are key to developing strong, long-term, grassroots support.
- *Is everyone clear on the ethical guidelines?* Make sure that every person who represents you (employees, your PR agency, etc.) is on the same page as you.
- *Are people in your company spreading the word?* Does everyone know what your company stands for? Do people feel part of it? Are they motivated to spread the word?
- *Are you thinking in terms of networks?* Thinking of markets, segments, and categories can be useful. But when you think of buzz, think of customers as part of an interpersonal information network. Your objective is to maximize the number of positive comments about your product.
- *Does your product or company have a story that is easily told?* What's the main idea of your organization? Can people easily pass on that idea?

Are You Listening?

You need to listen to buzz. The best way to do that is by talking to people. Every time you use another person—an interviewer, a reseller, a focus group moderator—as a messenger, you are adding a filter. Get out and talk to people directly.

- *Know what customers are saying.* What advice are people seeking in your product category? What do they tell their friends about your company? About your competitors? How satisfied are they with current solutions in the marketplace?

- *Are you measuring word of mouth on an ongoing basis?* Do you know your Net Promoter Score? What percentage of people hear about you through friends? What percentage of your buzz is positive and what percentage negative? How much of it is experience-based and how much is secondhand?

- *Are you talking with your customers?* What kind of response are they getting from your company? Is it marketing jargon or real dialogue? Are you having a real conversation with your customers?

- *Are you showing customers that you're listening?* The best way to do this is to act. Are you fixing what customers are complaining about? Do you accept suggestions? If you just listen for the sake of listening, customers may stop talking.

- *When are people recommending your product?* Right after they buy it? When they start noticing its benefits? Try to stimulate discussion at the critical points when people have a natural inclination to talk.

- *Use all possible approaches for listening to buzz.* Do you read what is being said about your company on different blogs, newsgroups, and other online forums?

- *Track visual buzz.* Do you visit Web sites such as Flickr, YouTube, and others and search for your brand? Your competitors' brands?

- *Track what the industry is saying.* It's important to listen not only to customer buzz but also to industry buzz. Customer buzz tells you what users are talking about *today*. Industry buzz can give you insight into what customers will be talking about *tomorrow*.

- *Talk to people who are in direct contact with your customers.* In addition to talking to customers on an ongoing basis, talk to people who are in direct contact with them—your call center employees, customer service, retailers, technical support. Ask them, What are people saying about us? Are they happy? What can we do to serve them better?

- *Is anyone else in your company doing something interesting with word-of-mouth marketing?* If you're working for a large organization, pay attention to what others are doing. (Check out the Intuit case study for additional ideas.)

- *Talk to company veterans.* Many companies initially grow through word of mouth and possibly have done things to stimulate it. You may hear about strategies and a general attitude that helped your company in its early years. How can you replicate that success?
- *What are you expecting people to say?* In his book *Word-of-Mouth Marketing*, Andy Sernovitz suggests you do the "pass-in-the-hall test." What will customers tell each other about your product in a few seconds? "You should try _____, it's _____." "Can you believe _____ did _____?" "There's nothing better than _____ for _____."

Are You Working with Network Hubs?

Hubs are people who talk more than most people, so finding and influencing them is important in building buzz.

- *Identify your network hubs.* Who are the network hubs in your category? Which are expert hubs and which are social hubs? What do you know about your hubs and how to reach them?
- *Use all available techniques to find even more hubs.* Are you listening when hubs identify themselves? Can you think of categories of people who might become network hubs for your product—people who, by virtue of their position, have many ties with people you would like to reach? Have you used surveys to identify potential hubs? Have you looked for hubs within your own company—an executive with the contacts and charisma to be a hub, or potential champions or activists from engineering, marketing, or R&D?
- *Who are the most influential bloggers in your field?* Do they know about you? Are you keeping them up-to-date?
- *Have you considered blogging?* You can become a hub yourself if you have something new to say, can commit to posting frequently, and know how to keep it interesting. Encourage others at your company to

do the same (within some guidelines that define what can and what cannot be disclosed; see, for example, how Sun Microsystems does it at www.sun.com/communities/guidelines.jsp).

- *Track your hubs.* Do you keep good records of them? Is your database accessible to others in the organization so they can draw on the information and update it?

- *Give your hubs what they need.* Do you provide hubs, especially expert hubs, with relevant facts? Are you putting the product in their hands?

- *Can you find people with an agenda?* Who are the people who will use your product/ideas/service to promote their own agenda? Can you link to that passion?

- *Can you find hubs in an existing structure?* For example, sometimes government or NGO officials or business leaders can give you access to lots of people.

"You've Got to Know the System"

Sometimes you find your hubs by working through the system. To spread the word about family planning methods in Thailand, Mechai Viravaidya first secured the support of the Thai government. Armed with a letter from the Ministry of Health, he was introduced to the district offices by governors of several provinces. He knew that these offices held a monthly meeting with all the village headmen, so Viravaidya and his staff went out to these meetings. "You've got to know the system," he says. To work with teachers, he went to the teachers' union and to the medical council of the teachers' union. "We trained them during the summer holidays, when they came for a special course to upgrade their qualifications," he explains. This way Viravaidya's group was able to train 320,000 teachers, who spread the word in their villages.

Have You Considered All Possible Techniques for Building Buzz?

Creating buzz is an active process: You have to work at it. Have you thought of everything you can do to make it happen?

- *Have you planned your grassroots seeding efforts?* Does your plan go beyond the "usual suspects" of your industry?

- *Are you ensuring experience?* You sent advance copies of your book to one thousand people? Good. But what can you do to ensure that they actually read it? When Grove/Atlantic promoted *Cold Mountain* to bookstores, it followed up the initial seeding with regional dinners where bookstore owners were invited to meet the author.

- *Can you limit access to your product* so that scarcity builds interest at the outset? (This tactic should be used selectively. It works best when there's significant anticipation for the product.)

- *Can you use a sneak preview* to capture the imagination of a selected group of customers?

- *What can you do that will surprise people?* People talk about the un- expected.

- *What's the most outrageous idea you can think of?* Write down several ideas like this, but read them again the next morning after drinking a good cup of coffee and answering the next question.

- *Can implementing this idea hurt anyone?* If the answer is yes, don't do it.

Will It Blend?

Watching a shiny new iPhone being dropped into a blender, where it is reduced to black powder, is something that lots of people will talk about. Proof: The blending iPhone video has been viewed more than 4 million times on YouTube. In his video series, Tom Dickson, the CEO of BlendTec, uses the company's blender to grind up items such as marbles, golf balls, iPhones, glow sticks—anything you can think of. Okay, the videos are funny and outrageous, but do kids who watch them on YouTube buy blenders as a result? Does the buzz translate into sales? As it turns out, it does. George Wright, the director of marketing for the company, reports that retail sales went up 500 percent in 2007. Part of the reason is that adults use YouTube too. In fact, 61 percent of YouTube users are over thirty-five (about half are women). Another reason it works is that the conversation hook (a guy blends unbelievable stuff) leads directly to the product benefit (this is one robust blender!). Viewer interaction is encouraged through comments and a special form that lets people suggest what Dickson should blend next. When the first videos ran, Wright was on the road, and he had the suggestions directed to his BlackBerry. In the next few days he got a very literal taste of buzz, thanks to the nonstop vibration of his BlackBerry! To date, BlendTec has gotten hundreds of thousands of suggestions from viewers and the videos have been watched more than 60 million times.

■ *Can you take your customers behind the scenes?* Can you show them how your product is made, who is making it, and why its producers are excited about it? (Even if you make a "boring" product, there must be something interesting in the way it's produced or in the way you came up with the idea.)

- *Does your story include a hero?* Is there a human drama behind your product? Is there a charismatic leader in your company? Can he or she blog?

- *Can you stage an event* that will feature your product and get people talking?

- *Can you create a simple (paper) pass-it-on promotion?* Does your Web site have a pass-it-on mechanism? Is it easy to use? Is it presented in a friendly, polite way?

- *Go beyond just "Tell a friend."* Encourage people to stop and think of people in their lives who might benefit from your product.

- *Can you create a conversation piece?* An item that people will carry around and that will trigger a conversation?

- *Can you create a specific message that's easy to pass along?* Here's an example from freerice.com, a site that helps you improve your vocabulary: "For each word you get right, we donate 20 grains of rice through the UN World Food Program to help end hunger." Notice how specific this message is.

- *Does it make sense to encourage your customers to post content?* Can they post pictures on Flickr? Videos on YouTube? Their experience on blogs?

- *Are your customers talking to one another?* The more your customers interact, the more involved they will become with your product and the more they will have to tell others. Can you find ways to help them socialize or exchange comments? Can you arrange face-to-face meetings, such as through special events?

- *Do you have a referral awards plan?* If so, do your customers like it and respond to it? Have you asked them for their feedback?

- *Is your product being given as a gift?* Can you stimulate your customers to do this more often?

Give a Brita. Plant a Tree.

For years Brita in Australia tried to stimulate recommendations by offering a free replacement filter cartridge to the purchaser if he or she passed on a card to a friend who subsequently bought a Brita too. The mechanics of this were cumbersome, though, and the results were mixed. In recent years the company started reaching for a higher cause while encouraging gift-giving. If you received your Brita as a gift, you could plant a tree in honor of another person. "We came to the belief that if a recommendation was made with good altruistic intent, rather than for personal material gain, it would be better received and more sincerely communicated on," says Michael Fisher of Brita Australia. "The results to date surely validate this insight." The promotion is done in partnership with a nonprofit organization, Greening Australia, as part of its River Recovery Program, so it ties nicely to the product benefits.

Are You Engaging People?

The more people think about your brand, the more likely they are to talk about it.

- *Can you encourage your customers to create something?* You can involve people in the creation of your advertising, your product, or anything else, really.
- *Can you encourage people to participate?* You can invite people to participate in something where the rules are well defined. The Bob Dylan video and the Monk-e-Mail are two excellent examples.
- *People love to include themselves.* Do you let people post their pictures or their names? Can people customize your product in a way that inspires them to share it with others?

- *Can you expand the duration of the experience?* (Without boring the user, of course.)
- *Can you create an experience that people will talk about?* For example, the Jeep Jamboree left a lasting impression because it engaged enthusiastic Jeep owners.

Are Your Ads Building Buzz?

The techniques for generating buzz don't necessarily end the need for conventional advertising. The challenge, though, is to advertise in a way that helps to build buzz, not dampen it.

- *Do your ads help people articulate what is unique about your product?* If your customers can't explain what is new or special about your product, they might be less effective when they tell their friends about it.
- *Can you use advertising to jump-start buzz for your product?*

Was Your Father a Thief?

BBNT is a fast-food chain with a handful of stores in Melbourne, Australia. To encourage young people to try its burgers, the company ran a campaign that's based on bad pickup lines. The staff was instructed that if anyone came in and said, "Was your father a thief?" they were to respond, "No, why?" Then if the customer replied, "Well, who stole the stars and put them in your eyes?" they were to give him or her a free cheeseburger. Twenty people around Melbourne were told about the promotion, and pretty soon the word got out. "What was really exciting about it was that people had to be a little bit brave," says Nick Cummins at Sputnik Agency, which ran the promotion. "Some people came in and chickened out halfway, fearing their friends were having a joke on them, especially when the staff answered 'No, why?' " But soon the campaign got so popular and so many free burgers were being handed out that the bad pickup line had to be changed to "Are you from Jamaica?" (Answer: "Cause Jamaican me crazy.") With only word of mouth, the campaign drove lots of young people to sample the burgers and positioned BBNT as a fun and irreverent brand.

- ■ *If you're using testimonials, are they credible?* Check with your customers: Their opinion may not be the same as yours.
- ■ *Do your ads help your customers,* such as by giving them useful information or by giving them facts that reinforce their reasons for buying?
- ■ *Can your ads be made clever enough to create buzz?* Think of the white milk mustaches or the catchphrase "What happens in Vegas stays in Vegas."
- ■ *Are your ads written in "marketing speak"?* Switch to plain English.

Are Your Resellers Building Buzz?

Some retailers can play a major role in spreading the word about your product.

- ■ *Have you identified the channels that are most promising in terms of buzz?* These are the channels that are most trusted by their customers.
- ■ *Are you in direct contact with the frontline people in these channels?* Build direct relationships not only with executives but with the people who talk to customers every day.

- *Have you seeded the channel?* And again, have you made sure that your seed products have reached the people who are actually talking with customers?
- *Can salespeople articulate what's new and special about your product?* Do you train them? Recognize them? Can they learn from your packaging what's special about your product?

How Can You Keep the Buzz Alive?

Buzz is mostly about newness. It's hard enough to get buzz going, and harder still to maintain it. What can you do?

- *Are you actively looking for new customers who haven't yet been exposed to your product?* Are there new market segments or new geographic areas you haven't yet reached? If your product is "old," has a new generation of potential users come along?
- *Are you supplying the networks with a constant flow of innovations that people can talk about?* The biggest enemy of buzz is routine. To keep buzz going over a long period of time, even a five-star restaurant has to change its menu and decor. Are you adding enhancements that will be worth talking about? Are you letting people know what's new and improved?
- *Are you keeping customers involved?* If your customers buy your product and never think about it again, you can't expect them to talk about it too much. However, if you involve them, engage them, make it interesting for them, they will talk.
- *Are you weaving buzz into your offering?* For example, by letting customers post reviews along with your product listings?

Is there a formula to creating buzz? When I talked to Dr. Yossi Vardi, who has invested in several companies that spread virally (including the widely successful ICQ), he made the point that there's usually an element of genius involved. "And there is no book for how to become Leonardo in three easy steps," Vardi said.

I agree. And this book can't give you the idea of the decade, or teach you how to be in the right place at the right time. But there are principles that can be learned and are worth repeating. In the same way that great art schools can't make you the next Leonardo but can teach color, composition, and perspective, I hope that this book has offered you a wealth of ideas that just might put your product into more conversations, more minds, and more shopping carts.

Notes

Web sites mentioned in the Notes can be accessed online at www.anatomyofbuzz.com.

Introduction

Everett Rogers is no longer here: See: Arvind Singhal and James W. Dearing, eds., *Communication of Innovations: A Journey with Ev Rogers* (New Delhi: Sage, 2006), and Everett Rogers, *The Fourteenth Paw: Growing Up on an Iowa Farm in the 1930s: A Memoir by Everett M. Rogers* (Singapore: AMIC, 2008).

1. Trigger

During the first few days of October: Interviews with Bruce Palmer, July 30, 2007, and Nov. 20, 2007; Amy Rathke, Nov. 1, 2007, and Nov. 20, 2007; Kary Sommers, Oct. 4, 2007; Matthew Copeland, Oct. 2, 2007; Brad Christensen, Nov. 20, 2007; Riley, Anne, and Sarah, Nov. 20, 2007. On Oct. 27, 2007, I spent a day with the bus crew—Andy Bassett, Paige Chambers, and Matt Celesta—in upstate New York. This is also where I interviewed alumni Randy, David, and Luke. On Nov. 20, 2007, I visited NOLS headquarters in Lander, WY, where I met students attending the fall semester. The bus blog can be accessed atnols.blogs.com; the bus story was described in NOLS's publication *The Leader*, available at www.nols.edu/alumni/leader/04fall/alumprofile_thomas_hand.shtml. Also see Bruce Palmer, "National Outdoor Leadership School: Have You Seen This Bus? The Intersection of Word of Mouth and Event Marketing," paper presented at WOMMA's Word of Mouth Basic Training, Jan. 19–20, 2006, Orlando, FL.

Before I go on, I need to define: For definitions of the different flavors of word-of-mouth marketing, see www.womma.org/wom101. In this book

I refer to everything a company does in order to stimulate talk among customers as word-of-mouth marketing. The firm's objective is to maximize the number of positive comments exchanged among customers.

The encounter reminds us: Mollie Conway's quote is from Blayne Cutler, "Hot Dog! (Oscar Mayer Marketing Efforts)," *American Demographics*, Dec. 1989, p. 39.

In the opening segment: Interview with Owen Matthews, Jan. 15, 2008; Steve Gorman, "Bob Dylan Has 'Homesick' Net Message," USAToday.com, Sept. 27, 2007.

In the last months of 1999: Interviews with Sandra B. Lawrence, Sept. 24, 2007, and Brian Poggi, Oct. 25, 2007. See Alec Klein, "The Techies Grumbled, but Polaroid's Pocket Turned into a Huge Hit," *Wall Street Journal*, May 2, 2000, p. A1; Cara Beardi, "I-Zone; Sandy Lawrence," *Advertising Age*, June 26, 2000, p. S8; and Todd Wasserman, "Re-Imaged Image Maker," *Brandweek*, Mar. 13, 2000, p. 22.

What prompted these comments?: Regarding the idea that experience is the deepest driver of buzz, see the Nielsen study in Pete Blackshaw, *Satisfied Customers Tell Three Friends, Angry Customers Tell 3,000* (New York: Doubleday, 2008), p. 124.

Here's how this idea works: Interview with Katie O'Brien, Sean Greenwood, and Liz Brenna, June 13, 2008. The quote is from Elaine Wong, "Ben & Jerry's, Sunkist, Indy Jones Unwrap Facebook's 'Gift of Gab,' " *Brandweek*, June 1, 2008, p. 7.

2. "I Haven't Read This Book, but . . ."

Robert East is a professor at Kingston: Interview with Robert East, Oct. 4, 2007. See Robert East, Kathy Hammond, and Malcolm Wright, "The Relative Incidence of Positive and Negative Word of Mouth: A Multi-Category Study," *International Journal of Research in Marketing* 24, 2 (2007): 175–84.

A good starting place is to look: The idea can be summarized in a simple matrix with two questions: "Did the recommender have the experience?" on one

		NEGATIVE	POSITIVE
EXPERIENCE	**YES**	*Experience-based detractors* "It sucks."	*Experience-based promoters* "I tried it. It's great."
	NO	*Secondhand detractors* "Joe says it sucks."	*Secondhand promoters* "Jeff says it's great."

OPINION

axis and "Was the recommender's opinion positive or negative?" on the other.

What about the secondhand promoters?: The statement that experience-based comments are more likely to bring sales is based on research from the Keller Fay Group, which found that 53 percent of the people who listen to *experience-based* positive word of mouth mark 9 or 10 on a 0–10 scale of likelihood to purchase the product. In the case of secondhand positive word of mouth, the percentage of people who mark the top boxes on likelihood to purchase drops from 53 percent to 33 percent.

Before you get too upset: Interview with Brad Fay, Oct. 26, 2007. The numbers were later updated by Keller Fay for the full year of 2007. Research on online reviews also shows that positive reviews outweigh negative reviews at a ratio of 8 to 1. See www.bazaarvoice.com/industryStats.html.

One explanation is that negative word of mouth: Interview with Barak Libai, Aug. 6, 2007. I described the case of Momenta in *The Anatomy of Buzz.*

Another explanation is that word of mouth is about solutions: Interview with Jon Berry, Sept. 13, 2007.

A third explanation has to do with the simple fact: Multiple sources, including interview with Andrea Wojnicki, Nov. 22, 2007, and Robert East, Oct. 4, 2007.

It's not enough to have "good word of mouth": The quote is from Robert East et al., *Consumer Behaviour: Applications in Marketing* (London: Sage, 2008), chap. 11.

3. The New Buzz

Sharing everyday experiences online: The report from Pew, "Teens and Social Media," is available at www.pewinternet.org/pdfs/PIP_Teens_Social_Media _Final.pdf.

At this point, it makes sense to return: Interviews with NOLS staff, as noted for Chapter 1. To see NOLS pictures on Flickr, go to www.flickr.com and type the word "NOLS" in the search items or click on the tag NOLS. To view activities on the NOLS alumni group on Facebook (you need to have a Facebook account), go to www.facebook.com/group.php?gid=2204758547.

It was Amy's job: Regarding the tech-savvy generation: A survey among 1,300-plus students at the University of Illinois, Chicago, showed that only 1.9 percent of respondents used Flickr sometimes or often; presentation by Dr. Eszter Hargittai at the "Beyond Broadcast" conference at Harvard Law School, May 12, 2006.

This is the other side of the new buzz: Interview with Bruce Ertmann, Nov. 7, 2007. The Toyota blog postings can be found at blog.toyota.com/2007/ 10/post.html. The Edmunds.com postings are from townhall-talk.edmunds. com. See also Steve Miller, "Q+A: Toyota CGM Exec Monitors the Good, the Blog, and the Ugly," *Brandweek*, Sept. 3, 2007, p. 8.

When Ruth Reichl moved from Los Angeles: Interview with Nina and Tim

Zagat, Oct. 29, 2007. The king of Spain story appears in Ruth Reichl, *Garlic and Sapphires: The Secret Life of a Critic in Disguise* (London: Penguin, 2005), pp. 35–53. For Sirio Maccioni's comments, see Sirio Maccioni and Peter Elliot, *Sirio: The Story of My Life and Le Cirque* (Hoboken, NJ: Wiley, 2004), p. 281.

In his book The Wisdom of Crowds: James Surowiecki, *The Wisdom of Crowds* (New York: Anchor, 2005), p. 10.

We see the world through filters: A report that demonstrates the focus of different filters was released by the Project for Excellence in Journalism. For one week in June 2007, the researchers monitored the news in mainstream media as well as in several user-news sites. While the mainstream press concentrated during that week on Iraq and immigration, the leading user-news sites—reddit, Digg, and del.icio.us—concentrated on the release of the iPhone and the fact that Nintendo had surpassed Sony in net worth. For more, see www.journalism.org/node/7493.

These tools are far from being ubiquitous: The data regarding Digg and Yelp are from research by Dr. Eszter Hargittai from Northwestern University. Hargittai reported on her 2006 study of more than 1,300 students at the "Beyond Broadcast" conference at Harvard Law School, May 12, 2006. She presented her 2007 data, on 1,060 students, at the Berkman Center for Internet and Society at Harvard Law School in October 2007, and she e-mailed some additional results to me. The facts that one in four Americans who use the Internet have read a review online and that 11 percent post ratings and reviews were reported in Charlene Li and Josh Bernoff, *Groundswell: Winning in a World Transformed by Social Technologies* (Boston: Harvard Business Press, 2008), p. 27.

In 2007 a marketing research company: Interview with Rex Briggs, Dec. 17, 2007. The full report, "Never Ending Friending," is available at www.myspace.com/neverendingfriending. The study was commissioned by Fox Interactive Media, Isobar, and CaratUSA. The research was conducted by TNS, TRU, and Marketing Evolution. See Abbey Klaassen, "What's Making 'Friends' with a MySpace User Worth?" Adage.com, Apr. 23, 2007. For a critical view of brands on MySpace, see Wade Roush, "Fakesters," *Technology Review*, Nov.-Dec., 2006, pp. 72–74.

4. Why Is Buzz on the Rise?

Why do we hear so much: The research about face-to-face word of mouth vs. online and telephone was done by the Keller Fay Group. Interview with Brad Fay, Oct. 26, 2007.

Something similar happened with the spread of Hotmail: "We would notice the first user from a university town or from India, and then the number of subscribers from that region would rapidly proliferate": Steve Jurvetson and Tim Draper, Viral Marketing, May 1, 1997, available at www.dfj.com. Similar wording can be found in Steve Jurvetson, "Turning Customers into a Sales Force," *Business 2.0*, Nov. 1998, pp. 102–108. This information is also based on my interviews with Jason Feffer, Aug. 15, 2007, and Steve Jurvetson, Dec. 4, 1998. For a description of the early days of Facebook, see John Cassidy, "Me Media: How Hanging Out on the Internet Became Big Business," *The New Yorker*, May 15, 2006, pp. 50–59.

In any area in life, there's someone: James C. Collins and Jerry I. Porras, *Built to Last: Successful Habits of Visionary Companies* (New York: HarperBusiness, 1994).

"Lockdown" is a song: Matthew J. Salganik, Peter S. Dodds, and Duncan J. Watts, "Experimental Study of Inequality and Unpredictability in an Artificial Cultural Market," *Science* 311 (2006): 854–856.

Who is considered the most credible source: The information on trust is based on the Edelman 2007 Trust Barometer, p. 7, available at www.edelman.com/trust/2007. In the 2008 study, "A person like me" was at the top, with 58 percent, followed closely by financial or industry analyst, academic, and doctor or health care specialist. See also Yankelovich press releases: "Consumer Resistance to Marketing Reaches All-Time High: Marketing Productivity Plummets, According to Yankelovich Study," Apr. 15, 2004, and "Consumer Trust Deficit Remains, Retailers Plan New Strategies," June 8, 2004.

There are other factors behind the increased attention: Interview with Piers Hogarth-Scott, Aug. 8, 2007.

How then do you engage people?: Interview with Jean-Louis Laborie, Jan. 28, 2008. Also see Ed Keller, "Unleashing the Power of Word of Mouth: Creating Brand Advocacy to Drive Growth," *Journal of Advertising Research* 47 (Dec. 2007): 448–452.

Yet another factor contributing to the increased attention: Interview with Paul Marsden, Oct. 11, 2007. Information about the Net Promoter Score can be found at www.netpromoter.com; Frederick F. Reichheld, "The One Number You Need to Grow," *Harvard Business Review* (Dec. 2003): 46–54; Fred Reichheld, *The Ultimate Question: Driving Good Profits and True Growth* (Boston: Harvard Business School Press, 2006); Paul Marsden, Alain Samson, and Neville Upton, "Advocacy Drives Growth," *Brand Strategy* (Dec. 2005): 45–47. For more on the debate regarding the predictive power of NPS, see, for example, Timothy L. Keiningham et al., "A Longitudinal Examination of Net Promoter and Firm Revenue Growth," *Journal of Marketing* 71 (July 2007): 39–51. Also see Paul Marsden, "Net Promoter: The Ultimate Debate on Customer Loyalty," Mycustomer.com, Sept. 17, 2007.

Indeed, research from all over the world validates: Nielsen's research found significant national and regional differences regarding the importance of word of mouth. The level of trust in other consumers is very high in certain places, such as Hong Kong (93 percent) and Taiwan (91 percent), and is lower in other places, such as Denmark (62 percent) and Italy (64 percent). An announcement of the study can be found atwww.nielsen.com/media/2007/pr_071001.html.

5. Can Buzz Be Measured?

Seven years later, I'm walking: The section about Keller Fay is based on interviews with Brad Fay, Sept. 13, 2007, and Oct. 26, 2007, and Jon Berry, Sept. 13, 2007. Numbers reported by Keller Fay were later updated for the full year of 2007; see Louise Story, "What We Talk About When We Talk About Brands," *New York Times*, Nov. 24, 2006, p. C7.

"When you do something significantly different": Ed Keller and Jim Kite, "When Words Speak Louder Than Actions: The Power of Conversation and How to Measure It," paper available at kellerfay.com.

With all the chatter on blogs: Interviews with Jonathan Carson, Aug. 13, 2007, and Kate Niederhoffer, Jan. 18, 2008. This section is also based on presentations at Nielsen's CGM Summit 2007, New York City, Oct. 25, 2007. BuzzMetrics's Web site is www.nielsenbuzzmetrics.com.

Why are marketers interested?: An example of underreporting of online activities was given by Nielsen/NetRatings in 2005. One of its studies found that almost 65 percent of individuals in an Internet panel who were observed visiting blog sites by the company in a thirty-day period responded that they had never visited a blog, had never heard of blogs, or had heard the term but were not really sure what it meant. See Charles Buchwalter, "The Blog Universe: Influencers, Early Adopters and Online Tenure Rolled into One," paper presented at WOMMA's Measuring Word of Mouth Conference, July 13, 2005, Chicago, IL.

Exploring online conversations: Interestingly, there are signs that smaller companies are ahead in monitoring word of mouth. In 2006, Jupiter Research reported that "sixty-six percent of small companies monitor [word of mouth] on an ongoing basis, compared to only 33 percent of large companies." See www.jupiterresearch.com/bin/item.pl/press:press_release/2006/id=06.06.12-word_of_mouth.html.

Measuring online buzz can also help in forecasting: Interview with Jonathan Carson, Aug. 13, 2007; Jonathan Carson, "Utilizing the WOMMA Framework to Build a Syndicated Buzz Tracking Product," *Measuring Word of Mouth* 1 (Summer 2005): 71–76.

Another study conducted by BuzzMetrics and BASES: Kate Niederhoffer et al., "The Origin and Impact of CPG New-Product Buzz: Emerging Trends and Implications," *Journal of Advertising Research* 47 (Dec. 2007): 420–426. The researchers also noted: "Even though both the aggregate data and the number of products that achieved strong buzz levels within this experiment were limited, this pattern was encouraging. The two products that received the strongest buzz levels were originally being under-forecasted on the basis of their consumer scores and marketing information alone; but the addition of buzz volume corrected this problem."

In recent years we've seen detailed studies: Interview with Dina Mayzlin, Sept. 21, 2007. The study is described in David Godes and Dina Mayzlin, "Firm-Created Word-of-Mouth Communication: A Field-Based Quasi-Experiment," Harvard Business School Marketing Research Paper No. 04–03, July 2004. The campaign is also described in Dave Balter and John Butman, *Grapevine: The New Art of Word-of-Mouth Marketing* (New York: Portfolio, 2005), pp. 93–101.

Some measurement efforts have gone beyond: Interview with Walter Carl, July 27, 2007. Names and specific locations have been changed to protect the identity of participants. For more details on the methodology, go to www.chatthreadscorp.com. (Dr. Carl is the founder and chief research officer at ChatThreads.) The study was described in Matt McGlinn and Walter Carl, "Measuring the Ripple: Creating the G2X Relay Rate and an Industry Standard Methodology to Measure the Spread of WOM Conversations and Marketing," *Measuring Word of Mouth* 3 (Autumn 2007): 37–46.

In the past few years: The Carnegie Mellon University study is Jure Leskovec, Lada A. Adamic, and Bernardo A. Huberman, "The Dynamics of Viral Marketing," *ACM Transactions on the Web* 1, no. 1 (2007). The numbers quoted are for a specific referral program: When a person bought an item, he or she could send e-mails recommending it to friends. The first person to purchase the same item through a referral link in the e-mail got a 10 percent discount and the sender got a 10 percent credit on the purchase. The study for the telecommunication company was reported in V. Kumar, J. Andrew Peterson, and Robert P. Leone, "How Valuable Is Word of Mouth?" *Harvard Business Review* (Oct. 2007): 139–146.

Other examples that involve buzz measurement: See Steve Hershberger, "The Evangelist Effect: Fact-Based Advocacy Measurement and Management," *Measuring Word of Mouth* 2 (Autumn 2006): 97–105; William L. Mosher, "Combining Several Metrics from the WOMMA Terminology Framework to Manage Consumer Expectations," *Measuring Word of Mouth* 2 (Autumn 2006): 43–52.

6. Insight and Buzz

When Shirley Polykoff was a kid: Shirley Polykoff, *Does She . . . Or Doesn't She? and How She Did It* (New York: Doubleday, 1975).

Fifty years later, a marketing team: Details on this case are available at business.tremor.com/work/herbalEssences.html. This section is also based on Steve Knox's closing address at the Duke University MBA Marketing Conference, Apr. 25, 2006, Durham, NC.

For Steve Knox, the CEO of Tremor: Interview with Steve Knox, Aug. 2, 2007. See also Todd Wasserman, "Q+A: P&G Buzz Program Tremor Moving on to Mothers," *Brandweek*, Sept. 26, 2005, p. 15.

Sculpting with clay is one: The Cranium story was told by Richard Tait at WOMMA's Word of Mouth Marketing Summit, Nov. 14–17, 2007, Las Vegas, NV.

In the case of Richard Tait: The information about Intuit's "follow me home" approach is from David Kirkpatrick, "Throw It at the Wall and See If It Sticks," *Fortune*, Dec. 12, 2005, pp. 142–150.

There are so many ways to listen: For more information on setting up a private online community, see Charlene Li and Josh Bernoff, *Groundswell: Winning in a World Transformed by Social Technologies* (Boston: Harvard Business Press, 2008), pp. 82–88, or visit companies such as www.communispace.com and networkedinsights.com.

Anyone who's run an online survey knows: Interviews with Laurent Florès, Sept. 10, 2007, and Sept. 28, 2007. Also see Thomas Crampton, "Consumers Vote for the Best Slogan," *International Herald Tribune*, Mar. 18, 2007; Laurent Florès and Mark Whiting, "What Can Research Learn from Biology?" *Admap* (Nov. 2005): 45–48; Laurent Florès, "Measuring the Impact of Word of Mouth," paper presented at WOMMA's Word of Mouth Basic Training, Jan. 19–20, 2006, Orlando, FL; Olivier Toubia and Laurent Florès, "Adaptive Idea Screening Using Consumers," *Marketing Science* 26 (May-June 2007): 342–360.

And another thought about listening: To get a sense of some stories that people share about customers, visit www.retailhell.info or www.customerssuck.com.

When Jackie Huba and Ben McConnell: Interview with Jackie Huba and Ben McConnell, Oct. 23, 2007.

7. Why We Talk

When Jimmy Carter was growing up: Jimmy Carter, *An Hour Before Daylight: Memories of a Rural Boyhood* (New York: Simon & Schuster, 2001), p. 59. Hobo signs can be found in Henry Dreyfuss, *Symbol Sourcebook: An Authoritative Guide to International Graphic Symbols* (New York: McGraw-Hill, 1972), pp. 90–91.

A hint to the answer can be found: The section about ravens is based on an interview with Bernd Heinrich, May 8, 1998, and on Bernd Heinrich and John Marzluff, "Why Ravens Share," *American Scientist* 83, no. 4 (1995): 342–349.

Another explanation for talking is our need: See Robin I. M. Dunbar, *Grooming,*

Gossip, and the Evolution of Language (Cambridge, MA: Harvard University Press, 1996).

While it's true that leaving these signs: Jonathan Frenzen and Kent Nakamoto, "Structure, Cooperation, and the Flow of Market Information," *Journal of Consumer Research* 20, no. 3 (Dec. 1993): 360–375.

In other cases we use products to send messages: Interview with Susan Fournier, Dec. 1998. See also Susan Fournier, "Consumers and Their Brands: Developing Relationship Theory in Consumer Research," *Journal of Consumer Research* 24, no. 4 (1998): 343–373.

This hidden agenda or mission helps explain: The quotes from readers of *Cold Mountain* are from interviews conducted in 1999.

"It all started in one of those little clothing factories": Charles W. Stevens, "Kmart Has a Little Trouble Killing Those Phantom Snakes from Asia," *Wall Street Journal*, Oct. 20, 1981, p. 29.

What does this mean?: In the first edition of this book, I wrote that venting our anger is the most common motivation behind negative word of mouth. I'm no longer sure that's true. People say negative things about a brand not only out of anger. They sometimes share an assessment that happens to be negative. See Dorothy Leonard-Barton, "Experts as Negative Opinion Leaders in the Diffusion of a Technological Innovation," *Journal of Consumer Research* 11 (Mar. 1985): 914–926.

Competitors often benefit: The information about the gas industry, FedEx, and Kodak are taken respectively from James M. Utterback, *Mastering the Dynamics of Innovation: How Companies Can Seize Opportunities in the Face of Technological Change* (Boston: Harvard Business School Press, 1994), p. 65; Robert A. Sigafoos, *Absolutely, Positively Overnight!: Wall Street's Darling Inside and Up Close* (Memphis: St. Luke's Press, 1983), p. 105; Douglas Collins, *The Story of Kodak* (New York: Abrams, 1990), p. 51.

When Andrea Wojnicki started working: Interview with Andrea Wojnicki, Nov. 22, 2007. The ten one-on-one interviews with consumers were conducted using the Zaltman Metaphor Elicitation Technique, developed by Dr. Jerry Zaltman. Also see Andrea C. Wojnicki and David Godes, "Word-of-Mouth as Self-Enhancement," Harvard Business School Marketing Research Paper No. 06–01, Apr. 25, 2008, available at ssrn.com/abstract=908999.

8. Hubs

Sean O'Driscoll knows not to refer: Interviews with Sean O'Driscoll, Sept. 28, 2007, and Nov. 14, 2007.

MVP Susan Bradley is such an expert hub: Interview with Susan Bradley, Feb. 1, 2008. Other MVPs interviewed are David Chin, Feb. 11, 2008, and Blaine Deal, Feb. 11, 2008.

So I went looking: Interview with Jia Shen, Aug. 21, 2007.

This is why I prefer the term "hub": The limitation of the word "leader," as in "opinion leader," was pointed out back in 1955. See Elihu Katz and Paul F. Lazarsfeld, *Personal Influence: The Part Played by People in the Flow of Mass Communications* (Glencoe, IL: Free Press, 1955), p. 138. Maven refers to "individuals who have information about many kinds of products, places to shop, and other facets of the market"; see Lawrence F. Feick and Linda L. Price, "The Market Maven: A Diffuser of Marketplace Information," *Journal of Marketing* 51, no. 1 (Jan. 1987): 83–97.

Peter Kellner is another MVP: Interview with Peter Kellner, Feb. 1, 2008.

The MVPs are an example: The information about Tremor's teen connectors is from Steve Knox's closing address at the Duke University MBA Marketing Conference, Apr. 25, 2006, Durham, NC. Note that the average number of names in an instant-messaging buddy list changes over the years.

Why are hubs so important?: Interview with Barak Libai, Aug. 6, 2007.

Ahead in adoption: For example, in 1997, 40 percent of influentials owned a cell phone, versus 24 percent of the total public. See Ed Keller and Jon Berry, *The Influentials: One American in Ten Tells the Other Nine How to Vote, Where to Eat, and What to Buy* (New York: Free Press, 2003), pp. 62–66. Regarding the positive correlation between innovativeness and opinion leadership, see Thomas W. Valente, *Network Models of the Diffusion of Innovations* (Cresskill, NJ: Hampton, 1995), p. 36; Gabriel Weimann, *The Influentials: People Who Influence People* (Albany: State University of New York Press, 1994), p. 175; and Everett M. Rogers, *Diffusion of Innovations,* 5th ed. (New York: Free Press, 2003), p. 27.

Travelers: The study of medical innovation is James Samuel Coleman, Elihu Katz, and Herbert Menzel, *Medical Innovation: A Diffusion Study* (Indianapolis: Bobbs-Merrill, 1966). Another classic study found that innovative farmers were more cosmopolite, as measured by their number of trips to the largest city in their state; see Rogers, *Diffusion of Innovations,* p. 34. His definition of cosmopoliteness is on p. 290. His assertion that opinion leaders are more cosmopolite is on p. 317.

Vocal: The data are from Keller and Berry, *The Influentials,* p. 146.

Exposed to the media: CRM Metrix found that 30 to 40 percent of visitors to brand Web sites happen to be category opinion leaders (interview with Laurent Florès, Sept. 10, 2007). The data about financial opinion leaders are from Barbara B. Stern and Stephen J. Gould, "The Consumer as Financial Opinion Leader," *Journal of Retail Banking* 10, no. 2 (1988): 43–52. For information on fashion, see John O. Summers, "The Identity of Women's Clothing Fashion Opinion Leaders," *Journal of Marketing Research* 7 (May 1970): 178–185.

How does Microsoft find its MVPs?: Interviews with Sean O'Driscoll, Sept. 28, 2007, and Nov. 14, 2007.

Identifying hubs through surveys: See Rogers, *Diffusion of Innovations,* pp. 308–312; Weimann, *The Influentials,* p. 35; and Tom Valente and Patchareeya Pumpuang, "Identifying Opinion Leaders to Promote Behaviour Change," *Health Education & Behavior* 34, no. 6 (Dec. 2007): 881–896. On identifying category-specific opinion leaders, see Laurent Florès, "A 10 Point Road Map to Planning and Measuring the ROI of WOM," *Measuring Word of Mouth* 1 (Summer 2005): 113–121, also available at www.crmmetrix.com.

Is there a way to avoid the bias: Interviews with Patrick Thoburn, Sept. 28, 2007, and Karen Stenner, Aug. 21, 2007.

Just one example: Interview with Patrick Thoburn and Matthew Stradiotto, Aug. 21, 2007.

Then a group of experts: Interview with Marc Schiller, July 17, 2007. In September 2007 I visited several of the sites in Chicago that participated in the campaign. Also see Lisa Leff, "Berkeley Church Tops List of Favorite Bay Area Landmarks," USAToday.com., Nov. 2, 2008. The campaign Web site is www.partnersinpreservation.org.

Judy Porta is part of the Friends: Interview with Judy Porta, Aug. 5, 2007.

Passion and interest should not be ignored: Interview with Paul Marsden, Oct. 11, 2007.

In 2007, Dr. Duncan Watts: Duncan J. Watts and Peter S. Dodds, "Influentials, Networks, and Public Opinion Formation," *Journal of Consumer Research* 34 (Dec. 2007): 441–458; Duncan Watts et al., "Breakthrough Ideas for 2007," *Harvard Business Review* (Feb. 2007): 20–54; Todd Wasserman, "Buzz-Kill: Columbia Prof Blasts Influencer Model," *Brandweek,* Mar. 5, 2007, p. 9; Matthew Creamer, "What's Plaguing Viral Marketing; Sorry, Malcolm, But the Tipping Point Might Be More Myth than Math," *Advertising Age,* July 16, 2007, p. 1; Clive Thompson, "Is the Tipping Point Toast?" *Fast Company,* Feb. 2008, pp. 74–78.

So what is Watts arguing?: The quote about how some people are more influential than others is from Duncan Watts, "Challenging the Influentials Hypothesis," *Measuring Word of Mouth* 3 (Autumn 2007): 204.

Threshold models have been used: Watts's "almost comically simple" comment is from "Word of Mouth Marketing: How It Works and the Role of 'Influencers,' " discussion at the Avertising Research Foundation, Sept. 26, 2007, New York, NY.

Still, there are many examples from the trenches: Brian Maxwell's quote is from an interview on Nov. 19, 1998.

Another example of the effectiveness of hubs: I don't want to oversimplify things and attribute the success of *The Purpose-Driven Life* solely to the hub strategy. Other factors played a role in this success story, but Warren clearly used his established connections with pastors to launch the book. This example is based on Greg Stielstra, *PyroMarketing: The Four-Step Strategy to Ignite Customer Evangelists and Keep Them for Life* (New York: HarperBusiness, 2005), pp. 78–79, 96. In his discussion, Stielstra doesn't focus on the pastors as hubs or opinion leaders but on their role as "the driest tinder," which is his term to describe the people most likely to buy. See also Greg Stielstra, "Up in Flame," *Advertising Age* Dec. 2005, pp. 14–18. Rick Warren's quote about the influence of pastors is from Linton Weeks and Alan Cooperman, "Faith, Moving Mountains of Books; Rick Warren's Spiritual Bestseller Is a Nontraditional-Marketing Miracle," *Washington Post*, Feb. 22, 2004, p. D1; Warren is also quoted in this article, describing the spread of his book: "I did not do a book tour, all the things you normally do to promote a book. What I did was, I created a new distribution channel—I went direct to these pastors who have loved me and trusted me for years." Indeed, Warren's credibility among pastors is significant. When 614 pastors of Protestant churches were asked in 2005 to identify up to three individuals whom they believe have the greatest influence on churches and church leaders in the United States, 26 percent named Rick Warren, who was second only to Billy Graham, with 34 percent. See www.barna.org.

Prior to the publication of Stielstra's book, Warren issued a statement that reads in part: "The worldwide spread of the purpose-driven message had nothing to do with marketing or merchandizing. Instead it was the result of God's supernatural and sovereign plan, which no one anticipated." While Warren didn't question the effectiveness of "pyromarketing," he asserted that it didn't create the *Purpose-Driven Life* worldwide phenomenon and that no one, including Zondervan and he himself, can claim credit for the book's success. See Juli Cragg Hilliard, "Purpose-Driven Interference?" *Publishers Weekly*, July 25, 2005, pp. 14–15; Juli Cragg Hilliard, " 'Pyro' Goes Ahead; Warren Weighs In," *Publishers Weekly*, Aug. 29, 2005, p. 9.

When I asked Steve Knox: Interview with Steve Knox, Aug. 2, 2007.

In the mid-1980s, Canadian physicians: Interview with Jonathan Lomas, July 5, 1999. Also see Jonathan Lomas et al., "Do Practice Guidelines Guide Practice? The Effect of a Consensus Statement on the Practice of Physicians," *New England Journal of Medicine* 321, no. 19 (1989): 1306–1311; and Jonathan Lomas et al., "Opinion Leaders vs. Audit and Feedback to Implement Practice Guidelines. Delivery After Previous Cesarean Section," *Journal of the American Medical Association* 265, no. 17 (1991): 2202–2207.

Watts's work reminds us: And yes, I need to be reminded of this occasionally too. I got carried away in one place in *The Anatomy of Buzz* and wrote that hubs are "the key to influencing the network" (although I had several examples of buzz created without their help).

9. It's a Small World. So What?

Even in the most familiar environments: Interviews with David Krackhardt, June 15, 1999, and Stacy Horn, June 4, 1998. See David Krackhardt and Jeffrey R. Hanson, "Informal Networks: The Company Behind the Chart," *Harvard Business Review* (July-August 1993): 104–111; and Stacy Horn, *Cyberville: Clicks, Culture, and the Creation of an Online Town* (New York: Warner, 1998), p. 231.

Okay, but is this still true today?: The Facebook group, "Facebook, stop invading my privacy!" can be found at www.facebook.com/group.php?gid= 5930262681. Mark Zuckerberg's apology is at blog.facebook.com/blog. php?post=2208562130. Zuckerberg discussed Beacon during an interview with Kara Swisher at D: All Things Digital conference, Carlsbad, California, May 28, 2008; interview with Harald Katzmair, Jan. 9, 2008.

As innocent as this principle may sound: The information about PowerBar is based on an interview with Brian Maxwell, Nov. 19, 1998.

The homophily principle: The Nintendo case is described in David Sheff, *Game Over: How Nintendo Zapped an American Industry, Captured Your Dollars, and Enslaved Your Children* (New York: Random House, 1993). I also interviewed Shef on Apr. 22, 1998. The quote from Helen Rockey is from an interview my assistant, Kerry Shaw, conducted with her in Apr. 1999.

Why do Hell's Angels travel in packs?: For why churches, clubs, and professional organizations are so homogeneous, see Pamela A. Popielarz and J. Miller McPherson, "On the Edge or In Between: Niche Position, Niche Overlap, and the Duration of Voluntary Association Memberships," *American Journal of Sociology* 101, no. 3 (1995): 698–720.

Clusters and cliques are so common: The jail story is told briefly in two places: H. Russell Bernard and Peter Killworth, "The Search for Social Physics," *Connections* 20, no. 1 (1997): 16–34; and Dan Seligman, "Me and Monica," *Forbes*, Mar. 23, 1998, pp. 76–77.

Clusters can informally adopt: The Korean villages study is from Rogers, *Diffusion of Innovations*, p. 333. For comprehensive coverage of this study, see Everett M. Rogers and D. Lawrence Kincaid, *Communication Networks: Toward a New Paradigm for Research* (New York: Free Press, 1981).

The social psychologist Stanley Milgram: Stanley Milgram, "The Small-World Problem," *Psychology Today,* May 1967, pp. 60–67.

Incidentally, in 2002 researchers from Columbia: Peter S. Dodds, Roby Muhamad, and Duncan J. Watts, "An Experimental Study of Search in Global Social Networks," *Science* 301 (2003): 827–829.

Ronald Burt of the University of Chicago: Ronald S. Burt, *Structural Holes: The Social Structure of Competition* (Cambridge, MA: Harvard University Press, 1992), p. 18. For a review of Burt's work as it applies to marketing, see Peter

H. Reingen, "Structural Holes: The Social Structure of Competition," book review, *Journal of Marketing* 58 (Jan. 1994): 152–155.

Imagine a woman from California: Interview with Margot Fraser, Dec. 22, 1998. The sales figures for Birkenstock are from Michael Lewis, "The Irresponsible Investor," *New York Times*, June 6, 2004, p. 68.

Shortcuts that connect clusters: The idea is discussed in several sources: Duncan J. Watts and Steven H. Strogatz, "Collective Dynamics of 'Small-World' Networks," *Nature* 393, June 4, 1998, pp. 440–442; James J. Collins and Carson C. Chow, "It's a Small World," ibid., pp. 409–410; and Duncan J. Watts, *Six Degrees: The Science of a Connected Age* (New York: Norton, 2003).

Another example of people who: The concept of venture capitalists as connectors was described in Everett M. Rogers and Judith K. Larsen, *Silicon Valley Fever* (New York: Basic Books, 1984).

Barry Wellman and David B. Tindall: Barry Wellman and David B. Tindall, "How Telephone Networks Connect Social Networks," *Progress in Communication Science* 12 (1993): 63–94, and Thomas J. Allen, *Managing the Flow of Technology: Technology Transfer and the Dissemination of Technological Information within the R&D Organization* (Cambridge, MA: MIT Press, 1977). At a 2008 roundtable organized by McKinsey, Bo Cowgill, who manages Google's prediction markets, shared some insights about how information moves around the company: "Beliefs are clustered, and these clusters are made up of individuals who physically sit and work close to each other, not only at the level of city and country, but at the microlevel of the office floor, measured in feet or meters between desks." See Renée Dye, "The Promise of Prediction Markets: A Roundtable," *McKinsey Quarterly*, July 1, 2008, available at www.mckinseyquarterly.com.

In the same way that regional dialects: See "U.S. Dialects Persist by Both Region and Race," *Science* 279, Feb. 27, 1998, p. 1311.

In the late 1960s, Mark Granovetter: Interview with Mark Granovetter, June 11, 1999; Mark Granovetter, *Getting a Job: A Study of Contacts and Careers*, 2nd ed. (Chicago: University of Chicago Press, 1995); Jacqueline Johnson Brown and Peter H. Reingen, "Social Ties and Word-of-Mouth Referral Behavior," *Journal of Consumer Research* 14, no. 3 (1987): 350–362. Barak Libai pointed out to me that the strength of weak ties effect is also at work in spreading *bad* news, as shown by him and his colleagues in Jacob Goldberg et al., "The NPV of Bad News," *International Journal of Research in Marketing* 24, no. 3 (Sept. 2007): 186–200.

Strong-tie buzz has a different impact: Interview with Brad Fay, Oct. 26, 2007. The numbers were updated by Keller Fay for the full year 2007.

It's easy to maintain weak ties on the Internet: Interview with Valdis Krebs, Aug. 10, 1999. Also see Barry Wellman and Milena Gulia, "Net-Surfers Don't Ride Alone: Virtual Communities as Communities," in *Networks in the Global*

Village: Life in Contemporary Communities, ed. Barry Wellman (Boulder, CO: Westview, 1999), pp. 331–366.

This explosion in weak ties: See Robin I. M. Dunbar, *Grooming, Gossip, and the Evolution of Language* (Cambridge, MA: Harvard University Press, 1996).

It is difficult to determine how many links: Ibid., pp. 76–77. As to the number of acquaintances, scholars are reluctant to come up with an exact number. The numbers I mention here are rough estimates mentioned in the literature.

In the late 1980s a company called Gojo: Hanna Rosin, "America's Obsession with Germs," *New Republic,* Nov. 10, 1997, p. 24; Jack Neff, "Purell: Sandor Katz," *Advertising Age,* June 28, 1999, p. S28; Michael J. Dolan, "Can a Category-Defining Brand Be Created with No Portfolio Management, No Stage-Gate, and Back-of-the-Envelope Calculations?" Paper presented at the annual international conference of the Product Development and Management Association, Oct. 12–16, 2002, Orlando, FL.

10. How Buzz Spreads

I should make one point: Gabriel Tarde, *The Laws of Imitation* (New York: Holt, 1903); Gabriel Weimann, *The Influentials: People Who Influence People* (Albany: State University of New York Press, 1994).

Charles Frazier first heard: The section about *Cold Mountain* is based on interviews with Leigh Feldman, Feb. 1, 1999; Elisabeth Schmitz, May 1, 1999; Morgan Entrekin, Jan. 29, 1999; Mike Barnard, May 17, 1999; and Patricia Kelly, Apr. 30, 1999. I also interviewed about a dozen readers of *Cold Mountain,* including Mike Jordan, Jan. 29, 1999; Jo Alice Canterbury, May 24, 1999; and Lynne Jenkins, Jan. 28, 1999. Additional sources include Steven M. Zeitchik, "PW's Rep of the Year: Patricia Kelly, Publishers Group West," *Publishers Weekly,* Apr. 5, 1999, pp. 41–45; Martin Arnold, "A Success a Year Later," *New York Times,* May 27, 1999, p. B3.

Based on the model I've described: We are not only motivated by wanting to be like everyone else. We also want to be special. So it may be that after hearing all the buzz about *Cold Mountain,* you will object to reading the book. For more on this "crowding effect," see Mark Granovetter and Roland Soong, "Threshold Models of Interpersonal Effects in Consumer Demand," *Journal of Economic Behavior and Organization* 7 (1986): 83–99. In some cases, unsolicited advice that contradicts the consumer's initial impressions may create a backlash. See Gavan J. Fitzsimons and Donald R. Lehmann, "Reactance to Recommendations: When Unsolicited Advice Yields Contrary Responses," *Marketing Science* 23 (Winter 2004): 82–94.

This last point has not gotten too much attention: Jonah Berger and Chip Heath, "Where Consumers Diverge from Others: Identity-Signaling and

Product Domains," *Journal of Consumer Research* 34, no. 2 (2007): 121–134. The wristband study is described in Jonah Berger and Chip Heath, "Who Drives Divergence? Identity-Signaling, Outgroup Dissimilarity, and the Abandonment of Cultural Tastes," *Journal of Personality and Social Psychology* 95, no. 3 (2008) 593–607. Berger's quote is from "From Cool to Passé: Identity Signaling and Product Domains," Knowledge@Wharton, the online business journal of the Wharton School of the University of Pennsylvania, Sept. 5, 2007.

The higher the monetary or psychological risks: See Rogers, *Diffusion of Innovations*, Chap. 7, about adopter categories.

Why are the two types of buzz different?: Michael E. Porter, "Clusters and the New Economics of Competition," *Harvard Business Review* (Nov.-Dec. 1998): 77–90.

11. Contagious Products

"Gale and Lida, you are genius goddesses": Interviews with Gale Epstein and Lida Orzeck, Oct. 29, 2007, and Wendy Bounds, Dec. 10, 2007. See also Gwendolyn Bounds, "A Tiny Scrap of Fabric Wins a Huge Following," *Wall Street Journal*, June 18, 2004, p. A1.

In fact, Hanky Panky's founders: The section on Kodak is based on Douglas Collins, *The Story of Kodak* (New York: Abrams, 1990).

Hawkins knew exactly what: See Andrea Butter and David Pogue, *Piloting Palm: The Inside Story of Palm, Handspring, and the Birth of the Billion-Dollar Handheld Industry* (New York: Wiley, 2002). Karl Townsend's quote is from p. 86. Information here is also drawn from interviews with Ed Colligan, Apr. 23, 1998, and Mar. 18, 1999.

Fear, of course, is an emotion that evokes: The case of 20Q is discussed in Matt McGlinn, "Measuring BzzCampaign Word-of-Mouth Activity Using the WOMMA Terminology Framework," *Measuring Word of Mouth* 1 (Summer 2005): 157–161.

Sometimes the feeling of delight is achieved: The Palm case is based on interviews with Ed Colligan, Apr. 23, 1998, Mar. 18, 1999; Andy Reinhardt, Aug. 17, 1999; and Rafe Needleman, Aug. 16, 1999. I also interviewed several Palm users in 1999.

Colligan sounds almost apologetic: It's amazing how many times Palm users I talked to mentioned this simple fact: "The Palm does exactly what it's supposed to do." Seybold's quote is from an interview, May 28, 1998.

What happens next depends on cultural norms: Lida Orzeck's story and Gale Epstein's quote are from my interview with them, Oct. 29, 2007.

Social learning of this kind plays a major role: Barry Schwartz's quote is from a 1999 interview with him.

Another product that has spread this way: Interview with Dave Kapell, Apr. 30, 1999.

One interesting part of this network effect: Interview with Jason Feffer, Aug. 15, 2007.

Researchers theorize that: In an article on viral sentences, Douglas Hofstadter mentions the work of the biologist Jacques Monod, who wrote in 1970 about the "spreading power" of ideas that may depend upon "preexisting structures in the mind." See Douglas R. Hofstadter, *Metamagical Themas: Questing for the Essence of Mind and Pattern* (New York: Basic Books, 1985), p. 50.

Compatibility often is a matter: See Rogers, *Diffusion of Innovations*, p. 41. Rogers mentions the French sociologist Gabriel Tarde in this regard, who in 1903 pointed out that innovations similar to ideas that have been already accepted are more likely to be adopted; see p. 249. The boiling water story appears on pp. 1–5.

Keep in mind that the beliefs: See, for example: "More Cities Join Anti-Bottled Water Movement," www.msnbc.msn.com/id/21214017.

12. Accelerating Natural Contagion

Linda Pezzano was really after: Interview with Linda Pezzano, Oct. 24, 1998; Louise Bernikow, "Trivia Inc.: It's a Simple Board Game, but for Its Founders the Prize Was Joy, Sorrow, and a Multimillion-Dollar Conglomerate." *Esquire*, Mar. 1985, p. 116; Philip H. Dougherty, "Advertising; Trivial Pursuit Campaign," *New York Times*, July 17, 1984, p. 47; Douglas Martin, "[Obituaries] Linda Pezzano, 54, Marketer Who Aided 'Trivial Pursuit,' " *New York Times*, Oct. 28, 1999, p. C24. The case is also described briefly in Thomas L. Harris, *The Marketer's Guide to Public Relations: How Today's Top Companies Are Using the New PR to Gain a Competitive Edge* (New York: Wiley, 1991).

Imagine that you're a buyer at a toy store: Answers to Trivia questions: The largest city between Ireland and Canada is Reykjavik, Iceland. John Wayne played football at USC. Elvis Presley's middle name was Aaron. A nonagon has nine sides. Al Capone's nickname was Scarface. The word "Mafia" was intentionally omitted from the screenplay of *The Godfather*. George Washington Carver invented peanut butter.

Another part of the promotion: More answers to Trivia questions: Queen Elizabeth II was *Time*'s Man of the Year for 1952. Before World War II, World War I was known as the Great War. J&B stand for Justerini & Brooks.

Chris Byrne was in his twenties: Interview with Chris Byrne, Oct. 26, 2007.

Or someone like Ted Sartoian: Interview with Ted Sartoian, Jan. 12, 1999. Also see Robert A. Sigafoos, *Absolutely, Positively Overnight!: Wall Street's Darling Inside and Up Close* (Memphis: St. Luke's Press, 1983).

13. The Envelope and the Line

Waiting for a movie to start: This section is based on Justin Foxton's article "Live Buzz Marketing" in Justin Kirby and Paul Marsden, *Connected Marketing: The Viral, Buzz and Word of Mouth Revolution* (Oxford: Butterworth-Heinemann, 2006), pp. 32–34; interviews with Justin Foxton, July 29, 2007, and Vanessa Pike, Jan. 17, 2008; video clip of the theater event, available at www.commentuk.co.uk/tflmotorsaftey.html.

People in London certainly talked: The quote is from John Wigram, "Shocking, but Is It Relevant?" *Financial Times*, Feb. 18, 2003, p. 32.

Let's look at another example: More about the *60 Minutes* program, "Undercover Marketing Uncovered: Hidden Cameras Capture Salespeople Secretly Pitching Products," which aired on July 25, 2004, can be found at www.cbsnews.com/stories/2003/10/23/60minutes/main579657.shtml.

I was happy to see: WOMMA's code of ethics is available at www.womma.org/ethics/code. See also Jim Nail and Steve Hershberger, "Solid Ethics for a Changing Landscape," paper presented at WOMMA's Word of Mouth Marketing Summit, Nov. 14–17, 2007, Las Vegas, NV.

I don't really think that the question: For example, as of May 2008, undercover marketing is illegal in the U.K. See Emma Hall, "U.K. Cracks Down on Word-of-Mouth with Tough Restrictions," *Advertising Age*, Apr. 28, 2008, p. 132.

BzzAgent requires its members: BzzAgent's guidelines are available at www.bzzagent.com. Steve Knox's quote is from an interview Aug. 2, 2007. See also Rob Walker, "The Hidden (In Plain Sight) Persuaders," *New York Times Magazine*, Dec. 5, 2004, pp. 68–75.

There are also special questions: Roshan D. Ahuja et al., "Teen Perceptions of Disclosure in Buzz Marketing," *Journal of Consumer Marketing* 24, no. 3 (2007): 151–159.

I believe that marketers who get involved: Regarding the point that agents who disclose their affiliation with the company are not less effective than the ones who don't, see "To Tell or Not to Tell?: Assessing the Practical Value of Disclosure for Word-of-Mouth Marketing Agents and Their Conversational Partners," 2006, available at www.waltercarl.neu.edu/downloads. The research showed that the pass-along rate was actually higher when the conversational partner was aware that he or she was talking with a participant in an organized word-of-mouth program, but Dr. Carl said in an interview (July 27, 2007) that other factors may have contributed to this. "I think that the most important takeaway from it is that it's not lower," he said. Another point to keep in mind is the fact that most BzzAgents and their conversation partners are friends, coworkers, or acquaintances with an initial level of trust. This means that disclosure may not work the same way with complete strangers. The academic version of this paper is Walter Carl, "The Role of Disclosure in Organized Word-of-Mouth Marketing Programs," *Journal of Marketing Communications* 14, no. 3 (2008); 225–241. For a game theoretic model of the issue, see Dina Mayzlin, "Promotional Chat on the Internet," *Marketing Science* 25, no. 2 (Mar.-Apr. 2006): 155–163.

People have a wide range of attitudes: E-mail from Scott Cook, Jan. 28, 1999.

But incentives can work: Two researchers, Jochen Wirtz and Patricia Chew, argue that incentives may be an effective way to get satisfied customers to recommend a firm. See Wirtz and Chew, "The Effects of Incentives, Deal Proneness, Satisfaction and Tie Strength on Word-of-Mouth Behaviour," *International Journal of Service Industry Management* 13, no. 2 (2002): 141–162.

In 2005, Creative Commons: A good starting point for this story can be found at lessig.org/blog/2005/05/bzzzz_seeking_advice.html.

Unfortunately, there are plenty of examples: For more on the reaction to the Aqua Teen Hunger Force campaign, see Michael Levenson et al., "Marketing Gambit Exposes a Wide Generation Gap," *Boston Globe*, Feb. 1, 2007, p. A1. For some of the consequences (which included $1 million paid by Turner), see Jenna Russell et al., "Criminal Charges Dropped in Marketing Stunt— Two Men Apologize for January Scare," *Boston Globe*, May 12, 2007, p. A1.

14. Active Seeding

In 2001 Miramax hired: Interview with Marc Schiller, July 17, 2007. For details on the Christina Aguilera campaign, see Erin White, " 'Chatting' a Singer Up the Pop Charts—How Music Marketers Used the Web to Generate Buzz Before an Album Debuted," *Wall Street Journal*, Oct. 5, 1999, p. B1.

How did a movie that got such positive: See David Godes and Dina Mayzlin, "Using Online Conversations to Study Word-of-Mouth Communication," *Marketing Science* 23, no. 4 (2004): 545–560; interview with Dina Mayzlin, Sept. 21, 2007.

To accelerate the rate: Barak Libai et al., "The Role of Seeding in Multi-Market Entry," *International Journal of Research in Marketing* 22 (Dec. 2005) 375–393.

Numbers make a difference: See Greg Stielstra, *PyroMarketing: The Four-Step Strategy to Ignite Customer Evangelists and Keep Them for Life* (New York: Harper-Business, 2005), pp. 68, 78–79, 96. Based also on Greg Stielstra, "How to Create a Best-Selling Book with WOM," paper presented at WOMMA's Word of Mouth Basic Training, Jan. 19–20, 2006, Orlando, FL. For additional sources, see notes to an earlier mention of this case in Chapter 8.

Tom Peters also attributes: Tom Peters, *Thriving on Chaos: Handbook for a Management Revolution* (New York: HarperPerennial, 1987); interview with Edward Burlingame, Jan. 8, 1999. Regarding Harper & Row's concern,

Edward Burlingame said, "Peters might be right about H&R's concern about their giving away 15,000 of the report, but I don't remember this."

Because information can get stuck: Seeding wasn't necessarily the main reason Microsoft sent out these copies. Fifty thousand were distributed as part of the beta testing program. The other 400,000 copies were distributed to enable IT professionals to plan their move to the new operating system. Regardless of the motivation, there was an enormous number of advance copies out there.

Here's a little riddle: Duncan J. Watts and Jonah Peretti, "Viral Marketing for the Real World," *Harvard Business Review* (May 2007): 22–23. A more detailed version of the article (with an additional author, Michael Frumin) is available at cdg.columbia.edu/uploads/papers/watts2007_viralMarketing.pdf.

The seeding that took place: Interview with Matthew Stradiotto, Aug. 21, 2007. The Sonicare campaign is described in Matt McGlinn and Walter Carl, "Measuring the Ripple: Creating the G2X Relay Rate and an Industry Standard Methodology to Measure the Spread of WOM Conversations and Marketing," *Measuring Word of Mouth* 3 (Autumn 2007): 37–46.

15. Story

The author Stephen Denning argues: See Stephen Denning, *The Leader's Guide to Storytelling: Mastering the Art and Discipline of Business Narrative* (San Francisco: Jossey-Bass, 2005), p. 62. For a good discussion of stories, see Chip Heath and Dan Heath, *Made to Stick: Why Some Ideas Survive and Others Die* (New York: Random House, 2007), pp. 204–237.

So let me tell you a story: Interview with Blake Mycoskie, Feb. 12, 2008; Nadia Mustafa, "The Shoe That Fits So Many Souls," *Time*, Feb. 5, 2007, p. C2; Jennifer Irwin, "Alpargata's New Step," *International Herald Tribune*, Jan. 18, 2007, p. 12.

Here's how that story unfolded: Booth Moore, "They're Flipping for *Alpargatas*," *Los Angeles Times*, May 20, 2006, p. E1.

Remember, facts alone don't do the trick: Regarding the persuasiveness of stories, see Joanne Martin, "Stories and Scripts in Organizational Settings," in A. H. Hastorf and A. M. Isen, eds., *Cognitive Social Psychology* (New York: Elsevier-North Holland, 1982), pp. 225–305. See also Heath and Heath, *Made to Stick*, pp. 272–273, on how stories affect jury decision-making.

Luigi Pirandello, the Italian playwright: I first came across this quote in Annette Simmons, *The Story Factor: Secrets of Influence from the Art of Storytelling* (Cambridge, MA: Perseus, 2001), p. 49. It comes from Luigi Pirandello, *Six Characters in Search of an Author* (London: Penguin. 1995), p. 25 (a slightly different translation).

A lot of good business stories: Interviews with Blake Mycoskie, Feb. 12,

2008; Brian Maxwell, Nov. 19, 1998; and Dave Kapell, Apr. 30, 1999. Regarding stories within a brand community, see Albert M. Muniz Jr. and Thomas C. O'Guinn, "Brand Community," *Journal of Consumer Research* 27, no. 4 (Mar. 2001): 412–432.

You don't have to be a giant company: More about Schaub's can be found in Stett Holbrook, "Little Shop on the Corner," *San Francisco Chronicle,* Feb. 5, 2003, p. FD 1.

Ask your customers to tell their stories: From the Coca-Cola Web site, www. thecocacolacompany.com/heritage/pdf/stories/Heritage_CokeStories _ROMANCE.pdf. More stories can be found at www.thecoca-colacompany. com/heritage/stories/index.html.

16. Give Us Something to Talk About

One day in 1974: Interviews with Mechai Viravaidya, Sept. 22, 2007, and Arvind Singhal, Aug. 17, 2007; Thomas D'Agnes, *From Condoms to Cabbages: An Authorized Biography of Mechai Viravaidya* (Bangkok: Post, 2001); Glenn A. Melnick, "From Family Planning to HIV/AIDS Prevention to Poverty Alleviation: A Conversation with Mechai Viravaidya," *Health Affairs* 26, no. 6 (2007): w670–w677; Mechai Viravaidya, "The Population and Community Development Association in Thailand," in Anirudh Krishna et al., eds., *Reasons for Hope: Instructive Experiences in Rural Development* (West Hartford, CT: Kumarian, 1997), pp. 203–215. Also see Arvind Singhal and Everett M. Rogers, *Combating AIDS: Communication Strategies in Action* (New Delhi: Sage, 2003).

Outside observers have taken: Daulaire's quote is from the Gates Foundation Web site, www.gatesfoundation.org/GlobalHealth/Announcements/ Announce-070529.htm. Rosenfield and Potts's quote is from their foreword to D'Agnes, *From Condoms to Cabbages*.

Mechai Viravaidya is not only: D'Agnes, *From Condoms to Cabbages*, p. 279. The statistics about population growth are from PDA's Web site, www. pda.or.th/eng.

"Put the pedal to the metal!": Of course, the "volunteer" may have been a BMW person, but this did not change the impact of the presentation.

As with everything else, some publicity stunts: Candice Fuhrman, *Publicity Stunt!* (San Francisco: Chronicle, 1989). I had the opportunity to watch a recorded interview with the late Marty Weiser in which he described this publicity stunt.

Moss Kadey, who introduced Brita: Interview with Moss Kadey, Sept. 6, 2007.

Contrast these examples to a publicity stunt: Interview with Linda Pezzano, Oct. 24, 1998.

Can a top executive be a conversation hook?: The study about celebrity CEOs is from James Hamilton and Richard Zeckhauser, "Media Coverage of CEOs:

Who? What? Where? When? Why?" Working Paper, 2004, available at www.stanford.edu/~wacziarg/mediapapers/HamiltonZeckhauser.pdf.

The woman who wrote this: James Dyson, *Against the Odds: An Autobiography* (New York: Texere, 2003); Iain Carruthers, *Great Brand Stories: Dyson: The Domestic Engineer—How Dyson Changed the Meaning of Cleaning* (London: Cyan, 2007).

There's also a category: The tax rap site is at turbotax.intuit.com/taxrap.

In 2006, White Castle: Andy Sernovitz, *Word of Mouth Marketing: How Smart Companies Get People Talking* (Chicago: Kaplan, 2006), p. 15.

These are the exceptions: Viravaidya's quote is from Melnick, "From Family Planning to HIV/AIDS Prevention," p. w676.

17. The Power of Participation

Anders Søborg built a candy machine: Interview with Anders Søborg, Dec. 20, 2007. His Web site is www.norgesgade14.dk.

Lego benefits greatly: There are several Mindstorms robots that solve the Rubik's Cube. This one is "Danny's Mindstorms NXT Rubik Cube Solver," at www.youtube.com/watch?v=3QOvEG27Gt4.

Lego faced a dilemma: Interview with Søren Lund, Jan. 31, 2008.

The interaction and the sharing: Brendan I. Koerner, "Geeks in Toyland," *Wired*, Feb. 2006, pp. 104–111.

The Oxford English Dictionary: Of course, there are significant differences between the making of the *Oxford English Dictionary* and today's collaborative and much more democratic projects. For more on the role played by volunteer readers in the making of the dictionary, see Simon Winchester, *The Meaning of Everything: The Story of the Oxford English Dictionary* (Oxford: Oxford University Press, 2003).

This type of customer participation: Interviews with Paul Marsden, Oct. 11, 2007, and Søren Lund, Jan. 31, 2008.

CareerBuilder knew it had: Interview with Adi Sideman, Dec. 2, 2007.

I'm not trying to set a rule: See Ben McConnell and Jackie Huba, *Citizen Marketers: When People Are the Message* (Chicago: Kaplan, 2007), pp. 31–38.

Some participation can be created: Interview with Piers Hogarth-Scott, Aug. 8, 2007.

Dr. Paul Marsden and Martin Oetting: Interviews with Paul Marsden, Oct. 11, 2007, and Martin Oetting, Oct. 18, 2007. Also see Paul Marsden and Martin Oetting, "Consumer Empowerment Reloaded: Why Your Customers Should Drive Your Marketing," MarketingProfs.com, Nov. 29, 2005.

Marsden has been explaining: See Justin Kirby and Paul Marsden, *Connected Marketing: The Viral, Buzz and Word of Mouth Revolution* (Oxford: Butterworth-Heinemann, 2006), pp. 5–6. For the history of the Hawthorne effect, see www.library.hbs.edu/hc/hawthorne.

Toward the end of our meeting: Interview with Jia Shen, Aug. 21, 2007.

The next time you go to YouTube: Interview with Arielle Reinstein, Bill Nee, and Jason Freidenfelds of Google, Nov. 27, 2007.

A few months ago I downloaded: Interview with Tom Fugleberg of Olson, Aug. 21, 2007; "MarketingSherpa's Viral Marketing Hall of Fame 2007: Top 10 Efforts & Results Data to Inspire You," available at www.marketing sherpa.com/article.html?ident=29947.

18. Uneven Distribution

The children emerging: The Nintendo case is based on David Sheff, *Game Over: How Nintendo Zapped an American Industry, Captured Your Dollars, and Enslaved Your Children* (New York: Random House, 1993). I also interviewed Sheff on Apr. 22, 1998.

The psychological principle: The quote from a Tremor member is from Melanie Wells, "Kid Nabbing," *Forbes*, Feb. 2, 2004, p. 84.

One campaign used this concept: The Kern quote is from an e-mail interview with him, Feb. 5, 1999.

The people at BMW understood: The BMW case is based on interviews with James McDowell, June 21, 1999, and Jeff Salmon, Apr. 29, 1999. Also see Susan Fournier and Robert J. Dolan, "Launching the BMW Z3 Roadster (N9-597-002)," Harvard Business School Case Study, 1997.

Not every customer who: The section is based on interviews with about ten early owners of BMW Z3s. My assistant, Kerry Shaw, interviewed six BMW dealers around the country.

In his book Influence: See Robert B. Cialdini, *Influence: The Psychology of Persuasion* (New York: Morrow, 1993), p. 237.

Marketers love the game: Interview with Jim Nail, Nov. 14, 2007. Also see Jim Nail, "Visibility versus Surprise: Which Drives the Greatest Discussion of Super Bowl Advertisements?" *Journal of Advertising Research* 47 (Dec. 2007): 412–419.

But even for older products: In-N-Out Burger's "secret" menu can be seen at www.in-n-out.com/secretmenu.asp.

19. More of a Café than a Subway Station

In 2007, Red Bull introduced: Interview with Charles Hull of Archrival, Sept. 24, 2007. Social interaction plays an important role in other Red Bull marketing activities. For a good case study about the company, see Nirmalya Kumar et al., "Red Bull: The Anti-Brand Brand," London Business School Case Study 04-006, 2004.

The second comment at the beginning: Interview with Virginia Miracle, Aug. 2, 2007. The Web site is www.fiskateers.com.

Ten years ago Steve Jurvetson: The quote is from Steve Jurvetson and Tim Draper, "Viral Marketing," May 1, 1997, available at www.dfj.com. It also appears in Steve Jurvetson, "Turning Customers into a Sales Force," *Business 2.0* (Nov. 1998): 102.

The third comment: The Thorn Tree community is at www.lonelyplanet. com/thorntree.

Community forums like this: Interview with Scott Wilder, Dec. 6, 2007.

If you start a club: The information about MySpace is from an interview with Jason Feffer, Aug. 15, 2007.

20. The *Wall Street Journal* and the Lingerie Business

Lida Orzeck was on vacation: Interviews with Gale Epstein and Lida Orzeck, Oct. 29, 2007, and Wendy Bounds, Dec. 10, 2007. See also Gwendolyn Bounds, "A Tiny Scrap of Fabric Wins a Huge Following," *Wall Street Journal*, June 18, 2004, p. A1.

To examine the relationships: Interview with Shereen Usdin, Oct. 8, 2007; Shereen Usdin et al., "Achieving Social Change on Gender-based Violence: A Report on the Impact Evaluation of Soul City's Fourth Series," *Social Science & Medicine* 61 (2005): 2434–2445; Shereen Usdin et al., "No Short Cuts in Entertainment-Education: Designing Soul City Step-by-Step," in Arvind Singhal et al., eds., *Entertainment-Education and Social Change: History, Research, and Practice* (Mahwah, NJ: Erlbaum, 2004), pp. 153–176; Arvind Singhal and Everett M. Rogers, *Combating AIDS: Communication Strategies in Action* (New Delhi: Sage, 2003), pp. 303–316; Arvind Singhal and Everett M. Rogers, *Entertainment-Education: A Communication Strategy for Social Change* (Mahwah, NJ: Erlbaum, 1999), pp. 212–217.

Arvind Singhal, a professor: Interview with Arvind Singhal, Aug. 17, 2007.

This may explain in part: The source for the product placement spending is a press release announcing a study by the research company PQ Media, Feb. 12, 2008, available at www.pqmedia.com.

As a practitioner, Shereen Usdin: To get a sense of the magnitude of the problem, here are some numbers from Usdin's paper "Achieving Social Change," cited above: "A 2003 antenatal survey in one city found 38 percent of women had experienced domestic violence at some point in their lives; 35 percent of women during their current pregnancy [. . .] A prevalence study across three of nine provinces found that 9.5 percent of women had been physically abused in the previous year. In one province 28.4 percent of women reported ever being physically abused, and over 50 percent of women reported emotional abuse in the previous year." p. 2434.

Strong reactions continued: The quote is from Ed O'Loughlin, "Blair in South Africa: Township Visit Rouses Emotions," *Independent*, Jan. 8, 1999, p. 6.

Then something totally unexpected happened: Interview with Shereen Usdin, Oct. 8, 2007; Usdin et al., "No Short Cuts."

Did the campaign cause actual change?: The numbers are from Usdin et al. "Achieving Social Change," cited above. Regarding the helpline: "Eight months after it had been established, 41 percent of respondents nationally had heard of the Helpline. This is entirely attributed to the SC4/NNVAW intervention as the line was established specifically for this purpose. 16 percent of people with no exposure to SC4 compared to 61 percent of respondents with exposure to 3 SC4 media knew about the Helpline." p. 2442. Regarding the perception of domestic violence as a private matter: "An increase (from 37 percent to 59 percent) was observed from baseline to evaluation on the item 'my community feels that violence between a man and a woman is not a private affair.' 53 percent of respondents with no exposure to SC4 radio compared to 63 percent of respondents with high exposure to SC4 radio held this view." p. 2438.

The political scientist Bernard Cohen: Bernard Cohen, *The Press and Foreign Policy* (Princeton, NJ: Princeton University Press, 1963), p. 13. Also see Gabriel Weimann, *The Influentials: People Who Influence People* (Albany: State University of New York Press, 1994), p. 279. The data about the percentage who talked about domestic violence are from Usdin et al., "Achieving Social Change," p. 2441: "More than 1 in 3 respondents talked about domestic violence while SC4 was on air [. . .]Men with high exposure to SC4 radio were less likely to never talk about domestic violence (35 percent) than men with no exposure to SC4 radio (62 percent)." Additional data and reports are available at *Soul City*'s Web site: www.soulcity.org.za.

21. Does Madison Avenue Still Matter?

A headline in a 2007 Advertising Age *article:* Jack Neff, "Want Online Buzz for Your New Product?" AdAge.com, May 16, 2007. The print edition of the article was published under the headline "The key to Building Buzz Is . . . Advertising," *Advertising Age,* May 21, 2007, p. 12.

The Nielsen study mentioned in Advertising Age *looked:* See Kate Niederhoffer et al., "The Origin and Impact of CPG New-Product Buzz: Emerging Trends and Implications," *Journal of Advertising Research* 47 (Dec. 2007): 420–426, also available as a white paper from www.nielsenbuzzmetrics.com/white papers; interview with Kate Niederhoffer, Jan. 18, 2008.

A good ad can help: For more on the way that word of mouth complements and extends the effect of advertising, see John E. Hogan, "Quantifying the Ripple: Word-of-Mouth and Advertising Effectiveness," *Journal of Advertising Research* 44 (Sept. 2004): 271–280.

Advertising is also a fairly effective way: See, for example, Eric Vernette, "Targeting Women's Clothing Fashion Opinion Leaders in Media Planning: An Application for Magazines," *Journal of Advertising Research* 44 (Mar. 2004): 90–107; Gabriel Weimann, *The Influentials: People Who Influence People* (Albany: State University of New York Press, 1994), p. 178.

Messages that spread among people: The source for the Alar story is Thomas L. Harris, *The Marketer's Guide to Public Relations: How Today's Top Companies Are Using the New PR to Gain a Competitive Edge* (New York: Wiley, 1991), p. 187.

Advertising content shows up in buzz: Interviews with Brad Fay, Sept. 13, 2007, and Oct. 26, 2007. See also Ed Keller and Brad Fay, "Single Source WOM Measurement," Nov. 2006, p.8, white paper available at www.keller fay.com.

Sometimes ads generate buzz: The Taco Bell data were provided to me by TBWA Chiat/Day.

Back in 1966, Ernest Dichter: Ernest Dichter, "How Word-of-Mouth Advertising Works," *Harvard Business Review* (Nov.-Dec. 1966): 147–166.

Bringing real customers into an ad: Interviews with John Yost, Dec. 6, 1998, and Paul Huber, Feb. 3, 1999.

A lot of customers say that they don't like advertising: "Consumer Resistance to Marketing Reaches All-Time High. Marketing Productivity Plummets, According to Yankelovich Study," press release, Apr. 15, 2004.

One word that comes to mind is "honesty": Interview with John Yost, Dec. 6, 1998.

4. Ask your customers to articulate: Interview with Jim Callahan, Feb. 7, 1999.

In 1990 a study estimated: Glenn A. Melnick, "From Family Planning to HIV/AIDS Prevention to Poverty Alleviation: A conversation with Mechai Viravaidya," *Health Affairs* 26, no. 6 (2007): 672; Thomas D'Agnes, *From Condoms to Cabbages: An Authorized Biography of Mechai Viravaidya* (Bangkok: Post, 2001), p. 342. The quote is from my interview with Mechai Viravaidya, Sept. 22, 2007.

A massive campaign that worked: Helene Gayle, "Mechai Viravaidya," *Time*, Nov. 5, 2006; Arvind Singhal and Everett M. Rogers, *Combating AIDS: Communication Strategies in Action* (New Delhi: Sage, 2003), pp. 99–110.

Companies are usually very proud: The quote is from an interview with Piers Hogarth-Scott, Aug. 8, 2007.

22. Buzz in Distribution Channels

But then I heard about Dave Nichol: Interview with Moss Kadey, Sept. 6, 2007.

Nichol started gaining the trust: Anne Kingston, *The Edible Man: Dave Nichol, President's Choice & the Making of Popular Taste* (Toronto: Macfarlane Walter &

Ross, 1994); John Dalla Costa, "Lessons in the Rearview Mirror." *Strategy Magazine*, Dec. 13, 1993, p. 4.

One thing that made the newsletter interesting: The statistics regarding the newsletter readership are from Dave Nichol, *The Dave Nichol Cookbook* (Toronto: Loblaw, 1993), p. 24.

People are overwhelmed by too much choice: Sheena S. Iyengar and Mark Lepper, "When Choice Is Demotivating: Can One Desire Too Much of a Good Thing?" *Journal of Personality and Social Psychology* 79 (2000): 995–1006. Nichol's quote is from an interview in *Progressive Grocer*, Nov. 1995, p. 24.

About twenty years before Nichol: John Markoff, *What the Dormouse Said: How the Sixties Counterculture Shaped the Personal Computer Industry* (New York: Viking, 2005).

In a 1971 edition of the catalogue: The Last Whole Earth Catalog: Access to Tools (Menlo Park, CA: Portola Institute, 1971).

Word of mouth was woven into: Nichol left Loblaw in the early 1990s. I recently learned that Loblaw now includes customer reviews in its newsletter and on its Web site. See Charlene Li and Josh Bernoff, *Groundswell: Winning in a World Transformed by Social Technologies* (Boston: Harvard Business Press, 2008), p. 191.

In early 1991 about five thousand: Maria Heidkamp, "Creating Word-of-Mouth for Literary and Midlist Fiction," *Publishers Weekly*, Apr. 26, 1991, pp. 34–35.

As always, numbers make a difference: Interview with Carl Lennertz, May 19, 1999.

Forget for a moment the physical flow: Interviews with Kary Sommers, Oct. 4, 2007, and John Holden, Oct. 22, 2007.

When Margot Fraser decided to market: Interview with Margot Fraser, Dec. 22, 1998.

23. Putting It Together

"A Hotel with a Pillow Menu": Interview with John Moser, Oct. 29, 2007; Michael Milligan, "Pillow Talk: The Benjamin Offers Sleep Amenities," *Travel Weekly*, Sept. 27, 2004, p. 26; Terry Trucco, "Pillow Talk for the Weary," *New York Times*, Sept. 17, 2007, p. H1; Anthony Ramirez, "Sleepless in New York? Not at This Hotel," *New York Times*, Oct. 8, 2007, p. A20. See also www.trip advisor.com.

"The Evolution of Seeding": Interviews with Mavis Fraser, Oct. 24, 2007; Patrick Thoburn, Sept. 28, 2007, and Aug. 21, 2007; Matthew Stradiotto, Aug. 21, 2007; Krista Dayman, Nov. 1, 2007; and Lauren White, Nov. 1, 2007. White's blog is at raymitheminx.com/. See also Pia Musngi, "Coty Prestige's Mavis Fraser: CK Invites Netgen in2 Brand Conversations," *Strategy Magazine*, June 2007, p. 22. For more about the product launch in the

United States, see Eric Wilson, "How to Bottle a Generation," *New York Times*, Mar. 8, 2007, p. G1.

"Are Barbers Influential?": Interviews with Virgil Simons, Aug. 2, 2007; James Coleman, Sept. 20, 2007; Joe Harrington, Sept. 18, 2007; Sharon Morgan, Sept. 18, 2007; Rahman Williams, Sept. 17, 2007; Craig Atkins, Sept. 18, 2007; and Samuel Smith, Sept. 18, 2007. See also Virgil Simons, "Prostate Net: Barber-Based Grassroots Outreach for a Non-Profit," paper presented at WOMMA's Word of Mouth Basic Training, January 19–20, 2006, Orlando, FL.; Kari Lydersen, "Cancer Effort Enlists Barbers; Prostate Awareness Program Focuses on African American Men," *Washington Post*, Mar. 28, 2005. p. A3; Jonathan E. Briggs, "Shave, Haircut and a Few Prostate Tips; Health Educators Reach Out to the African American Community in an Unconventional Way," *Chicago Tribune*, Feb. 4, 2005, p. 1. For more on African-Americans and the medical community, see Vanessa Gamble, "Under the Shadow of Tuskegee: African Americans and Health Care," *American Journal of Public Health* 87 (Nov. 1997): 1773–1778.

"Tasting Yogurt with Your Friends": Interview with Vicki Foster, Jo Schultz, and Karen Stenner, Aug. 21, 2007. The data about Vaalia yogurt were provided by the Word Of Mouth Company.

"Will People Talk about Chewing Gum?": Interviews with Christian Basten, Dec. 27, 2007, and Martin Oetting, Oct. 18, 2007; e-mail interview with Gabriela Froehlich, Apr. 24, 2008.

"Putting Word-of-Mouth Marketing on the Agenda": Interviews with Kira Wampler, Aug. 20, 2007, and Scott Wilder, Dec. 6, 2007. Also see Kira Wampler and Scott Wilder, "Winning at Word of Mouth Within Your Company: 'The Tipping Point,' " paper presented at WOMMA's Word of Mouth Basic Training 2, June 20–21, 2006, San Francisco.

"The Secret of Finding a Plumber": Interview with Angie Hicks, July 23, 2007. See also Damon Darlin, "Let's Say Your Toilet Backs Up: How Do You Find a Good Plumber?" *New York Times*, Aug. 5, 2006, p. B1. For additional discussion see Bruce Mohl, "Consumers Find New Voice in Taking Gripes Online; Wounded Targets Fight Back, but with Little Success," *Boston Globe*, Sept. 9, 2007. Angie's List can be found at www.angieslist.com.

24. Buzz Workshop

"You've Got to Know the System": Interview with Mechai Viravaidya, Sept. 22, 2007; Thomas D'Agnes, *From Condoms to Cabbages: An Authorized Biography of Mechai Viravaidya* (Bangkok: Post, 2001).

"Will It Blend?": Interview with George Wright, Apr. 22, 2008; Jennifer Alsever, "Puree a Rake for Fun and Profit," *FSB*, Apr. 2008, p. 51. The demographic data about YouTube can be found at www.youtube.com/advertise.

"Give a Brita. Plant a Tree": Conversation with Michael Fisher, Apr. 2, 2007.

"Was Your Father a Thief?": Interview with Nick Cummins, Jan. 30, 2008.

Is there a formula to creating buzz?: Interview with Yossi Vardi, Sept. 14, 2007.

Bibliography

Balter, Dave, and John Butman. *Grapevine: The New Art of Word-of-Mouth Marketing*. New York: Portfolio, 2005.

Barabási, Albert-László. *Linked: The New Science of Networks*. Cambridge, MA: Perseus, 2002.

Bhargava, Rohit. *Personality Not Included: Why Companies Lose Their Authenticity and How Great Brands Get It Back*. New York: McGraw-Hill, 2008.

Blackshaw, Pete. *Satisfied Customers Tell Three Friends, Angry Customers Tell 3,000*. New York: Doubleday, 2008.

Brodie, Richard. *Virus of the Mind: The New Science of the Meme*. Seattle, WA: Integral, 1996.

Brown, Duncan, and Nick Hayes. *Influencer Marketing: Who Really Influences Your Customers?* Oxford: Butterworth-Heinemann, 2008.

Bueno, Bolivar J. *Why We Talk: The Truth Behind Word-of-Mouth*. Kingston, NY: Creative Crayon, 2007.

Carl, Walter J. "What's All The Buzz About? Everyday Communication and the Relational Basis of Word-of-Mouth and Buzz Marketing Practices." *Management Communication Quarterly* 19 (2006): 601–634.

Christensen, Clayton M. *The Innovator's Dilemma: When New Technologies Cause Great Firms to Fail*. Boston: Harvard Business Press, 1997.

Cialdini, Robert B. *Influence: The Psychology of Persuasion*. New York: Morrow, 1993.

Coleman, James Samuel, Elihu Katz, and Herbert Menzel. *Medical Innovation: A Diffusion Study*. Indianapolis: Bobbs-Merrill, 1966.

Dawkins, Richard. *The Selfish Gene*. Oxford: Oxford University Press, 1976.

Denning, Stephen. *The Leader's Guide to Storytelling: Mastering the Art and Discipline of Business Narrative*. San Francisco: Jossey-Bass, 2005.

Dunbar, Robin I. M. *Grooming, Gossip, and the Evolution of Language*. Cambridge, MA: Harvard University Press, 1996.

Dye, Renée. "The Buzz on Buzz." *Harvard Business Review*, November-December 2000, pp. 139–146.

Dyson, Esther. *Release 2.1: A Design for Living in the Digital Age*. New York: Broadway Books, 1998.

Gillin, Paul. *The New Influencers: A Marketer's Guide to the New Social Media*. Sanger, CA: Quill Driver, 2007.

Gladwell, Malcolm. *The Tipping Point: How Little Things Can Make a Big Difference*. Boston: Little, Brown, 2000.

Godes, David, et al. "The Firm's Management of Social Interactions." *Marketing Letters* 16, no. 3 (December 2005): 415–428.

Godin, Seth. *Unleashing the Ideavirus*. Dobbs Ferry, NY: Do You Zoom, 2000.

Harris, Thomas L. *The Marketer's Guide to Public Relations: How Today's Top Companies Are Using the New PR to Gain a Competitive Edge*. New York: Wiley, 1991.

Heath, Chip, and Dan Heath. *Made to Stick: Why Some Ideas Survive and Others Die*. New York: Random House, 2007.

Hogan, John E., "What Is the True Value of a Lost Customer?" *Journal of Service Research* 5, no. 3 (2003): 196–208.

Hughes, Mark. *Buzzmarketing: Get People to Talk About Your Stuff*. New York: Portfolio, 2005.

Iacobucci, Dawn, ed. *Networks in Marketing*. Thousand Oaks, CA: Sage, 1996.

Katz, Elihu, and Paul F. Lazarsfeld. *Personal Influence: The Part Played by People in the Flow of Mass Communications*. Glencoe, IL: Free Press, 1955.

Kawasaki, Guy. *Selling the Dream: How to Promote Your Product, Company, or Ideas and Make a Difference Using Everyday Evangelism*. New York: HarperBusiness, 1991.

Keller, Ed, and Jon Berry. *The Influentials: One American in Ten Tells the Other Nine How to Vote, Where to Eat, and What to Buy*. New York: Free Press, 2003.

Kirby, Justin, and Paul Marsden. *Connected Marketing: The Viral, Buzz and Word of Mouth Revolution*. Oxford: Butterworth-Heinemann, 2006.

Lazarsfeld, Paul F., Bernard Berelson, and Hazel Gaudet. *The People's Choice: How the Voter Makes Up His Mind in a Presidential Campaign*. 2nd ed. New York: Columbia University Press, 1948.

Leonard-Barton, Dorothy. "Experts as Negative Opinion Leaders in the Diffusion of a Technological Innovation." *Journal of Consumer Research* 11 (March 1985): 914–926.

Li, Charlene, and Josh Bernoff. *Groundswell: Winning in a World Transformed by Social Technologies*. Boston: Harvard Business Press, 2008.

Lynch, Aaron. *Thought Contagion: How Belief Spreads Through Society*. New York: Basic Books, 1996.

Mancuso, Joseph R. "Why Not Create Opinion Leaders for New Product Introduction?" *Journal of Marketing* 33 (July 1969): 20–25.

McConnell, Ben, and Jackie Huba. *Citizen Marketers: When People Are the Message*. Chicago: Kaplan, 2007.

———. *Creating Customer Evangelists: How Loyal Customers Become a Volunteer Sales Force*. Chicago: Dearborn, 2003.

McKenna, Regis. *Relationship Marketing: Successful Strategies for the Age of the Customer*. Reading, MA: Addison-Wesley, 1991.

Misner, Ivan R. *The World's Best-Known Marketing Secret: Building Your Business with Word-of-Mouth Marketing*. Austin, TX: Bard & Stephen, 1994.

Moore, Geoffrey A. *Crossing the Chasm: Marketing and Selling Technology Products to Mainstream Customers*. New York: HarperBusiness, 1991.

Ogilvy, David. *Ogilvy on Advertising*. New York: Vintage, 1985.

Peters, Thomas J., and Robert H. Waterman, Jr. *In Search of Excellence: Lessons from America's Best-Run Companies*. New York: Harper & Row, 1982.

Reichheld, Fred. *The Ultimate Question: Driving Good Profits and True Growth*. Boston: Harvard Business Press, 2006.

Reingen, Peter H., and Jerome B. Kernan. "Analysis of Referral Networks in Marketing: Methods and Illustration." *Journal of Marketing Research* 23 (November 1986): 370–378.

Robertson, Thomas S. *Innovative Behavior and Communication*. New York: Holt, Rinehart and Winston, 1971.

Robertson, Thomas S., Joan Zielinski, and Scott Ward. *Consumer Behavior*. Glenview, IL: Scott, Foresman, 1984.

Rogers, Everett M. *Diffusion of Innovations*. 5th ed. New York: Free Press, 2003.

Roper Starch Worldwide. *Influential Americans: Trendsetters of the New Millennium*. 4th ed. New York: Roper Starch Worldwide/*Atlantic Monthly*, 1995.

Schelling, Thomas C. *Micromotives and Macrobehavior*. New York: Norton, 1978.

Scott, David Meerman. *The New Rules of Marketing and PR: How to Use News Releases, Blogs, Podcasting, Viral Marketing, and Online Media to Reach Buyers Directly*. Hoboken, NJ: Wiley, 2007.

Sernovitz, Andy. *Word of Mouth Marketing: How Smart Companies Get People Talking*. Chicago: Kaplan, 2006.

Seybold, Patricia B., and Ronni T. Marshak. *Customers.com: How to Create a Profitable Business Strategy for the Internet and Beyond*. New York: Times Business, 1998.

Silverman, George. *The Secrets of Word-of-Mouth Marketing*. New York: Amacom, 2001.

Singhal, Arvind, and Everett M. Rogers. *Entertainment-Education: A Communication Strategy for Social Change*. Mahwah, NJ: Erlbaum, 1999.

Singhal, Arvind, Everett M. Rogers, and Meenakshi Mahajan. "The Gods Are Drinking Milk." *Asian Journal of Communication* 9, no. 1 (1999): 86–107.

Stern, Barbara B., and Stephen J. Gould. "The Consumer as Financial Opinion Leader." *Journal of Retail Banking* 10, no. 2 (1988): 43–52.

Stielstra, Greg. *PyroMarketing: The Four-Step Strategy to Ignite Customer Evangelists and Keep Them for Life*. New York: HarperBusiness, 2005.

Tapscott, Don, and Anthony D. Williams. *Wikinomics: How Mass Collaboration Changes Everything*. New York: Portfolio, 2006

Thorstenson, Göran. *People Influence People: On Friends and Word-of-Mouth in PR and Communication*. Stockholm: Springtime, 2006.

Underhill, Paco. *Why We Buy: The Science of Shopping*. New York: Simon & Schuster, 1999.

Valente, Thomas W. *Network Models of the Diffusion of Innovations*. Cresskill, NJ: Hampton, 1995.

Valente, Thomas W., and Rebecca L. Davis. "Accelerating the Diffusion of Innovations Using Opinion Leaders." *Annals of the American Academy of Political and Social Science* 566 (1999): 55–67.

Valente, Thomas W., and Patchareeya Pumpuang. "Identifying Opinion Leaders to Promote Behaviour Change." *Health Education & Behavior* 34, no. 6 (December 2007): 881–896.

Wasserman, Stanley, and Katherine Faust. *Social Network Analysis: Methods and Applications*. New York: Cambridge University Press, 1994.

Watts, Duncan J. *Six Degrees: The Science of a Connected Age*. New York: Norton, 2003.

Weimann, Gabriel, *The Influentials: People Who Influence People*. Albany: State University of New York Press, 1994.

Wellman, Barry, ed. *Networks in the Global Village: Life in Contemporary Communities*. Boulder, CO: Westview, 1999.

Whyte, William H., Jr. "The Web of Word-of-Mouth." *Fortune*, November 1954, p. 140.

Wilson, Jerry R. *Word-of-Mouth Marketing*. New York: Wiley, 1991.

Word of Mouth Marketing Association. *Measuring Word of Mouth*. Vols. 1–4. Chicago: WOMMA, 2005–2008.

Acknowledgments

Thanks to the people who were willing to share their ideas and insights. I learned a great deal from every one of them. Here they are, in no particular order: Steve Hershberger, Arvind Singhal, Bill Mosher, Adi Sideman, Kira Wampler, Michael Fisher, Dan Johnson-Weinberger, Jia Shen, Jonathan Carson, Angie Hicks Bowman, Jason Feffer, Steve Knox, Justin Foxton, Virgil Simons, Bruce Palmer, Geno Church, Tom Fugleberg, Tom Valente, Rick Anguilla, Gale Epstein, Lida Orzeck, Sandra B. Lawrence, Vicki Foster, Jo Schultz, Karen Stenner, Paul Francis, Walter Carl, Dina Mayzlin, Marc Schiller, Barak Libai, Patrick Thoburn, Matthew Stradiotto, Jon Berry, Virginia Miracle, Piers Hogarth-Scott, Judi Porta, Laurent Florès, Vanessa Pike, Kate Niederhoffer, Søren Lund, Nick Cummins, Jean-Louis Laborie, Peter Kellner, Susan Bradley, David Chin, Blaine Deal, George Wright, Rahman Williams, Mechai Viravaidya, Shereen Usdin, Moss Kadey, Andy Bassett, Paige Chambers, Matt Celesta, Yossi Vardi, Andrea Wojnicki, Robert East, Brad Fay, James Coleman, Joe Harrington, Sharon Morgan, Craig Atkins, Samuel Smith, Sean O'Driscoll, Matthew Copeland, Brad Christensen, Harald Katzmair, Christian Basten, Owen Matthews, Kary Sommers, Paul Marsden, Jackie Huba, Ben McConnell,

Martin Oetting, Gabriela Froehlich, Tim Zagat, Nina Zagat, John Moser, Chris Byrne, John Holden, Dave Balter, Lauren White, Krista Dayman, Amy Rathke, Bruce Ertmann, Jim Nail, Arielle Reinstein, Bill Nee, Jason Freidenfelds, Scott Wilder, Rex Briggs, Anders Søborg. Thanks to Duncan Watts, who commented on sections related to his research. And thanks to everyone who helped with the first edition!

In the past ten years I talked to lots of people before, during, and after my presentations about buzz, and I learned a lot from their questions and comments. Readers like Louis Gray, Jacqueline Moreno, Dan Johnson-Weinberger, Michael Rubin, Danny Kennedy, and so many others gave me feedback on the first edition. And thanks to people who were willing just to chat with me about the topic: Alex Chu and her friends, who talked about buzz over pizza; Riley, Anne, and Sarah and the folks from NOLS's fall semester; NOLS alumni David, Luke, and Randy. And special thanks to Jeanne O'Brien, Max Kalehoff, Claus Moseholm, and many other people who gave me access to even more information and people.

My agent, Daniel Greenberg, of Levine Greenberg, has been instrumental in getting this book published. And many thanks to Monika Verma and Melissa Rowland for their ongoing help and support. Meredith Alexander did a superb job in editing the book. Sarah Rainone at Doubleday was enormously helpful in tightening the manuscript and turning it into a real book. Many thanks also to Roger Scholl for his confidence and to Liz Duvall, Talia Krohn, and everyone at Doubleday. Thanks to Paul Romano, who designed the book cover. I smiled the first time I saw it, and I still do every time I look at it.

Finally, I would like to thank the five people to whom I've dedicated this book: Daria, Noam, Yonatan, Maya, and Mika, who all served simultaneously as my editors, research assistants, coaches, and family. Thank you.

Index